REFLECTIONS ON SOCIOLOGY
AND THEOLOGY

Reflections on Sociology and Theology

DAVID MARTIN

CLARENDON PRESS • OXFORD
1997

Oxford University Press, Great Clarendon Street, Oxford OX2 6DP

Oxford New York

*Athens Auckland Bangkok Bogota Bombay
Buenos Aires Calcutta Cape Town Dar es Salaam
Delhi Florence Hong Kong Istanbul Karachi
Kuala Lumpur Madras Madrid Melbourne
Mexico City Nairobi Paris Singapore
Taipei Tokyo Toronto*

*and associated companies in
Berlin Ibadan*

Oxford is a trade mark of Oxford University Press

*Published in the United States
by Oxford University Press Inc., New York*

*British Library Cataloguing in Publication Data
Data available*

*Library of Congress Cataloging in Publication Data
Data available*

ISBN 0–19–827384–3

1 3 5 7 9 10 8 6 4 2

*Typeset by Best-set Typesetter Ltd., Hong Kong
Printed in Great Britain
on acid-free paper by
Biddles Ltd, Guildford and King's Lynn*

PREFACE

THIS is a book of essays written for various 'emergent occasions' but all having to do with the relationship between sociology and theology (or sociology and religion). They are not all at the same analytic level and that in part arises because some were given to lay audiences. One writes so as to be heard at a particular time and place by a specific group of people.

One also writes under the pressure of the moment and of controversies in which one may be personally involved. Thus, the essay on ecclesiology makes assertions I should now express more tentatively, and with proper balancing comment. I have similar reservations about the essay on ecumenism. Nevertheless, I do not wish to repudiate what I have written in these two pieces. I believe the sociological standpoint often places one in a creative tension with what theologians characteristically argue, and the tension should not be allowed to go slack.

Perhaps I might mention for the sake of completeness that I have attempted other work cognate with what is included here, in particular the Sarum Lectures given at Oxford in 1995 and to be published under the title *Does Christianity Cause War?* by OUP. The Sarum Lectures were not precisely about the relation of sociology to theology (or rather, religion) but they did aim to take a particular issue in the standard critique of religion, the relation of religion to war, and show what difference might be made by adopting a sociological approach. The lectures were dedicated to the proposition that Christian apologetics can apologize too much. Here, as elsewhere, my basic perspective is Niebuhrian and can be traced back to Niebuhr's classic work *Moral Man in Immoral Society*.

The structure of the book is as follows. The initial essay picks up the kinds of theme covered in the rest of the book and is intended as an Overture. Then in Part I there follows a group of essays with a strong methodological content, concerned with the nature of sociology or theology and their inter-relationship. The two essays which focus most directly on that inter-relationship are chapters 4 and 5, to do with differing maps of the same ground and how the sociological mode bears on the theological vocabulary. Chapters 3 and 6 are both relatively simple pieces for lay audiences.

Part II has to do with sociology and practical issues of interest to theologians, such as peace, unity among Christians, and the nature of religious comment on politics.

Part III is made up of socio-theological addresses to colleagues and to clergy. The first was to a mixed audience and can be regarded as a *feuilleton* directed against the notion of collective guilt and the kind of socio-theology resting on such categories as nation, colour, or ethnicity. The second was to an audience comprised entirely of clergy. It sets out the empirical situation of contemporary religion and suggests a socio-theological response.

I should perhaps add that all these essays, except the first, were written before I encountered the remarkable book by John Milbank *Theology and Social Theory* (Oxford: Blackwell, 1990). If I understand him rightly, Milbank is saying that sociology and theology are incommensurable discourses, both rooted in fundamental presuppositions. He is also saying that sociology is ideological and does not add to a theological 'account'. That there is an ideological shadow thrown over much sociological theorizing I would not deny, but I do believe there is a sociological mode of analysis which may add dialectically to a theological account, and which offers a context which needs to be confronted rather than philosophically elided. How the different modes and accounts may be related seems to me excellently presented in the book by Peter Clarke and Peter Byrne *Religion Defined and Explained*.

I should make a concluding apology. There are several distinguished people writing in this field whose contributions are barely mentioned. I have in mind scholars like Peter Berger, Robin Gill, William Pickering, Kieran Flanagan, and David Lyon. This is because my own way of working is to go for the issue in hand rather than to survey the field exegetically. It goes without saying that I have gained enormously from the writings of others.

The 'emergent occasions' calling forth these essays were:

Chapter 1 (initial sections) was given originally to teachers meeting at the University of Trondheim and printed in Norwegian by the University of Trondheim Press in *Religionsfag–Samfunnsfag* edited by Gustav Karlsaune in 1994.

Chapter 2 was written originally for a book edited by Michael Banner on *Theology in a Scientific Culture*. The essay here was to have been the social scientific contribution, but the whole project fell through.

Chapters 3 and 6 were both given as contributions to conferences held in Dallas, Texas on 'Theism and the Sciences'.

Chapter 4 was a contribution to *Sociology and Theology* edited by D. Martin, W. Pickering, and J. Orme-Mills OP, and published in 1980 by Harvester Press.

Chapter 5 was a contribution to a conference at Christchurch, Oxford in 1979 which was published in 1981 as *The Sciences and Theology in the Twentieth Century* by the University of Notre Dame Press, under the editorship of Arthur Peacocke.

Chapter 7 was to have been a contribution to a conference on 'lawfulness' to be held in Germany in 1990 which failed to take place due to lack of funds.

Chapter 8 was a contribution to the Anglo-Scandinavian Theological Conference held in Finland in 1985.

Chapter 9 was the Annual Public Lecture in Theology, given at Flinders University, Adelaide, Australia in 1986.

Chapter 10 was the Sir Roger Madgwick Lecture, given at the University of New England, Armidale, NSW, Australia in 1986.

Chapter 11 was a lecture given to the Centre for the Study of Religion and Society at the University of Kent at Canterbury, 1984.

Chapter 12 appeared originally in Eileen Barker (ed.), *New Religious Movements* published by the Edwin Mellen Press, New York, 1982.

Chapter 13 was given originally at King's College, London in November 1995 as part of a series on 'Harmful Religion'. It appears in a volume on that topic edited by Lawrence Osborn and Andrew Walker.

Chapter 14 was an address in two parts given at the opening and closing of the Guildford Diocesan Clergy Conference held at King Alfred College, Winchester in September 1994.

ACKNOWLEDGEMENTS

Grateful acknowledgements are made to the following:

TAPIR (Trondheim University Press) for sections of Chapter 1;

Simon and Shuster for Chapter 4, originally printed by the Harvester Press;

The University of Notre Dame Press for Chapter 5;

The University of New England, NSW for the Sir Robert Madgwick Lecture—Chapter 10;

The University of Kent (Centre for the Study of Religion and Society, Pamphlet Library No. 7) for Chapter 11;

Edwin Mellen Press for Chapter 12;

SPCK for Chapter 13.

CONTENTS

1

Sociology and Theology:
An Introduction to Themes

IN the pages that follow I want to engage in a survey of themes which have concerned me over the past several years. Initially I offer a fairly abstract account of the sociological mode of procedure. I then offer two illustrations of that procedure in relation to religion. The first has to do with civil conflict and ethnic cleansing. The second has to do with the way in which tribal 'marginals' on the border between two South American states pick up a universal religious message which enables them to step out of their local situation and step over the pressure of local nationalism. Then I offer two further illustrations designed to bring out the relation between sociological and theological vocabularies: the rite of Christian initiation—baptism, and the rite of sacrificial costing—the eucharist.

THE SOCIOLOGICAL MODE OF PROCEDURE

Sociology seeks to give an account of the patterns and sequences of social action. Human activity is not random. It gives rise to observable regularities which are susceptible to systematic statement and so allow modest anticipations concerning what is likely to happen next.

In ordinary colloquial language we acknowledge these regularities when we say that things 'happen as a rule'. However, our rule-governed activity as humans is not part of a closed system within which clearly identifiable elements are constantly rearranged in different combinations. Instead it belongs to an open-ended semi-system moving forward in time and so constituting history. Hence sociology deals in the located, the particular, and the idiographic as well as the general. It is a hybrid enterprise weaving together accounts in terms of processes with partially recurring characteristics, and accounts which embody a narrative of human motivations and their consequences. This does not mean that sociology is unscientific, provided we understand by science simply the kind of knowledge best designed to elicit maximum sense from its material. Of course, given that the material is human interaction in all its existential variety rather than (say) the abstract, slimmed down version of 'the human' represented by 'economic man', the models deployed are messy. They are loaded with the freight of cultural meanings and of everyday vocabularies. They cannot, for the most part, be cleaned up to allow mathematical quantification, nor can they be set to work in an abstract world, drained of its grain and colour, and removed from concrete situations.

In short, sociology is a human science which seeks regularities within the specific densities and local character of culture as that unfolds over time in an understandable narrative. It is a mode of telling 'the story', and so its vocabulary overlaps the vocabulary of the participants and the actors in the story. It also subjects the inwardness of human culture to a certain amount of external redescription.

That said, it is useful to illustrate what kinds of recurrence in human affairs are discerned by sociology. For example, a sociologist might be interested in what are commonly labelled 'revolutions' and that would initially mean defining and delimiting revolutions in terms both of an adequately large number of shared characteristics and some sort of postulated relation between these characteristics. Indeed, this preliminary act of definition is in itself an initial act of generalization, because it suggests that characteristic A, say violence, and characteristic B, say a reversal and overturning of previous hierarchies, do in fact go together. It is this repeated coincidence which constitutes the recognizability of a revolution as being such. From that point on the sociologist endeavours to account for differences, for example, why in one case a revolution is very bloody and in another virtually bloodless.

SOCIOLOGICAL TREATMENT OF RELIGION: AN EXAMPLE FROM ETHNIC CLEANSING

That particular example is very simple in order to bring out what is involved in defining such a phenomenon as 'a revolution'. The next example needs to be more concrete and for the purposes of this essay it needs to include religion. So, the example selected is that of civil war and 'ethnic cleansing' in Bosnia. Ethnic cleansing in Bosnia exhibits some widely familiar characteristics, such as the emergence of small and fissiparous male mafias, their arming by outside agencies which use them as proxies, and the perpetration of truly horrible deeds visited on other people merely because they are identified as belonging to a rival group. There are many other connected characteristics, but those just indicated go together more often than not. They happen 'as a rule'.

At any rate, once an identification of elements has been achieved on the basis of their frequent con-currence, it becomes possible to formulate comparisons, let us say, between Bosnia and Northern Ireland or the Lebanon. It is these comparisons which enable such matters as the precise role of religious conflict in relation to ethnic conflict to receive adequate scrutiny. The sociologist has identified a subset of roughly comparable situations and proceeds to ask what general conditions bring them about. One relevant condition is clearly that places like Bosnia and Northern Ireland exist at a border between major civilizations and between major imperial systems, and that a group constituting the majority on the right side of the border finds itself a minority on the wrong side of the border. Thus, in Northern Ireland the Catholic minority, which is a majority in the Irish Republic, and in western Europe as a whole, finds itself modestly disadvantaged *vis-à-vis* a Protestant majority, which is also a majority in the British Isles though a minority in western Europe. Such a situation is not in itself sufficient for the ignition of conflict but it makes conflict relatively likely if other aggravating circumstances emerge, amongst which might be the financing of terrorism by Libyans and by Irish-American agencies, the existence of a large number of unemployed young males, and the turning of working-class districts into adjacent hostile ghettos.

The sociologist then notes parallel elements in Bosnia, which may, however, in particular instances be more or less important than in Northern Ireland. But certainly Bosnia exists at a crucial border of the Slavic, Austro-Hungarian, and Ottoman spheres of influence and that border overlaps another border between Latin and Eastern Christianity and Islam. The precise aggravating circumstances leading to conflict do not matter here, though they include the breakdown of centralized control in the 'south Slav' state and the retention of its military arsenal by Serbia.

The role of religion in this situation, as in Northern Ireland, will be fixated on the identity of the rival groups and the evocation of their mutually hostile historic myths. That means that, although the Serbian Orthodox and Croatian Catholic churches will show an initial ambivalence towards conflict and even a preference for peace, as warfare gets under way they may well declare some sort of solidarity with the national cause, and that solidarity will be the more marked the closer they are to the actual scene of action.

This particular example has been chosen because it introduces and illustrates so many issues at once, all of them relevant to the relationship between sociology and theology. Clearly it shows what is meant by things happening 'as a rule' and also how comparison between roughly similar situations enables the sociologist to elicit the standard dynamics of ethnic cleansing as well as the special local dynamic, which may exacerbate or ameliorate the degree of violence. It shows, too, how a particular *kind* of religion rooted in national identity, history, and attachment to an (ill-defined) territory will be sucked into a process of inter-ethnic polarization. This will in turn influence theological pronouncements by Serbian leaders, the Vatican, and so on. Furthermore, the example serves to illustrate the issue of freedom and determinism as it arises in the context of sociological analysis. This is of major interest in the relationship between sociology and theology and requires a succinct account.

In general one may say that the things which happen 'as a rule' in situations like those in Northern Ireland and Bosnia (or

Cyprus, or Armenia, or Lebanon, or Sri Lanka) are likelihoods. Other things being equal, they are 'on the cards' i.e. definite probabilities which in social scientific terms we can formulate as 'average tendencies'. When we speak of the likely actions of human beings in the aggregate, we envisage a spread of possible responses, but circumstances being what they are we also recognize that most responses will cluster in a particular 'average' response. This response will be entirely intelligible once the circumstances are understood and once you have entered into the cast of mind built up historically in the course of previous hostile encounters. However, this has no special implication for individual freedom, beyond the intelligible nexus discernible between a given circumstance and a likely intelligible response. Some people will reject the 'average' response, though as a sociologist one may observe that they are likely to pay certain costs for that rejection. That cost, too, will surprise nobody, because such costs also are incurred 'as a rule'. The sociologist has not unearthed some hitherto unexpected 'determinate fatality' in human affairs, but merely articulated a common intelligent understanding of what generally happens to those who stand out against the standard response of their fellows. If we did not know about that through 'common experience' we would be deprived of the capacity both to understand and anticipate. It is the existence of standard likelihoods which allows intelligent anticipation and enhances freedom.

The examples just given all imply a modest but not necessarily extensive disjunction between the external account given by the sociologist and the internal understanding and imagery of events and situations entertained by participants. One could in principle imagine that a Bosnian Serb leader was also a sociologist and utilized a sociological articulation of 'common experience'.

A SECOND EXAMPLE: HOW MARGINALS RESPOND TO A UNIVERSAL MESSAGE

However, the issues are somewhat more complicated and they would benefit from a different example. The underlying issue here can be stated thus: is there a sufficient disjunction between the 'external' elements in a sociological account to throw some kind of ontological doubt on the internal account?

The example I use here comes from my own work on Pentecostalism in Latin America. I take this example in part because I have striven to avoid reductionist language and to listen seriously to the accounts given by participants, in part because the theology involved is part of group experience rather than the work of an individual theologian. A sociologist would normally begin by asking about what religious traditions are available to the Latin American environment, what social changes assist a break-up of the hitherto dominant traditions, and which areas are most vulnerable to break-up. Clearly, Pentecostalism is sufficiently close to Catholic Christianity and to Latin America for its message to be heard quite easily. So there is no problem about availability. Equally, contemporary social changes include a vast increase in every kind of mobility which is likely to disturb the automatic dominance of Catholicism. People are on the move from the countryside to megacities and across national and religious borders; they can aspire to new social roles, they can pick up new messages by cassette or television, and furthermore many of them are on the margin of the wider society as now constituted. And there is a discernible pattern of penetration which can be charted in time and place: Chile and Brazil are respectively 20 and 13 per cent evangelical, Guatemala 30 per cent, Mexico 6–7 per cent. The Andean republics are relatively resistant with the proportion of evangelicals at about 5 per cent. Naturally, there are specific variations in vulnerability within countries: the mountain peoples of Ecuador may convert very quickly, as may the Maya of Guatemala; and the South-east of Mexico is much more affected than the South-west. All these variations in time and place are to be understood in terms of social context.

Here I offer an individual case. A native people in the Andes on the Argentinian side of the Bolivian border responds initially to the national pressure exercised by the Hispanic state by relinquishing its own nature deities. But then marginals within that people adopt a faith associated with a wider evangelical faith community beyond the immediate provenance of Argentina. Though the local school and local Catholic church may act as powerful agents of the Hispanic state, nevertheless, the mobile marginals of tribal society in contact with the wider world outside may evade pressure from these agents.

Now, let us postulate that the universal tongue promised by Pentecost has a resonance in the ears of these marginals, because it 'corresponds' to an extension of their horizon of communication, because it provides a spontaneous release of spirit, and because it offers a link with sources of power wider and larger than the immediate and threatening power of the Argentinian state. It so happens this example is quite close to the details of a genuine instance but it is offered as a case of a typical sociological *procedure*. That being so, is the sociological statement of the environment conducive to the religious change inimical or not to the internal account offered by converts?

It will not be difficult to suggest further circumstantial aspects of the life of likely converts making Pentecostalism an attractive option. A typical suggestion would be that social changes had enabled those on the periphery of the group on the border to break free from the bonds hitherto holding them within the wider social and religious system, so that they were enabled simultaneously to secure both religious and social distinctiveness. A novel freedom in general became available and was made manifest in a freedom to select a new religious independence, and this might be particularly true of the mobile young men. Certainly there are a large number of instances all over the world from Mexico to Zimbabwe where the assertion of religious independence and rejection of the authority of the elders have gone together. But is there anything in these openings and the attractiveness of the options they bring into view which bears on the validity or otherwise of a Pentecostal theology? Pentecostal theology may stress participation, equality, and individual appropriation of the religious good but how can such things be rendered more (or less) true by the existence of circumstances which make them attractive and the existence of reasons which render that attractiveness intelligible?

One might even make a further imaginative leap in interpretation, stressing a lack of inward moral balance following recent social changes in Latin America which brought about a deep sense of moral deficit and 'indebtedness'. For many people this was put to 'rights' by the imputed righteousness of Christ and by the call to put 'right' a moral deficit through works of righteousness. This would undoubtedly be part of the appeal of some evangelical groups, particularly where actual debt had added further weight to the broad sense of being morally overdrawn and indebted. There would, therefore, be multiple resonances between message and situation, but it is once again difficult to see how a resonance invalidates a message. There is a seamless linkage between situation—the awareness of indebtedness—and response—the reception of grace and divine validation. The one dovetails into the other without the existence of indebtedness somehow impugning the existence of grace.

THEOLOGICAL AND SOCIOLOGICAL VOCABULARIES: THE EXAMPLE OF BAPTISM

At this point a sociological analysis of baptism can be offered to throw light on the intersection of theological and sociological vocabularies. There is also an ancillary objective in offering this example, which is to see what a sociological analysis of the 'surrounds' of contemporary baptism adds to a theological account. It may seem obvious that sociological analysis adds something, but in a recent brilliant study by John Milbank entitled *Theology and Social Theory* (1990) this is roundly denied. In his view the sociology of religion is a metaphysically based discourse which falsely claims an innocent scientific objectivity. So it is useful to take a concrete case to see whether or not sociology has anything to add.

A sociologist begins by identifying baptism as a rite of passage which accomplishes a transition from 'the world' to membership in the Christian body. The rite employs a symbolism of death through water and the emergence of a 'new creature' into life and light to signify initiation and incorporation. However, this sociological identification of baptism so far barely extends or amplifies the religious account at all. Maybe a Christian liturgist would not use a phrase like 'accomplishing a transition' but there is no major difference of substance.

So where, then, does a difference emerge? In part the difference lies in the way religious language embodies proclamation, announcement, invitation, reception, and an authoritative declaration of inclusion and acceptance. The child is ferried across the waters of baptism and received on the other shore. Clearly sociological language does not embody gestures of inclusion or involve personal 'address' in the name of transcendent divinity. But the difference of vocabularies also has to do with a wider sociological curiosity about all rites of initiation and inclusion. The sociologist seeks to place baptism as one variant of initiation alongside others which receive and incorporate for rather different purposes, such as communist youth ceremonies. It could be that such rites exhibit significant similarities in structure, in sequence, in kinds of requirement and demand, or in selection of symbols of fire and water. One particularly interesting similarity would be in the exaction of cost as a pre-condition of being received. In certain rituals there may be excoriation, subjection, and humiliation, or a painful process of marking, or a test of capacity or endurance. These costs can be viewed and re-viewed as corresponding to the manner in which the Christian child or adult undergoes symbolic or actual submergence. Once such parallels and correspondences have been reviewed a query can be put to the rite of baptism, for example—is this symbolic submergence a soft and gentle version of the genuinely painful rite of inclusion by circumcision? Could it be that a crucial difference between Christianity and Judaism is indicated by the difference between permanent biological incision on the genitals and a momentary gesture indicating and implying a mutation from doubt to commitment? Of course, that question can easily lead back once more to theology.

The argument would be that at the point where such questions arise the two languages of sociology and theology have set themselves different tasks. Theology as such has little interest in the structure of rites as a class or in the different kinds of cost that rites may exact. Its interest is in why this rite rather than that, or why in the Christian rite circumcision was abandoned in favour of baptism and confirmation.

Sociology, then, identifies structures, makes comparisons, and formulates probes and queries from the special viewpoint of orderly curiosity. In the case of baptism nothing is implied about the validity of the faith embodied in baptism. There is simply a widening of interest away from personal involvement towards curious and controlled observation of semi-comparable cases.

However, the area of interest can be widened further, though this does not prevent constant and fruitful return to theological understanding. A sociologist may be expected to show a particular kind of interest in the statistics of baptism, and one focus of that interest might be the decline in the numbers baptized in folk churches such as exist in England or Norway or, indeed, practically anywhere in Europe. The point about a folk church is that it receives all the folk, quasi-automatically, including children brought for initiation on the initiative of adults. These wide-open arms can be spoken of in theological terms as God's universal invitation or in sociological terms as the general availability of baptism at 'low cost'. Again, the alternative descriptions are not contradictory and can even perhaps be assimilated together.

But there is a further problematic lurking here, as follows. Folk churches belong by definition to the times of organic union between church and society. That means that they retain into the modern period a strong overlap between initiation into the church and initiation into civil society as such. Given that the modern period involves a fragmentation of organic unities and a loosening of connections between church and society, a strain may emerge in theological understandings of baptism. After all, one major support for baptism, i.e. the fact that it was understood as acceptance into civil society as such, has been removed. And as the numbers being presented for baptism decrease, theological concern heightens. Theologians may as easily observe the transition from the status of state church to voluntary association as do sociologists. At that point commissions may be appointed, not only to revise the rite but also to scrutinize the relationship between baptism and confirmation. Policy decisions by the church or by some of its clergy may result in greater stringency in the administration of baptism and a refusal automatically to accept parents who desire it for their children, with the further consequence that the numbers baptized decrease once again.

As a result of all this we see a whole series of changes. Those who compose liturgy and sit on commissions feel a pressure to be much more explicit about the nature of baptism and to require more active responses from the parents, the sponsors, and the Christian community. Adhesion to or incorporation in the church as a distinctive body occupies the mental foreground more than reception into the local community or the recognition of civil existence.

Now, of course, there was always a disparity between the strictly Christian understanding of the rite and the meanings mutely conferred on it by the natural or local community. That disparity was inherent in the very existence of a national or folk church, because the casket of Christian truth has been embedded or let into the good earth of automatic belonging in the family and the tribe. But now the partial severance of that ancient tie alerts the priestly guardians of Christian truth to the need for more precise definition and for a reconstitution of the whole theology of initiation. Indeed, initiation will emerge as a theme (or, as the Americans say, be 'thematized'). One response to the ensemble of changes—declining numbers, the partial loosening of the ancient organic tie, the pressure for more explicit meaning—will be a doubt about infant baptism itself and a more friendly survey of the Baptist position concerning voluntary adult commitment. There will also be a response from those outside the church, since the 'folk' will have lost a ceremony of entry into society as such, and may now seek to devise one. What was once joined together in a single ceremony is now separated out into an explicit Christian initiation and a newly devised ceremony for new arrivals in the human community. They lose their 'Christian' names and acquire 'forenames'.

But what was the object of that example with respect to the relationship between sociology and theology? In the first place the object was to select a signal of a fundamental shift away from organic unity of faith and community to voluntary association, rooted (so far as sociological theorizing is concerned) in a long-term process of differentiation of spheres. That process is not some metaphysical reduction of 'religion' to some underlying social base but an empirically observable and historically traceable set of changes. It does not mean that the relation of church to land or people is finally about to be severed or even that changes cannot occur in a reverse direction. It simply points to a 'fact', a social reality 'out there'.

But in the second place the object was to see how far the theological analysis of these changes differs in tone, focus, and purpose from the sociological analysis. Theologians may well make the same observations as sociologists, because there is nothing particularly mysterious or recondite about the sort of analytic sociological procedure just outlined. But insofar as theologians speak in their role of theologians, focused on their *opus proprium*, they treat the sociological analysis as a clarification of the context of their activity. It is not at the heart of their endeavour.

That heart has to do with the transition from darkness to light through the waters of death to the far shores of resurrection. It is a burying of the 'old Adam' and a celebration of a renewed humanity 'in Christ'. What in sociological terms is a rite of passage, analysable alongside other rites, is in Christian terms the great and singular change whereby 'this corruption puts on incorruption and this mortal puts on immortality'.

The two modes can be complementary but they are different. Nothing whatever follows for the validity of baptism or for the affirmation of the great change, except that infant baptism is accorded a particular social location so far as concerns its practice in folk churches. According a location to a practice does not itself undermine the theological reasons for infant baptism, although it does alert us to the problem of baptism in a society which changes its character.

SOCIOLOGICAL AND THEOLOGICAL VOCABULARIES: A SECOND EXAMPLE

So much for contextualization and so much for a particular attempt to place sociological and theological vocabularies in parallel facing columns. The question of different vocabularies is, however, even more complex than appears in that treatment of baptism. I want now to offer an example which amplifies the problematic of baptism in the context of the ancient union of church and land, faith and locality, religion and nation. If we have identified a lurking contradiction in Christian baptism being also a rite of entry into the local community, so there is a more ample contradiction in the Christian sign, the cross, being the emblem of national identity.

Why should the emblem of the Pilgrim People of God (so described by theologians) be also the emblem of a nation's identity, its history and its power? Plainly that is the case, and the cross is to be observed on the flags of England, Scotland, Norway, and a host of other countries. It is a sociological problem of some magnitude and (maybe) a theological offence as to how and why the emblem of redemptive sacrifice accompanies crusaders into bloody battle against infidels.

Since reference was made above to the key element of cost in baptism, so cost may be a key element in understanding this strange mutation in the practical theology of the cross. It may be that two fundamentally different kinds of cost have been juxtaposed and partially merged: first, the expense incurred by redemptive love in the redress of our indebtedness and chronic moral deficit, and second the expense incurred by soldiers in discharging duties of national survival. Let the question be rephrased to illuminate the relationship of sociology to theology.

The problem can be put thus. The cross is counterposed to the sword, the power of love to the love of power. The good news concerns peace, goodwill, and reconciliation. How is it, then, that the cross becomes the sword, both the sword of justice and the sword of national pride and imperial assertion? The cross stands on crusaders' shields and on national flags, as well as on hospitals and the vehicles of the International Red Cross. The cross as a sign of peace and of a non-violent individual sacrifice emerges in a thousand war cemeteries to commemorate mass sacrifice in war. Why?

There is another way to put this dialectic. Christianity rapidly came to constitute a universalization and spiritualization of fundamental social concepts: the land, the city, the kingdom, power, and warfare. Jerusalem and Zion are 'above' and God's kingdom is expanded not by force but by the sword of the spirit. But for reasons which have to do with the nature of social integration and regulation, with the struggle for survival and for just relationships within and between social groups, this message has *in part* to mutate back again to its temporal location, in fresh earthly cities, in new 'holy lands', in godly nations or, for that matter, in the temporal politics of social gospel or liberation theology.

The above example is entirely sociological, since it has to do with the mutation of ideas in the furnace of social processes. It lies at a junction where religion and politics, faith and community, are mutually and massively implicated together, and so illustrates the linkage of the religious and the political. But with only one shift of tonality it could provide the structure of a theological argument.

That example suggests that some of the basic elements dealt with by sociology overlap some of the basic elements of theological discourse. They both deal with land, city, exodus, exile, transition, entry, warfare, power, sacrifice, and so on, but whereas sociology traces webs of connection, theology reassembles these realities as a solid poetry concerned with imperatives of hope and necessary cost. These dramatic poles of hope and cost, vision and sacrifice, draw into their scope all the resources of emblem and image, for example, the sacrificial lamb and the visionary lion, crossings through waters of death and waters of life, journeys through wildernesses of testing to delectable mountains, the grass that withers and the rose that never fades. The primary emblems of light and darkness correspond almost exactly to hope and cost and to the underlying ground of everything—life and death, provided these are understood as complementary: the gift of life by a passage through death.

Perhaps this imagery begins to look as if it lies at some distance from sociology, but the common ground, in fact, remains even if treated in very different modes. Take, for example, the vocabulary of peace and violence central to both. Sociology and theology both recognize a creative turbulence occurring as the power of the flood waters of religion effects a junction with the mainstream of politics. Each discipline recognizes that peace and violence twist and turn in this maelstrom, the one turning into the other and vice versa. But sociology analyses the paradoxical interconnections while theology absorbs, dramatizes, and images the paradoxes themselves as they are worked out in the stuff of human existence. Thus the enactments of faith are the social and human realities of peace and violence cast into a condensed drama in the intimate company of hope and cost, light and darkness, life and death, presence and absence. Taking only the strand of peace and violence, the Eucharist is a representation of the unity of peace and the violence of the broken body: the body of Christ, the body of his people, the body of the polis and of the peoples of the world. To put it another way, it is a union of love's helpless expense in pursuit of peace and of the spirit's recuperative power after violence. Peace and violence, love and power: is there a more fundamental vocabulary? It is here, of course, where an entry may be effected from sociology to theology, should one so desire.

SOCIOLOGY AND THE TENSION BETWEEN HOPE AND LIMIT

The final set of themes covered in these essays has to do with confrontation between the religious vision carried by the Church (in all its forms) and the processes of social interaction with respect to power, wealth, and local solidarity and violence. Christianity brings forward 'on the books' and through icon and liturgical action a repertoire of hopes concerning the rule of God, meaning by that the meeting of all humans in the heavenly city and their shared pleasure in a common banquet. This vision of human unity is inevitably a hope of peace and harmony based on love, respect, fairness towards neighbours, and reconciliation.

Plainly 'the world' is not like that, and Christianity aims to 'overcome the world'. But there immediately arises a problem as to whether this victory can be achieved now on the contemporary time-scale, or is an option for the 'athletes of God', or is held over the world in temporal suspense as a criterion of judgement. Nor is that the only problem because the Church, in order to work within 'the world', assimilates some of its characteristics, including disunity, power, wealth, violence, and vengeance. It therefore has to elaborate codes of viable compromise, and in so doing raises up fresh witnesses to the pristine vision. In this way Christian civilization becomes simultaneously an infiltration of hope into the world and an overcoming of hope by the world. Such a civilization is disturbed and perturbed by its own hidden treasury of possibilities, embodied in icon and image, including the broken image of Christ who absorbed the tension in his own body. So the perturbation and the brokenness are represented and continually re-enacted at the heart of Christianity, often under conditions of incongruous splendour.

The problems which exercise such a civilization, insofar as it is Christian, have precisely to do with unity and its lack, including its potent absence among Christians, and with peaceability, and its lack. Christianity, therefore, generates a discourse about its own relation to the polis, both in the interim and in the long term, and this involves some understanding of the political and some conceptualization of 'the way of the world'. Given the nature of Christianity, its discourse about the political and about the world acquires a certain tonality and runs into characteristic paradoxes. It is here that sociology can be relevant as an empirical discourse about social and political process, because it can analyse how and why the paradoxes arise and penetrate their form. Sociology can help untangle a puzzle about the turbulence set up by religious vision, about the way it can be tamed or diverted within the church, and about the paradoxes set up by the special angle of Christian comment and witness. A sociology which helps untangle this puzzle can even be used in the armoury of Christian apologetic, since much that happens by way of divisions between churches or by way of violence between Christian peoples or through violence in general can be seen as deeply embedded in social nature and process. 'It needs be that offences will come.'

But what exactly is deeply embedded? In detail that turns on contrasts which are constant and inter-related. One is the contrast between 'Moral Man' and 'Immoral Society' as formulated by Reinhold Niebuhr. This contrast turns around the possibilities of love and forgiveness which exist at the personal level and the exigencies which govern different kinds of collective action, for example of nations or political parties or classes. These kinds of collective action all involve disciplines of solidarity, and leadership depends on observing these disciplines. In other words a leader is bound by the 'interested' character of the collectivity he represents. He—or she—simultaneously initiates and is subject to the disciplines required by loyalty, by survival, and the long-term pursuit of certain ends. Clearly, the linkages here are very complex and to articulate them is to anticipate the argument in Part II. The point to note here is the pervasive nature of the contrast between the personal and the collective.

The second and related contrast referred to above has to do with the diversity of moral roles available, depending on the kind of social space you occupy. The limits encountered by a solitary witness are not identical with those encountered by a religious leader and the limits encountered by a religious leader are (often) not identical with those encountered by someone actually exercising power and authority. One inserts the word 'often' because religious leaders may themselves be assimilated to this or that degree to the culture of the political classes or be semi-subject to them. There is, all the same, a certain complementarity and diversity of moral roles, and these roles offer varied rhetorical and practical possibilities. Of course, a religious leader may traverse the distance between roles and emerge as a fully fledged politician, but what then happens to him will illuminate the difference between the social space of religion and the social space of politics. One has only to consider, for example, the situation of Bishop Lazlo Tokes now that he is a political leader of the Hungarian minority in Romania as compared with his situation when he was (virtually) a lone prophetic voice. Previously he was imprisoned by the Romanian Securitate, but relatively free in what he said, but now he is imprisoned by his role and by the group dynamics of ethnic minority politics. He, therefore, has to adopt certain positions in the interests of personal and group survival.

Only one other general point needs to be made with respect to the essays in Part II. It is that limits are expressed above all in the varied costs attendant on alternative options and in the rather restricted range of options in practice normally available. One of the temptations of Christians and liberals (and therefore of Christian liberals and liberal Christians) is to assemble wish-lists of amiable desiderata, not asking how far these may exclude one another and what are their relative costs. Of course, 'opportunity cost' is a central concept of economics, but it is equally central to sociology and has to be deployed with unshrinking realism. Part of that realism is to understand things as they are and to follow the logic of social entailment. By that I mean that in social life one thing does follow from another in extended series of spiralling consequences. Socio-logic has to do with what follows from the pursuit of particular options, and that involves, so far as may be, pre-science and pre-vision. In that sense sociology is a practical science, and its understanding of 'practice' includes the dialectic of religious vision and social practicality. The five Chapters 8–12 are, therefore, explorations of that dialectic. There is no discipline more salutary to religious vision, or more helpful to understanding the empirical vicissitudes of vision than being forced to ask the basic question as to what is actually the case and what is most likely to follow from a given course of action. Sociology can, therefore, be part of a moral discipline imposed by reality. It also underscores the theological affirmation that the banquet is both here already and not yet. The good and the bad 'grow together to the harvest'.

PART I

Theoretical Considerations

2

Theology in a (Social) Scientific Culture

LET us suppose that sociology is indeed part of what is called scientific culture. As we shall see there are some complexities in making that supposition, certainly as regards the strictly scientific nature of some kinds of sociological work. But for the moment we need only hold that there is a long tradition of controlled thinking about social phenomena which aims at uncovering what elements coexist with what other elements and what pre-conditions lead to what consequences. That tradition seeks to accumulate instances which exemplify characteristic trends and tendencies, to provide persuasive rationales of those trends and tendencies, and to specify the circumstances under which they cease to operate. It is to that extent indubitably scientific.

Of course, the instances which sociology builds up cannot for the most part be acquired by controlled experiment and by the manipulation of variables. Rather they have to be carefully culled by a method of historical and cross-cultural selection and comparison. This means that conclusions are often no better than modestly persuasive and are even on occasion based on appeals to imaginative propriety. Some are intuitively correct, some counter-intuitive. At the same time, there are usually shared criteria to which researchers may appeal, and rational persons regularly contend with each other in terms of those criteria. The evidence adduced and the criteria appealed to may both be 'soft' but that does not in itself render the judgements arrived at unscientific. Nor for that matter does softness make the practice of sociology easy. It does not follow because materials are soft that they are easily handled. On the contrary the raw stuff of sociology is often very hard to handle, which may help account for the undoubted fact that a great deal of sociological work is jejune, confused, and ill-judged.

Sociology, then, is indeed a science, and one which is hard precisely because many of its materials and governing criteria are so soft. Theology, too, is hard and soft, and in a somewhat similar manner, though there are those, of course, who argue that the database of theology is so soft as to be conjured up solely by the imagination. At any rate sociologists and theologians both sift soft materials deploying the kinds of rigour which may be appropriate. And this similarity between them makes it difficult to establish how the one impinges upon the other. Those trying to relate the precarious to the precarious may well lose their footing.

There are other important similarities which also bear on the articulation of the relationship between sociology and theology. In the first place, neither sociology nor theology operates according to an undisputed paradigm. There exist a multiplicity of modes of operation and of kinds of procedure in each subject. These modes are linked by no more than a family likeness, which enables one to recognize that such and such piece of a work *is* sociological or theological.

Again, neither sociology nor theology has entirely abandoned its classical formulations. That, maybe, is not suprising so far as concerns theology, but it is also unexpectedly true of sociology. Aristotle and Machiavelli are not dead for contemporary sociology in the way that Kepler is dead for contemporary natural science. The point is a complex one, and if properly investigated could detain us for a long time, but it is at least clear that the natural scientists of the past are not part of the contemporary debate as are Marx, Durkheim, and Weber. In sociology even veins of enquiry which at one time seemed almost exhausted can be reopened and revisited.

Clearly, the lack of an undisputed paradigm and the frequency of revivals affects any attempt to relate the two subjects, since it is partly a question of which theological or sociological mode is under consideration, and which revival is currently under way. Indeed, it is not altogether certain that either sociology or theology can produce that which is entirely novel. There have been advances in the past, yet there is in both cases a query about the advent of 'the new'. Such a situation in which advance is possible and yet novelty uncertain may seem too paradoxical to be sustained, but it nevertheless appears correct.

From this it follows that just as the classical foundations of sociology and theology do not go dead and distant so the master metaphors of both are constantly being recovered and reused. These recoveries derive from a more fundamental shared characteristic, which is the inherently metaphorical character of sociological and theological discourse. In sociology, as also in theology, metaphorical language is endemic. Perhaps theology is more metaphorical than sociology but sociology is at least metaphorical. Of course, both subjects devise technical vocabularies, but these remain continuous with ordinary language and with its metaphorical character. Sociology and theology are equally capable of being understood by the ordinary literate person, which is precisely why ordinary literate persons complain about the opacity of their specialized usages.

This contention means that the relations between theology and sociology are such as hold between varieties of ordinary discourse, and may therefore be bedevilled by the extraordinary and uncontrolled richness of language. For example, a sociologist may use a metaphor from hydraulics or optics or from the general notion of mechanism which carries uncontrolled overtones. Ideas may be said to 'reflect' economic conditions. Weber, in a classic discussion, referred to ideas as 'switchmen' on a railway track, controlling the direction of social movements but not causing them. The usage is simultaneously illuminating and misleading, but insofar as it is misleading may appear to cause problems for theology where none exist.

The problem of relating two discourses rooted in ordinary language does not end there. The ordinary writing of ordinary language mixes modes almost as rapidly as music changes keys. A piece of writing, which in its general tenor is mostly sociological or mostly theological, may veer rapidly through several other kinds of logic and modality. (Similarly, writing which defines itself as primarily literature or history can rapidly veer towards sociology or theology.) So far as sociology and theology are concerned it is clear that it is even possible for theological discourse actually to incorporate sociology, though I am not sure how far the reverse may be true. I mean that theologians, especially those who at the present time declare themselves committed to a liberating mission (or an emancipatory project) engage in a variety of sociology. Their sociology is controlled by theological presuppositions usually operating at some distance from the analysis. Such mixtures of modes certainly make relationships between theology and sociology confusing. It means, among other things, that sociologists are sometimes criticizing theologians for having misconstrued their sociology.

When I say I am uncertain whether a sociologist may veer towards theology as easily as a theologian may veer towards sociology, I do not mean that sociologists never work within theological presuppositions. Some of them undoubtedly work with a theological limit set to what they are willing to regard as thinkable. They may, for example, baulk at the idea of total secularization because they hold Christianity or some other faith to be true and/or indestructible. Such sociologists are hardly in a majority, but they do exist. What is more frequent, perhaps even usual, is the importation of assumptions about the constitution of society and especially about social development and social ontology which are derived from secular metaphysics or ideology. For example, in discussions of social development, religion is assumed to be evanescent. This assumption in turn often rests on a social ontology which treats religion as inherently impotent and causally derivative. This means that when the relations between sociology and a theology are at issue it is important to tease out the kind of metaphysic or ideology in which the sociology may be embedded. The supposed problem for theology may lie in the remoter metaphysical underpinnings of the sociology.

Such a candid admission may seem to be yet another reason for discounting the claim of sociology to count as any kind of science at all. This is simply not the case. A sharper perception of the existence of ideological frames and assumptions is in itself an advance towards some less tainted form of observation. The argument about ideology cannot be further pursued here, beyond asserting that sociology does contain the possibility of autonomous discourse controlled by its specific subject-matter. The important point in this context is for theology to subject itself to examination solely with respect to that autonomous discourse and not to stay bemused by ideological and metaphysical underpinnings. Indeed, an acute and aggressive theologian may assist the sociological enterprise itself by noting the way sociologists 'frame' their understanding of social development and utilize their social ontology independently of what the subject-matter itself may demand. Unfortunately the theologians most inclined to use sociology are often least inclined to question its ideological underpinnings (or 'domain assumptions'). They too easily run along the historical trackways undergirding notions of social development and too rapidly accept dehumanizing accounts of the social realm or dogmas as to what social layers (economic, structural) are to be regarded as causally prior, efficient, or powerful.

DOING SOCIOLOGY

From these preliminary observations it may well appear that doing theology or doing sociology is already far too problematic without attempting to relate the two. I intend, however, to pursue that relationship unimpeded by too much inhibition. If Professors Hoyle and Wickramsinghe can adduce extraordinary 'external' sources for the constitution of our universe perhaps a sociologist need not feel bound hard and fast by the more restrictive canons about what is to count as 'science'. Indeed, in the formulation of hypotheses, and of imaginative frames and reconstructions of material, the sociologist should be simultaneously bold and cautious. If what he or she has to say is of any consequence the community of scientific peers will not be slow to provide comprehensive criticism and as many caveats as may be appropriate. So in what follows I intend to 'do sociology' boldly and on a large canvas in order to see what such uninhibited sociological activity may generate by way of theological worry. I proceed now to devise a connected set of sociological reflections specifically about religion to see to what extent a theologian may be made uneasy. Every now and then I may pause to indicate where I think uneasiness could occur, and in the final section I shall try to mark out the areas of unease more systematically.

In the following extensive tract of sociology I begin with the classical concepts of church and sect, concentrating on the former. This will immediately enable me to illustrate the proximity of sociological concepts to ordinary 'messy' language as well as the elements of theoretical distance and sociological purification. It will also enable me to sketch a sociological 'frame' for understanding ecclesiology. I then go on to analyse a historical mutation of 'church' and of collateral theological concepts which are to be found in the emerging relationship of religion to ethnic nationalism. The advantage provided here is the opportunity to use functional language about religion as it partially merges into ethnic nationalism and thus to raise the issue of when religion is still 'really' and 'effectively' religion. If religion is observed to retain social power only when associated with ethnic nationalism, what does that say to us about the 'real' social roots of 'faith'? This is part of the question just raised about the social ontology of religion. I conclude the sociological exposition by looking at one major consequence of the break-up of the Church as sociologically conceived. That consequence is the emergence of individually chosen spiritual biographies, and along with that a discernible pattern of conversion and revival. Certain problems presumably arise in attempting to order that pattern of conversion in terms of social roles, cultural slipways, and structured openings. Such a sequence of problem areas as I have outlined is fairly coherent and clearly enables a wide range of issues to be raised *en route*.

The concepts 'church' and 'sect' have, of course, received a classical formulation at the hands of Troeltsch and have undergone a prolonged process of refinement and extension through decades of discussion. I do not intend to expound either the classical formulation or the course of the subsequent debate. The reason for that lies in the way concepts take on different content according to who is using them and according to his or her analytic intention. They are for use not for reification. The sociological usages of 'church' derive from discrete sets of related phenomena which the analyst selects out of the range indicated by the ordinary usage of the word. Within that discrete set the sociologist assembles the internal linkages of his concept on the basis of proto-empirical connections. Or, to put it another way, the sociologist absorbs the characteristics of institutions ordinarily called 'churches' through a sociological filter, together with the specifically sociological usages of church, and then rearranges these varied elements according to his own analytic purposes and with respect to their own inner socio-logic.

In the sociological meaning of the term a 'church' emerges when the body of believers achieves a relation to the whole body politic whereby it is sucked into the vortex of social necessities, especially those pertaining to power and sovereignty. As the religious body becomes integrated with the body politic it receives the indelible stigmata of social stratification, of political necessity, and of preponderant power. The hierarchical elements which are already present in the church, as they are in all developed organizations, now receive strong reinforcement. At the same time the acceptance of legitimate violence is greatly accelerated. The hierarchy of the church now runs parallel to the social hierarchy and may well share some of its functions and sometimes recruit from identical cadres.

As this partial fusion occurs the membership of the church changes character and so do the rites of incorporation into membership. These changes are summarized in the shift from the voluntary to the involuntary. Thus baptism is now not so much an inner voluntary transition from darkness to light confirmed by fellow-believers but rather a recognition of civil status on the part of the whole society. It follows that to leave the church is to leave civil society as such, and to embrace heresy is also to embrace treason. The existence of an all-embracing institution means that the average sensual man is now willy-nilly within the ambit of 'the church', so that those who desire standards above the average must develop specialized institutions for that purpose. Ideal aspirations derived from the foundation documents of faith are shunted into monastic sidings.

These comprehensive changes inherent in the emergence of 'church' are signalled in the conceptual and iconic spheres. For example, the idea of 'lord' is partially assimilated to the idea of secular lordship. The whole spiritual armour of God materializes as the temporal sword, and the universal cross is converted into a symbol of local political identity. Reversals of the social hierarchy and critiques of wealth in the original gospel become almost invisible or else they are subject to hermeneutic manipulation and treated as marginal and vestigial. Those original potentials of the gospel which are not compatible with the ordinary systemic requirements of developed imperial societies, or for that matter with the institutions of a decentralized feudalism, are put into storage. Occasionally there will be attempts to establish the peace of the church or to outlaw a new weapon of frightfulness (like the crossbow) or to control personal profiteering, but such attempts either collapse or are gradually circumvented.

However, the idea of 'storage' is important, since the encapsulation of revolutionary potential either in mysterious images of political and economic reversal or in specialized institutions provides the basis for sectarian development. The church somnambulistically recites a thematic repertory, parts of which will be picked up as they come to resonate with the aspirations, needs, and interests of radical and other groups. The sects can be seen as embodying every kind of experiment in political and economic organization, in sexual reproduction, in peaceability, and in fraternity. They are often early platforms in consciousness which set before the general population new models and fresh possibilities, as well as providing exemplary warnings of what is involved in anarchic disintegration.

This leads to a paradoxical observation. Christianity is not a very promising religion as the ideological basis of an empire, given the degree of adjustment required to ensure what sociologists call the 'imperative coordination' of large social units. On the other hand the degree of adjustment required provides precisely those stored up energies which explode in every form of monastic or sectarian experimentation, including the radical reduction of hierarchy in small groups and the abolition of violence. Thus the sect is the necessary and fruitful vehicle of difficult angles of social and spiritual vision, built into the original Christian proclamation and stored by the church.

Now it may be that there are mild queries for theology or for certain theologies raised by such an account of church and sect, notably in the account given of rites of incorporation like baptism, and of sectarian development. But rather than break into the flow of sociological characterizations, I will hold such queries in reserve and proceed rather to trace two ways in which the social reality of 'church' may mutate. The first of these concerns the mutation of the church which occurs when it becomes a carrier for ethnic nationalism. The partial fusion of 'church' with ethnic identity allows a brief examination of the implications of functional language.

Over the last three or four centuries the Christian religion has undergone a partial fusion with the power of ethnic nationalism. Sometimes this has been associated with the emergence of an independent national church like the Church of England, and sometimes it has been associated with Gallicanism or its equivalents. In any event the consequences are much the same. The phenomenon is easily recognizable among Afrikaaners, Slovaks, Croats, Greeks, and Irish alike. Though the Church retains its credal and liturgical structures it begins also to act as a marker of identity, a vehicle of national consciousness, and a reservoir of historic memories and customs.

This momentous shift takes on special intensity where a superior and alien power exercises political sovereignty at the expense of local autonomy. Thus church attendance is unusually high and Catholic sentiment unusually intense among Croats, Poles, the Catholic Irish, the Basques, and so on. The same phenomenon may occur where the group concerned cherishes or acquires some marginal advantage which is threatened by another group of different faith and ethnic identity, as for example among the Maronites of Lebanon, the Ulster Protestants, and the Fiji Methodists. The precise mixtures of ethnicity and religiosity vary in each case, but variations on the theme of peoplehood and faith are to be observed almost universally from the English to the Maoris and the Afrikaaners.

Under pressure of conflict, especially wars of independence, ethnic religiosity comes over time to represent a faith which is only para-Christian. The key doctrines of classic Christianity are translated so as to ensure they serve the national cause and reinforce its militancy. Thus in the struggle of Ulster Protestants to retain the right to make an independent political choice the idea of the Covenant People becomes coextensive with their identity as a national group. Likewise in the earlier struggle of Catholic Irish for their independence, Ireland itself was identified as sacred and those who died in its cause were regarded as martyrs. In Poland the whole nation granted itself the status of suffering Messiah. Charles Péguy perfectly expressed this type of sentiment as it has developed in France by proclaiming 'Blessed are they who die for the Carnal City!' In this instance we see quite dramatically how external adhesion to Christianity may appear intense but the actual content of the faith turns out to be the reverse of Christian. Christian universality and inter-nationalism (like socialist and liberal internationalism) go down before the power of ethnic faith. The questions which then emerge with reference to (say) Polish Catholic nationalism are obvious: is it really religion and is it proper Christianity?

However, more is involved than the nationalization of Chris-tianity and the tuning of Christian symbols to subserve ethnic sentiment and solidarity. It is a matter of empirical observation that the redoubts of religiosity are most secure precisely in those areas, usually peripheral and often somewhat retarded eco-nomically, where the ethnic consciousness of a minority is or-ganized for cultural defence. What then does this imply? How far can it be taken to mean that the momentum and power of 'faith' in (say) Brittany or Wales, in Quebec or the Southern States of the USA, is mainly or in part derived from its function in maintaining ethnic solidarity?

This kind of explanatory move, in which ethnicity is designated a primary carrier for religion, is closely related to functional analysis. Functional analysis comes in many forms, some of them functional*ist*. In the Durkheimian version of functional*ism*, religion is accounted 'real' because it is 'essentially' the vehicle of group identity. Religion supposedly projects the idealized form of group consciousness which it then offers for the self-worship of the group.

However, this version of functionalism is not only theologically offensive but highly problematic. Religion is simultaneously accounted real and yet it is reduced to an emanation of Society with a capital 'S'. Such a view cannot be supported by sociological evidence since it derives from a social metaphysic. One cannot begin to imagine the mode of its verification or falsification. Yet oddly enough it creates a framework for understanding religion which generates insights. It is the randy progenitor of interesting truths without itself being true. To watch the rituals of political conventions in the United States is indeed to observe a self-communion with the idea of one's own collective transcendence focused in a human totem. So we have the curious phenomenon of an unverifiable and unfalsifiable sociological theory of religion which nevertheless offers fruitful understandings.

Apart from this strongly reductionist doctrine, functionalism offers other less speculative approaches to religion conceived as a carrier of ethnic identity. Group identity and survival are viewed as sucking religion inwards in order to provide fundamental social support. Religion 'functions' to assist the continuing maintenance of the social whole. Such language borrows from biological notions of the self-regulating organism and is part of a 'systemic' approach to society in which the whole exercises a constraining influence on the parts in the interests of survival, and in which there is a strain towards consistency among the various parts. But even this kind of functionalism is today adjudged highly problematic or else straightforwardly condemned for circularity. Yet there are phenomena which are usefully indicated by functionalism, notably the struggle to maintain the social fabric or to recover and revivify it. In this perspective religious revivals may be seen as part of 'revitaliza- tion' movements aimed at restoring social vigour.

But, of course, two dangers immediately present themselves, one minor, one major. The minor danger is that terms like 'revitalization' and 'restoration' easily acquire overtones of ethical approval, and these overtones need to be noted and bracketed. The major danger is that religious revival is easily characterized as 'just' a revitalization movement. Undoubtedly there is in some religious revivals a revivification of collective consciousness, for example in Wales in 1904. But it is again difficult to see by what criteria a revival can be unequivocally adjudged 'just' a revitalization movement. What possible basis can there be for such a reduction? We are once more confronted with a sociological theory for which the criteria of falsification or verification are hard to state, and yet, the underlying insight seems to have some imaginative truth in it. As always, the question is: 'How much?' And if there is a grain of truth in either the language of revitalization or even the broader func- tionalist frame, what kind of query could that possibly raise for theology?

At this juncture it may be worth noting a related variety of reductionism embedded in some interesting tricks of sociologi- cal rhetoric. This rhetoric depends on the transfer of terms from one kind of social movement to another in order to bring out unnoticed similarities. Thus black emancipation in America over the past quarter of a century, including its religious compo- nent, defines itself and is defined sociologically as a civil rights movement. That causes no problem. However, the present author would also describe the expansion of the free churches in mid-nineteenth-century Britain as part of a civil rights move- ment on the part of the upper working and artisan classes. I would point out, as have others, that the peak of Nonconformist membership came at the peak of the Liberal Party triumph and that the decline of Nonconformity ran parallel to the decline of Liberalism. As in all the previous instances the problem is to decide just how far the social thrust is crucial to the religious momentum. The parallelism between expansion and decline in the religious and in the political spheres does indeed suggest that there is some kind of linkage, which includes the capacity of group militancy and even resentment to impart extra energy to religious solidarity. It makes plausible sense to relate Nonconformist decline in part to the uncoupling of faith from the sources of energy deployed to achieve civil rights. 'Faith' freewheeling on its own after (say) the mid-1920s was not sufficient to sustain commitment and momentum. Yet to describe nineteenth-century Nonconformity as basically a civil rights movement would be entirely illegitimate. An insight would have been carelessly transformed into yet another false reduction.

I turn now to a second mutation of 'church' which involves the break-up of the all-inclusive and authoritative institution and the emergence of voluntary sectors where people exercise choice and exhibit inner religious biographies. Ecclesiastical monopoly gives way to a religious *laissez-faire* in which rival religious firms compete on the market for souls. The free market gives rise to multiple schism.

The development of inner religious biographies and of spiritual diaries in an atmosphere of religious choice makes possible individual conversion and mass conversion. For individual conversion to occur the all-inclusive ecclesiastical frame has to have collapsed. That constitutes a general pre-condition and is quite close to being tautological. Thus there were next to no 'conversions' in Latin America prior to 1850 except of the kind where Spain first incorporated whole populations politically and then incorporated them religiously. However, the way in which the inclusive frame breaks down and ceases to be 'natural' varies systematically from one society to another. This systematic variation can be codified in terms of five or six basic patterns. Two of these have now to be articulated in order to come at the phenomenon of revival and conversion.

There is a Southern European and South American pattern in which the ecclesiastical monopoly initially endeavours to tighten its grip and then suffers a catastrophic breakdown into warfare between a solidary group of clericals and a solidary group of anti-clericals. By contrast there is an Anglo-Saxon pattern in which a voluntary sector, appearing originally in

England, is transferred to America and there becomes the social norm. This means that revivals and conversions were likely in Des Moines and unlikely in Lyons or Asturias or Lima. The point is obvious, but the existence of an explicable social geography of conversion needs to be underlined. It is crucial to the purposes of this argument.

Of course, things may change and do so quite rapidly. A pattern which almost precludes conversion may mutate. Thus in contemporary Latin America from about 1960 onwards, a new pattern has appeared out of a combination of the Anglo-Saxon pattern and the Latin pattern. Conversions occur by the million, many of them within the Roman Catholic Church itself, and people begin to express their faith 'spontaneously'. This is where a social geography of conversion becomes clearly discernible. Few are saved in Uruguay or Venezuela and large harvests of souls are garnered on 'the other side of the boat' in Brazil and Chile. Variation of this kind is perfectly well known. It attracts explanations which I could offer were there space to do so, and maybe they contain no threat for theology or for classical accounts of the economy of salvation. (I mean by the 'economy of salvation' the way theology articulates the access which people have to saving grace, having proper regard to their varied situations.)

Yet the point may be pressed further at the micro-level and amounts to claiming that the sociology (or social geography) of conversion is able to give intelligible accounts of how persons ensconced in one social structural situation are more or less likely to respond to calls for conversion. The anthropologists Reina and Schwartz, for example, conducted a study of conversion in three towns of El Petén, Guatemala, and concluded that people were more likely to change their faith in town *B* at an interim level of development, than in town *A*, which was traditionally and organically sealed, or than in town *C*, which constituted a developed civic centre and regional market.[1]

For this geography of conversion to make complete sense

[1] Reina, Rubem E. and Schwartz, Norman B., 'The Structural Context of Religious Conversion in El Petén, Guatemala', *American Ethnologist*, 1/1 (1974), 157–91.

much more detail would be required, which is not really possible in such a discussion as this. However, it is worth referring to a further element in the analysis which is that in town *C*, the civic centre, the counter-élite of the place took up reformed Catholicism rather than evangelical Protestantism. Reformed Catholicism enabled them to distance themselves from the control exercised by the traditional élite in secular and in religious fora, and to satisfy their more individualized religious needs. Like Protestantism, it offered an activist and participatory faith and thus provided a 'functional equivalent' of evangelical conversion. The point is important because the sociology of conversion identifies certain basic psychological and social 'needs' in specific milieux and also suggests that various alternative religious or even political movements will serve as 'functional equivalents' with respect to their satisfaction.

Clearly the language of functional equivalents and of psycho-social 'needs' leaves considerable scope for inventive hypotheses, and many of these are based on the theory of deprivation, about which something needs to be said.

Undoubtedly theories of deprivation have been the stock in trade of sociologies of conversion. When one type of deprivation is inconveniently absent, sociologists have usually adduced another and yet another until it may be concluded that all humankind is in this way or that deprived or 'needy'. Of course, it is the case that in certain circumstances the poor find in religion a message which makes sense of their situation and which offers some personal deliverance or reversal of the current order. There are, to use Lanternari's phrase, 'Religions of the oppressed'. But one still cannot loosely extrapolate from such data to views which either specifically reduce the religions of the oppressed to epiphenomena of deprivation without remainder, or else roundly conclude that all religion is exhaustively described as compensatory. Distinguished sociological practitioners have come close to this, and it is a proper task for theologians to subject their concepts, their language, and their methodology to philosophical and empirical criticism. Charles Glock's theories as to the several kinds of deprivation and Rodney Stark's formulations as to religious 'compensators' offer themselves as interesting candidates for rigorous examination.

What has to be stressed is the varieties of vocabulary available, some of them carrying less far-reaching overtones than others. The language of 'compensators' used by Stark is certainly tough and far-reaching, and intended as such. Other writers, for example Smelser in his study of family, religion, etc. in the English Industrial Revolution, use a much softer language of strain and adjustment derived from functionalist premisses.[2] That language is, so to speak, less stark.

I, myself, in my current study of conversion in Latin America, use the language of disturbance and mobilization. After all, Methodism has been described as one of the earliest instances of mass mobilization: the coming of a group or of several groups to a certain degree of self-consciousness. The term is borrowed from political science, where it is used with respect to the emergence of socio-political self-consciousness, and in that context it apparently carries no overtone of epiphenomenalist reduction—partly because political movements are mostly (and mysteriously) exempted from the epiphenomenalist reduction. Such language as 'disturbance' and 'mobilization' represents the *sine qua non* of sociological understanding and as such presents theologians with the nub of whatever problem there is to be faced.

The only issue *au fond* is whether theologians are happy with the general supposition that movements of the spirit co-respond to lines of social fault emerging in upheavals of social structure. Or to put it more precisely: are theologians happy with the general supposition that the take-off of movements—and the degree of power exhibited in their expansion, minimally includes the ability of the message to resonate with parallel changes in social circumstance. Presumably theologians will want to articulate that general supposition in such a way that the originating power of the Word is *not* comprehensively subsumed in the language of social needs, compensations, and adjustments. It is a task they should now address.

---

[2] Smelser, Neil J., *Social Change in the Industrial Revolution* (Chicago: University of Chicago Press, 1959).

FORMS OF FRAMING

In what remains with respect to my own sociological exposition, I intend to change tack somewhat and offer examples of how sociological work on conversion may be set within linguistic and especially political frames. These frames have prima-facie implications for theology and should attract assessments and critiques from theologians.

The main object of adducing these theories is to indicate their imaginative character, and the extent to which they are seriously underdetermined by the evidence. Whereas Reina and Schwartz make detailed sense, the theories now to be examined, or at any rate parts of them, depend to a significant extent on intuitive appeal, or even on the half-hidden props about history and politics and progress to which we all almost automatically defer. That is not to say that they are necessarily wrong. It is simply to underline the problematic nature of the constructions now to be presented and by extension to indicate just how debatable is their import for theology.

The first construction is not really a fully articulated theory, but a tract of polemical text excerpted from David Stoll's *Fishers of Men or Builders of Empire*.[3] This excerpt concerns his account of the missionary effort made in Guatemala by the Wycliffe Bible Translators/Summer Institute of Linguistics (WBT/SIL). Stoll combines perspectives of a broadly sociological type with a strong overtone of political and moral disapproval. Such a combination is by no means unusual in sociological (or anthropological) texts, though in the brief account which follows I have not brought out the sharply critical overtone found in the book as a whole.

His account goes something like this. In Guatemala, some seventy years ago, the anti-clerical government then in power both encouraged Protestantism and colluded in the exploitation of the Maya Indians. In a parallel way the plantation-owners both welcomed the advent of the missionaries and encouraged slave-catchers to ply their victims with liquor. It was the view of

---

[3] Stoll, David, *Fishers of Men or Builders of Empire? The Wycliffe Bible Translators in Latin America* (Cambridge, Mass.: Cultural Survival, 1982).

the founder of WBT/SIL—Cameron Townsend—that the gospel could save masters and Maya alike. As soon as the Maya
abandoned vice and superstition they would become model
employees, and the masters for their part would replace debt
peonage with wages.

Stoll goes on to argue that the missionaries-cum-linguists associated with WBT/SIL inserted themselves in the process of
'internal colonialization', propagating the white man's power
and faith, yet siding with the Maya by saving their language,
creating their own indigenous churches, and, so far as they
could, preventing petty exploitation. Stoll briefly characterizes
the missionary perspective by saying that, 'Equations between
the power of antibiotics, prayer, literacy, and God's word, appealed to people comprehending tribulation and technology in
spiritual terms.'[4] From Stoll's point of view, the missionaries
were marshalling the Maya people for progress.[5]

Stoll describes this process as one in which Jesus pays the
debt, having been crucified by the Patrones of his own day, and
then himself becomes the new Patron. At this juncture we pause
only to note that we are presumably being offered an imaginative construct, which sets up certain equivalences between the
gospel story and the situation of the Maya, and which goes on to
suggest how that story works on them psychologically, as well as
hinting at why it is effective.

At any rate, as a result of conversion the Indian is now in-
wardly motivated to self-improvement and work, and simultaneously moves out of the *cargo* system with its saints, its
expenses, its folk healers and ritual alcoholism. Stoll quotes
Townsend as saying that when drink and superstition have
gone, 'health and happiness enter the door'.[6] The underlying
point here is that the institutions of folk Catholicism offered
small protection against those Ladinos who were manipulating
debt and alcoholism in order to extract yet more land and to
control yet more workers. In that situation some of the Maya
were able the better to help themselves in a modest way through
Protestantism. In Stoll's view this is how a newly Protestant

---

[4] Stoll, David, 23.   [5] Ibid. 29.   [6] Ibid. 34.

(and reformed Catholic) petty bourgeoisie emerged in the Guatemalan highlands, though he adds that its 'path of advancement soon closed for other Maya.'[7] The newly converted and newly educated Protestants were able to use their command of two languages to negotiate with Ladinos and create ties with Ladino groups.

Now this kind of account of conversion is clearly sociological in its general provenance and indicates a problem for theology of an odd kind, which I shall underline once again in the final sections. Logically the withers of the theologian faced by such an account are quite unwrung. Yet the activity of Christianity on the ground has been rhetorically framed. We are given to understand how missionary activity marshalls native peoples for progress within the context of internal colonialism. The narrative is so constructed that the missionaries appear to act almost like somnambulists. They may perhaps perceive certain limited consequences, but in the last analysis they are effectively helping to extend the domination of the established Hispanic groups. True, the Protestant Maya received certain benefits, but the Maya as a whole were not able to achieve these benefits. So one has a sense of something 'wrong', of a misguided and subconscious activity. Of course, some elements in this account can be straightforwardly backed by evidence. Others, like the account of Jesus paying the debt, are no more than intuitive speculation. Yet others may be plausible but are heavily framed in critical language and negative terminology.

The second construction is expounded by Jean-Pierre Bastian. It represents sociology at its most benign and rejects the usual battery of reductionist ready-mades.[8] In particular Bastian rejects the Marxist (or left liberal) view which reduces Protestantism to no more than the ideological vanguard of North American expansion. It is necessary, as he rightly points out, to set conversion to Protestantism in a wide historical and cross-cultural perspective. Once that is done it becomes clear that many Protestants in late nineteenth-century Mexico took

[7] Ibid. 36.
[8] Bastian, Jean Pierre, *Protestantismo y Sociedad en México* (Mexico City: CUPSA, 1983).

part in the revolutionary vanguard, and that in contemporary Nicaragua many Protestants supported the Sandinistas.

Bastian goes on to argue that one must distinguish between a kind of Protestantism which is progressive and reformist and a kind which is reactionary and supports the status quo. There is a variety of urban Protestantism dominated by clerical bureaucracies which constitutes a reactionary agency of internal colonization and reproduces traditional kinds of authority in a revised format. This urban Protestantism has links with the USA and it utilizes North American technology and techniques for merchandising religion. There is, however, also a rural Protestantism, found among marginalized *campesinos*, which repudiates traditional authority and campaigns for economic and social redress.

Bastian then distinguishes phases within the development of Protestantism which run parallel to the development of a dependent capitalism. The older missionary Protestantism, which was linked to the 'liberal project', went into crisis, and this was accompanied by the rapid expansion of a Protestantism which was more spontaneous and more autonomous. This new wave of Protestantism affected the alienated and anomic masses as they emigrated to the megacities, and it disseminated a great deal of Cold War propaganda through radio, cassette, and television. Bastian comments that the new converts acquired only a fragmentary and individualistic understanding of society, and that their dualistic theology often led to political passivity, though not universally so. In rural areas millennarian and magical versions of dualistic Protestantism generated political activism and protest, as also occurred amongst some Protestants in urban Brazil and Chile.

I have presented this particular 'benign' example of the sociological analysis of conversion in order to illustrate certain very general characteristics of sociological writing which have to do with the way religion is framed, and which could therefore affect theology at one remove. The controlling interest of Bastian's analysis at this point is the contribution which Protestantism makes to certain kinds of political movement. These movements are in turn organized in a frame of social development. It becomes possible therefore to fit different kinds (or phases) of religion into a developmental sequence, which in turn enables certain kinds to be adjudged behind and pre-political, while other kinds are in the vanguard. Religious actors are reduced to players in a plot controlled by the cunning of sociological reason and judged by their contribution to the long-term political direction of that plot. They are somnambulists walking a terrain which can only be properly illuminated by varieties of sociological theory. They themselves do not 'see' what they are about.

Of course, theology may actually incorporate this variety of sociological theory, even though this entails important shifts of perspective about the appropriate mission of the church and its social role. Alternatively, theologians could mount a critique of this whole mode of thinking as not required by the evidence and as emanating from the political ideology of the radical secular intelligentsia. Whichever path is chosen it is clear that the challenge which sociology offers to theology is somewhat different from the challenge offered by most other subjects. It is a challenge arising from modalities of apprehension and of intellectual ordering some of which are underdetermined by evidence and/or influenced by political standpoints and perspectives.

A SURVEY OF PROBLEM AREAS

It is now possible to set out in summary fashion problems that may arise for theology, or some varieties of theology, on account of sociology, or some varieties of sociology.

One set of problems noted in the 'Preliminary Considerations' derived from the continuity between sociological discourse and ordinary language. The language of sociologists is replete with metaphors and analogies whose implications are difficult to control and therefore appear to create queries for theology. Mechanistic metaphors applied to social processes are especially likely to carry loose implications. Thus if religious solidarity is described as a 'carrier' for ethnic consciousness it easily appears that the carrier is an empty shell and that the cargo constitutes the real substance.

A second problem for theology, or at any rate for ecclesiology, may arise as part of the spin-off from the sociological
conceptualization of 'church'. Examples were earlier provided
of how a sociologist might understand the emergence of
hierarchical ordering in the church and how he might articulate
the relationship between infant baptism and a social order
where civil and religious memberships were coextensive and
automatic.

The problem seems to be that the hierarchical stratification of
the organization of the church and the way it is legitimated by
reference to an inherently sacred character may bear a suspi-
cious resemblance to the kinds of stratification and legitimation
once current (say) in medieval society. In that case a specific
ecclesiology comes to look suspiciously like the most long-
lasting 'shell' of an earlier social order.

Supposing this to be true historically, it is difficult to see quite
what it implies logically. Perhaps there is nothing more dangerous here than a certain relativization. Nevertheless, if one goes
on to relate the form of Christian initiation, i.e. infant baptism,
to the type of connection between church and society obtaining
under pre-modern conditions, then perhaps the implications for
theology (or, at any rate, certain kinds of baptismal theology)
become more pointed. If the total overlap of an organic church
with an organic society results in (or is cognate with) a transfer
of the concept of automatic involuntary incorporation from
society to church, then when the church emerges from the social
cocoon to become a voluntary group the concept of baptism
should undergo a similar mutation. In other words, the shape of
the liturgy of initiation alters with the 'shape' of the society.
However, this is not quite how rites are usually conceived by
normative ecclesiology.

Another problem may arise for ecclesiology from the parallelism posited between schismatic eruptions in the Christian
body and the fragmentation of society in accordance with the
interests and aspirations of rival groups. If the iconographic
repertory of the church is seen as a store of explosive materials
capable of fissionable contact with social fragmentation then
schism is inevitable and is rooted in the nature of Christianity

itself as well as in the nature of society. At one level theology may properly deprecate breakages in fellowship and deploy the language of 'sin'. At another level theology might discern a process of creative variation which enables a vast range of experiments to be undertaken in solving fundamental 'system problems'. The consequence is the conscious adoption of a double or bifocal vision. Through the lower focals one assesses phenomena in terms of what is normatively prescribed and/or sees breakages of unity as sinful. Through the upper focals one sees an inevitability issuing in a greater range of richness and in different emphases in order to circumvent different system problems.

The problems raised by sociological accounts of the interpenetration of Christianity with ethnic nationalism are similar to those raised by accounts of the religion of the poor which root a faith in deprivation, or by the redescription of the role of a denomination under the head of a civil rights movement. All such accounts have in common the supposition that the motor, the effective propulsion, the fundamental sub-strate, is deprivation or the search for equal citizenship or the solidarities of the suppressed or disadvantaged group. To deploy the mechanistic metaphor these drive the religious movement forward. Here then we have a variant of reductionism which Arthur Peacocke has elsewhere described as 'nothing buttery'. The sociological observer claims to recognize what is really going forward. So doing he operates yet another hermeneutic of suspicion with regard both to reports from actual participants and the standard public language and self-understanding of the group.

Presumably in their strong form such theories must cause problems for theology. It is difficult to imagine a theologian who is entirely happy with a dogmatically epiphenomenal account of the role of religion whereby it is reduced to a function of solidarity, or of the self-projection of group consciousness and collective forms, or of the aspiration for redress of wrongs and deprivations. All that can be reiterated at this point is that such epiphenomenalism is more rooted in metaphysical presumption than in empirical inference. On the one hand it is clear that religion is implicated in the energies of social bonding (and indeed in the search for redress). On the other hand it is far from clear that it is only an impotent reflection of the energies and forms taken by those bonds. As suggested earlier, theologians may well apply themselves to creating accounts and devising language which avoid the reductionist implication.

I conclude by indicating what is involved in the political-cum-ideological framing of explanations. First of all the horizon of consequences is extended considerably beyond those articulated by the participants. The Wycliffe Bible Translators may speak of helping the Maya in particular ways but they assuredly do not conceive themselves as agents of internal or external colonialism. Second, religious activity is 'placed' in a framework of phases, as for example Bastian's placing of mainline Protestant Christianity within the scope of 'the liberal project'. If this project is then conceived not as a permanent option but as a phase predestined to be surpassed, then the religion associated with it is likewise just a 'moment' in social evolution. It 'fits' that moment and then ceases to fit. Religion has been subsumed in an evolutionary system.

Third, such evolutionary/political accounts engage in imaginative or imaginary imputations when dealing with religious symbolism. Thus they impute assonances between 'real' social relations and their mythic projection. Such imputations are not inherently outside the remit of science but they are centainly speculative and allow ample room for the use of hostile rhetorical frames and negative terminology. E. P. Thompson's well-known analysis of the hymns of Wesley is just such a frame.[9]

Fourth, religious actors are not only reduced to players in a plot directed by the cunning of sociological reason but are judged by their contribution to the long-term political direction of that plot as understood and approved of by the writer. Now, it is certainly the case that historical plots of all varieties are utilized by people of different political viewpoints. Evolutionary sociology is replete with plots with every kind of ideological underpinning. But the left-wing plot is peculiarly comprehensive and inclined to reduce religion to a subordinate or even a

---

[9] Thompson, Edward P., *The Making of the English Working Class* (Harmondsworth: Penguin Books, 1968).

malevolent role in the plot. The viewpoint of the author becomes quite god-like in his exalted perception of the plot and in his foreknowledge of the way in which the direction of the plot has been 'written in'. Indeed, one may add that many people find sociology satisfying precisely because it allows and even encourages such god-like pretensions. It could even be the case that theologians adopting the sociological mode do so in order to achieve a secular version of the 'God's eye view'. Natural scientists (who can predict in certain circumstances) think God's thoughts after him. Social scientists (who in most circumstances cannot predict) like to think God's thoughts before him.

It should be emphasized that these political/evolutionary accounts follow the reductionist line already discussed in that they discount culture in favour of structure. Religion is placed under the general rubric of culture, and culture is denied anything much by way of independent impact. To put it another way, transformations of the self or initiations of novel cultural practices are inconsequential. The contrary view holds that models of self, of practices, of organization, imagined and devised at the level of culture, provide precisely the platforms in consciousness from which far-reaching changes may take off.

Suppose now that all the reductions and subsumptions indicated above are properly criticized, and all careless use of mechanistic metaphors steadfastly abjured, what is the nub of the problem with which theologians should concern themselves? That nub is the presumption of intelligible relations between shifts in the strata of society and movements in the sphere of the spirit. The purpose of adducing the ethnological account by Reina and Schwartz of the pattern of conversion (and of congregational splits and new denominations) was to show religious changes varying intelligibly with concomitant social changes. This is not to say that the precise form of the religious message reflects the social circumstance, since several somewhat different messages may operate as functional equivalents. It is not to say that the first sparks of the spirit, or the initial ferments, may not be generated independently. It is not to say that once a message resonates with a set of circumstances it cannot alter those circumstances. Ideas once incorporated in movements have independent power and are consequential. People may be seized of the idea that their faith may take them from the dirt to the sky and as a result they may at least achieve a useful network for mutual support and economic advance. But the religious movements will take off in circumstances which can be specified and they likewise develop according to dynamics and circumstances which can be specified. In short, the movements of the spirit and of social dynamics are intelligibly connected. That is the sociological postulate, its *sine qua non*, with which theology should concern itself at two levels: first, is there any difficulty in accepting the assumption of intelligible social orderliness; and, second, does that assumption require a revision of the economy of salvation too costly for comfort?

3

Nature: Human, Social, Divine

NOBODY should expect that any particular, discrete sector of human enquiry will stumble upon the stealthy marks of an elusive Deity and finally track Him to his lair. God is not a variety of Abominable Snowman, whose existence has been long hinted at in myth and story, but whose footsteps we now urgently follow, almost expecting to see Him face to face. Not even by peering backward to the Big Bang and the first crucial moments of the universe do we expect to go one stage further and descry the lineaments of the Creator.

In another word, God is not some *thing*, existing side by side with other things either prior to them as their original cause, or as some kind of interacting variable to be fitted into the ensemble of other explanatory variables. No science, *qua* science, can delimit the God-slot, putting Deity in His place. It is not of the nature of God to be 'put in His place'.

This is true whether we speak of cosmology, biology, psychology, or sociology. 'No man has seen God at any time' say the Scriptures, and that holds for the sociologist in pursuit of his special project of understanding human society. There is an inherent cordon built not around God, but set up by our mode of enquiry. This ensures that Being itself cannot stray off-limits or constitute a kind of random quiver upsetting the steady action and interacton of human association.

So what is the cordon which we draw around what we see? What is the *modus operandi* to which we consciously restrict ourselves? I ask that question because I see science as a particular variety of human project which elucidates by systematically cutting out vast tracts of the world taken as totality and experienced by us directly in its wholeness. The first question is, how do we elucidate social reality by a process of rigorous limitation of our focus? That question enables us to ask whether the categories we need to investigate the human world are congruent with the categories in which grow from the roots of religion, such as freedom, and history as narrative. The second question is: does a limitation of focus forbid us to alter our angle of vision to take in other levels, aspects, even transformations, of what we can 'see' scientifically. Those questions are both very important because sociology, perhaps more than any other field of study, has been regarded as subverting any religious understanding of man and his world. It has been frequently held that once you are seized of the idea of man in his social relationships which is given by *homo sociologicus*, you cannot then adopt the viewpoint of *homo religiosus*.

Let me now set out with due economy the sociological understandng of man in society. Sociology sees man as developing a politico-cultural realm precisely because he lacks sufficient instinctual guidance and genetically given answers to the questions thrown up in the struggle for existence. There is a certain world-openness and absence of genetic programme about the stuff of humanity that makes the institutional order necessary. Out of a vast number of theoretical possibilities, combinations and recombinations, the institutional order carves out a limited sector, one that is adjusted in some degree to the level of technological and other resources of the society and the specific challenges of its particular environment.

The process of drawing out the human nature and specific potential of each human being, and of moulding persons in relation to the limited sector of possibilities embodied in the institutional order, is mediated by 'significant others'. Man becomes himself, indeed gains the sense of selfhood, by taking up the cues progressively offered to him in the course of the local human drama. He defines his act, and has it defined for him, through cues and offers from others, through the constraints and limitations they set on his initiatives, through the initiatives they set before him as worthy and appropriate. It is human nature to grow real in the mirror of other people's eyes. Of course, the constraints which emanate from other people are part of a necessary process of inhibition, which frees a man from immediate dependence on direct impulse. He has a horizon of possibilities and is also hedged about with restrictions which he gradually takes to himself, becoming free from the total sway of instinctual gratification. Not all these restrictions are necessary to his survival or to the survival of the group, but the existence of inhibition is, nevertheless, the pre-condition of freedom and control.

The cues and constraints settle into a pattern of habitual action. Prescription and proscription offer a pattern of traditional behaviour. This pattern makes for a vast saving of effort, in that human beings do not have to perch delicately and dizzily on the threshold of existential choice and creative variation every moment of the day. If the inward court of self received an appeal on matters of principle all the time then the whole process of being judicial—i.e. making judgements—would collapse. In fact, it is the wide dominion of habit which makes possible the process of re-consideration and re-flection. Man is reflexive: his mode of existence includes a *se*. There is a vital shift from the reflex of instinct to the cultural reflex of habit and thence to reasoning reflection. Reflex and reflection are complementary.

The world of human nature is thus not simply one of instinctual responses and stimuli but one which includes conscious reflection, and that reflection is exercised in relation to a symbolic order. The human world is one of language, conceptualization, and symbol, and it is ordered so as to constitute a framework of meaning. Each society is a world (or a set of closely overlapping worlds) in its own right, with a special grain and character. These overarching frameworks confer knowledge of what is believed to be the original charter of the society, its genealogy and tradition, its hagiology, axial moments, and trajectory.

Above all, the frame of symbolic order which envelops human beings embodies a claim to rightness. *This* line of conduct is seen as appropriate or even as natural; *that* line of conduct as inappropriate or unnatural. It is human nature to develop through the frames of action a sense of what is natural and unnatural, proper and improper, orderly and disorderly. Very likely this will also include an indication as to the sources of disorder and a statement about the relatonship between the social world of human nature and the external world. (As you will notice, the very constitution of society overlaps closely those social phenomena we identify as part of religion.)

Now sociology analyses the roles, habits, institutions, and symbols of rightness and legitimacy in terms of congruence and contribution to the maintenance of the overall framework, and in terms of interests. There is both a strain towards coherence and a conflict of interests and aims. Human behaviour in the aggregate builds the arch of communality, and is interested. Moreover, there is a very widespread tendency, maybe universal, to clothe interest in the garb of rectitude. Part of the role of sociology is to show the linkage between interest and claims to rectitude.

There is one further very widespread characteristic of human society, though perhaps more marked at some stages of cultural evolution than others, and that is to construct signs and monuments of the link between the local society and a more embracing meaning and purpose. Societies centre themselves, and in the major civilizations, place their concerns in a transcendent perspective. Perhaps this cannot be described as a universal characteristic of human nature, since after all human nature has the quality of openness. If religion is part of man's freedom it must not be written in as an invisible and universal instinct. But it is a very conspicuous potential deriving from human nature-in-society, to develop a sense of the relationship between the project of the group and wider powers, or transcendent possibilities.

However we may want to phrase the last point, it is clear, at least in my view, that the drama of human beings in society is inherently moral, having to do with the frames and motives of action, and their relationship to the right, the appropriate, and the orderly. All attempts to drain the moral aspect out of the sociological level of scientific activity simply reduce the power to understand. Or to put it another way, the ethical dimension in an emergent property of the sociological level of scientific concern.

That is not to say, of course, that sociologists simply work by the concepts given by society. But they do take off from them. They take the notions in common currency, and proceed to order and clarify them in terms of theory, and expose linkages that commonsensical ideas might obscure or hide. Sociologists develop a second language out of ordinary language which distances itself from taken-for-granted worlds, so as to uncover hidden springs of action, unanticipated consequences, obscure linkages, latent functions.

That critical distance for purposes of analysis is essential, otherwise sociologists would simply be repeating commonsense understandings and accepting interested and partial justifications of action. But though critical distance must be achieved in the deployment of sociological language, nevertheless that language must remain continuous with ordinary language. If it is to be true to the nature of its specific scientific *object* it must recognize and be part of the discourse generated by the human *subject*. Whereas a technical vocabulary generated for endocrinology remains within the determinate world of biology, and treats of man with respect to part of his biological constitution, the vocabulary of sociology has to derive from the human nature which is its special concern.

This is not merely a plea made in order to protect a particular approach. It is a matter of observation that the language of sociology retains a continuity with the life-world and with its categories. Indeed, one has to admit that not only does it treat of a world of reflective human beings but it is itself almost chronically inclined to import ethical comment into scientific description. All attempts to dehydrate the language of social analysis, to cut off the relationship to ordinary discourse and to drain out the humanity have ended up ludicrously inadequate.

Perhaps I may bring together much of what I have been saying up to this point by recourse to words of Eric Voegelin in his *The New Science of Politics*.[1] He says that it, i.e. human society,

[1] Voegelin, Eric *The New Science of Politics* (Chicago: University of Chicago Press, 1952), 27.

is illuminated from within by the human beings who continuously create and bear it as the mode and condition of their self-realization. It is illuminated through an elaborate symbolism, in various degrees of compactness and differentiation—from rite, through myth, to theory— and this symbolism illuminates it with meaning so far as the symbols make the internal structure of such a cosmion, the relations between its members and groups of members, as well as its existence as a whole, transparent for the mystery of human existence. The self-illumination of society through symbols is an integral part of social reality and one may even say its essential part, for through such symbolization the members of a society experience it as more than an accident or a convenience, they experience it as of their human essence. And inversely, the symbols express the experience that man is fully man by virtue of his participation in a whole which transcends his particular existence ... Hence when political science begins, it does not begin with a *tabula rasa* on which it can inscribe its concepts; it will inevitably start from a rich body of self-interpretation of a society and proceed by critical clarification of socially pre-existent symbols.

Apart from being concerned with the structure of an inner world mediated by symbols, and apart from the necessary continuity with ordinary language which this concern requires, we should recognize two other characteristics of social analysis. One is that there is a difficulty about achieving really powerful and universally applicable generalizations. The other is that there is a persistent tendency for sociological analysis to dissolve at a certain point into a unique historical narrative. If I were to borrow my terminology from Dilthey I would say that the nomothetic tends to dissolve at a critical point into the idiographic.

The point about generalization needs to be phrased quite carefully. We look, so far as we can, for regularities and for typical conditions leading to typical consequences. And we can, up to a point, construct a net of interconnected phenomena. We can say that when circumstances *A*, *B*, and *C* are present, then *N* is to this or that extent likely to occur. And this follows as an extension of the ordinary stabilities and plausible anticipations of the life-world. All political, economic, and personal action depends on a pragmatic sense, more or less toned up by theory or proto-theory, as to the likely consequences of events. Events do not rattle around and jump about kaleidoscopically. So there is nothing odd about proposing rules of coexistence and succession rooted in our everyday sense of normal connection and orderly sequence.

But the generalizing impulse seems to run into irreducible and resistant aspects of the human world. I am not referring to the enormous number of possible circumstances that enter into any given situation, so as to thwart any confident or stable prediction. That is true, but trivial. Nor am I referring to a notable characteristic of the framing of sociological generalizations, which is the rather bland nature of the small number of acceptable generalizations and the enormous size of the rubric of appropriate qualifications needed to apply them to any specific case.

I am interested rather in the difficulty of holding concepts still over historic time and cultural space and the way in which every element in what one investigates is refracted by ranges of interpretation. As to the problem with concepts, I am peculiarly conscious of this in the sociology of religion, since not even the concept of religion itself submits to being kept still. Translation of concepts from one cultural lexicon to another is not impossible, yet there are serious strains. The dictionaries cannot be lined up on a one-to-one basis. The circumstances *A*, *B*, and *C* which enter into a situation can be conceptually located, but they cannot automatically be transferred. Again, let me be careful. I am not saying that concepts are absorbed into a local *Gestalt* which is *sui generis*. This is not so, since I can go to the Lebanon, Cyprus, or even Sri Lanka and observe features which are partial replays of the situation in Northern Ireland. But the elements which compose the circumstances *A*, *B*, and *C* do have a chameleon quality. One's generalizations are not so easily rotated from one social *Gestalt* to another.

This problem is deepened by the issue of interpretation which must arise when you are dealing with universes of meaning. Once again, caution is appropriate. Interpretation of human situations and social symbols is not a free-for-all. There *are* criteria of interpretation, but the linguistic frames within which interpretations are set can be more or less comprehensive, and sometimes they 'frame' the material in the pejorative sense of that word. We proceed, then, by successive approximations, using each perception of relativity and of interpretive variation to push on an advance on the human subject which can never be complete.

Furthermore, the universes of meaning which we interpret are moving through time and this is part of their uniqueness. Human events tumble forward with their own difficult internal logic within a specific cultural frame and along the dimension of time. We are dealing with stories, undoubtedly possessed of common and partially recurrent features, but without precise repetition. Events in the physical world repeat themselves, or can be made to do so, but in the human world the whole story never comes back to the same place. We may say, wearily, 'here we go again', but the context is shifting nevertheless, and will, *in time*, dissolve. (Of course, there are still those who follow one of the major hopes of the Enlightenment which was to trace the immanent laws of history and—perhaps—by knowing them obey them. It seems to me that this hope, like so many of the hopes of the Enlightenment, has either collapsed or run into increasing difficulties.)

I have spent most of my space on the nature of sociology in order to show how the nature of its subject-matter demands that we use bifocals. One focus is on the recurrence, so far as it may be discerned, and the other focus is on the specific social *Gestalt* as it moves forward in the creation and recreation of its own narrative. That bifocal vision leads one to a crucial acknowledgement of certain emergent properties associated with the appearance of man: these are symbolic meaning (and therefore the need for interpretation) the sense of rightness attaching to social and personal order, the ability to reflect, and the narrative quality of human affairs as they alter over time. Now, it is far from unscientific to acknowledge such emergent properties and to devise ways of knowing which are appropriate to them. Indeed, science, i.e. the search for knowledge, requires that we do just that. Science can delimit what we see for the purposes of a distinctive project, but it is not a form of dogmatism which denies the specificity of a given level of study or insists that it be denatured to conform to some other level.

The sense of rightness and historicity are, of course, central aspects of the Jewish and Christian understandings of the world. It is important to stress that sociology does not forbid us to work within such categories. This is the right juncture to return to a point I raised very cautiously earlier in my discussion about the perception of the transcendent within the historical evolution of societies. In one sense the world retains a structure of settled mundane limits. In another sense there is a constant transcendence, a multitude of epiphanies, whereby previous symbolizations are re-viewed as inadequate. Inevitably, the transcendent is diversified through a whole vast range of potentialities, and is rephrased in secular as well as religious terms.

We may not conclude, of course, that because the transcendent can be discerned as powerfully operative in human affairs, that it exists. God is not validated by the existence of believers any more than He is invalidated by their variety or non-existence. In order to discuss such a question we have to enter a different frame of discourse, where the criteria of what is to count as persuasive are looser even than in interpretive sociology. A man casts his vote in one direction or another, and the reasons for responding to one epiphany rather than another cannot possibly attain the general acceptability attaching in principle to scientific statement. We come here to that alteration in the angle of vision which I referred to at the very commencement of my discussion.

As to that alteration there is nothing further which requires to be said here beyond asserting the irrelevance of sociology to the conclusions which we may arrive at. Of course, sociology (and history) may indicate that (say) the Nicene formula emerged in the course of a power struggle, or that male workers in primary industries in nineteenth-century Germany were so positioned as to respond to Social Democratic propaganda against the Lutheran Church. Nothing follows from the social anatomy of religion as to its truth.

The change in the angle of vision can be shown very rapidly.

If I observe a church in a particular community I can show its role in the social fabric, its linkages with other institutions, its unanticipated effects in terms of (say) social mobility, its specific constituency among people of a certain kind and status. I can also delineate the rites which are celebrated within it, and set forth the symbolic world by which it is sustained and which it in turn maintains in being. But whether a church 'refers' to any other horizon and whether spires, towers (or minarets for that matter) are oriented towards a luminous point beyond themselves, I cannot say. I cannot say, that is, *qua* sociologist with the criteria available to me in that specialized activity. Such questions are answerable only by human beings, and with the criteria of persuasion which are appropriate.

Human society, human history, and much of individual experience is characterized by markers, distinctive places, buildings, or artefacts carrying a heavier freight of meaning than utility. Some are institutionally designated, like the sacraments of the Catholic Church; others arise by a kind of communal consent; yet others involve the sudden burning of a bush in the proximity of some unsuspecting individual. The social sciences can elucidate the context of a marker, its meaning, provenance, and even some of its effects, but as to whether I should genuflect or take off my shoes before a luminous Presence they remain totally silent.

4

The Sociological Mode and the Theological Vocabulary

W H A T is theology? It is an attempt to make intellectual sense of a way of life. This does not mean that theology tries to provide the inner rationale for the life-style of a stockbroker or a computer technician, or attempts to explain why we should be in a society whose way of life generates brokers and technicians. Those two tasks belong respectively to descriptive and to analytic sociology. It means rather that human existence characteristically engenders ways of living and feeling which try to make comprehensive sense of the human environment and situation. Theology is one of the intellectual disciplines which articulates that comprehensive sense.

But in what sense do I use the word 'sense'? I am clearly not talking about every attempt to elucidate meanings. When I ask a lawyer about the general sense of a legal document his reply is not 'theology'. So I am talking about the articulation of a very particular sort of 'sense', that is, the comprehensive sort. To comprehend is not to grasp this or that, but to hold this and that together. I may grasp a process or note and classify a quality or property, but my cognitive apprehensions concern only finite, delimited sectors of happenings. No doubt those sectors can be linked theoretically and the inner dynamics of one sector compared with those of another sector. This kind of theoretical linkage is no more 'theology' than is a lawyer's account of a legal document.

Theology articulates a 'set' or frame which gathers together into one an approach to our personal and social being, a relation of temporal and eternal, a location or image or focus for harmony and perfection, a meaning which lies beyond our immediate apprehensions and which informs the world of natural and historic process. What is really accidental and what is really essential to my health, wholeness, and salvation? Where are true joys to be found? Where in the changing scene may a man properly rest his hope? On what may I—and we—be stayed? What remains? To what do all things in nature and history tend? Where shall we find the secret names of God and the inner story of his purposes? Is the Eternal City being built in time or do its towers lie over the temporal horizon? By what signs and in what signs may we transcend our mortal limitations? What emblems cover and uncover ecstasy? What are the limits that govern even our transcendence of limits? By what are we bound and how shall we be freed? Who or what can release us?

The queries just listed have not included any reference to God. This is because theological questions overlap the concerns of every systematic and comprehensive quest for meaning and purpose. Nevertheless, within this broad category of concern the theologian does have a peculiar role. He asks his questions in relation to a particular postulate and a special possibility, which is that the concentrated 'image' of meaning and purpose, striving and release, perfection and plenitude, is not merely a subjective construct evoking the energies of men, or an emergent property of the process, but is *there*, objectively present, already meeting the hopes of men, and creatively implicated in the whole from the beginning. So his task is not merely or mainly to explicate the limits and rules under which images are created and translated into social arrangements, but to brood upon the paradox of a plenitude and power which can only express itself creatively within strict limitations and rules, and which only achieves fullness in relation to that which is not itself.

I have pointed to an immense labyrinth of query; and theology is the fumbling attempt to find the connecting thread. In the end there are perhaps only a few basic 'ways' through the labyrinth, each with a specific set of axioms and a characteristic internal logic, including a logic of social relationships. I do not pretend to know exactly how many basic approaches there are, partly because that depends on what principles of categorization you prefer to employ, but I suspect they are strictly limited. The world religions, for example, comprise a very small fundamental set. You can reduce that set even further by proposing more and more comprehensive groupings, as for example the grouping which derives from the common Hebrew root and the grouping which derives from the common Indian root. You can also expand the set by tracing mutations, new combinations, and recombinations. And you can even devise formulae for coping with gaps, 'mess', and chaos. What matters in this context is that each ground or frame generates a group of intellectual, aesthetic, and social assonances and that these embody certain possibilities at the expense of certain constrictions and limits. They carve an arc out of the spectrum of possibilities. They even embody their own specific dissonances and antitheses. If the point may be put crudely, the labyrinth allows a limited set of connecting threads, and once one or other is grasped you have to accept a particular map of possible paths and close off another map. You can only move along the historic thread by successive acts of closure. The thread itself is not a strict logical progression, but a set of assonances and harmonic relationships springing up from the initial ground.

Theology is the semi-collective enterprise which follows the different threads through the whole labyrinth of query set out above. Normally the theologian works with other people who are bound in and on the same 'Way' and follows through one set of assonances, though he may from time to time compare the costs which attend his own tradition with those which attend another. But whether he follows through his own tradition or compares it with others, he is engaged in a normative discipline. He only describes a particular theo-logic in order to prescribe a Way. Ordinarily he does not amuse himself playing a game with pure internal relationships. He articulates a vision by which he is compelled, and he wishes to show why it is compelling. Of course, he will also have to give an account of how his vision relates to the kind of theoretical knowledge which links up the world as grasped empirically. Presumably that is what we are attempting to do now.

So where does the sociologist come in? Surprisingly enough,

right at the beginning. First of all, he has to grasp these 'genera-
tors' and assonances as a prelude to the task of explanation. He
has to understand the underlying structure of world-views. A
sociologist who has not grasped the logic of systems cannot see
any deviations there may be and has no framework for tracing
mutations or showing how a vision is bent and refracted by
social realities. He needs at least to grasp the general idea of
such a 'logic' to embark even on the task of confuting it. If, for
example, he were to maintain that all religions are pure mish-
mash or the plausible but *ad hoc* conjunction of chaotic elements, he would need to conceive and construct something
systematic against which the chaos and mish-mash might be
contrasted.

So far everything I have suggested implies that the roles of
theologian and sociologist overlap each other. Both are concerned with the structure of statements and world-views. The
theologian concentrates on the idea that the divine image is not
merely product but source and ground, and on the normative
implications of that idea. However, a peculiar problem emerges
with respect to the logic of religious statements insofar as they
relate to a socio-logic. Every religious way includes an approved
mode of life and implies a particular set of institutional options.
Christianity, for example, distinguishes power from truth, and
thereby implies a range of options in the relationships between
church and state. So long as the theologian broods with normative concern on the implications, say, of the distinction between
Caesar and God he is within his *opus proprium*. But he is bound
at some point to consider the historical forms in which that
distinction has been embodied. This means that he may ask
himself why the distinction was minimally observed in medieval
Russia but is maximally observed in modern America—and
why that maximal observance may be more apparent than
real. At this point he leaves his own sphere and enters the
spheres of historical and sociological explanation, of sequences
of event and motivation and the rules governing man's social
constructions.

Of course, this may be an unproblematic change of academic
headgear, or at any rate the theologian may treat it as such. One

moment he has a normative or metaphysical or theo-logical interest, and at another moment he operates *qua* historian or *qua* sociologist. But it is not quite so simple a matter. A theologian changing hats retains the same head, and cannot simply jettison the language in which he usually talks about the world. That language is partly normative and partly descriptive; and both the normative and descriptive elements appear to have a problematic carry-over into the doing of sociology and history.

Let me give examples which may bring out both the relation of sociology and theology and also highlight a central problem of language and level of description.

The first example contains endless ramifications, so I will state it simplistically. The theologian broods on the norms and images that guide and illumine his particular religious tradition. He observes that these images are embodied in historical reality according to rule-governed orderly processes, which distort or maim them. He observes too that his images of perfection are not merely subject to distortions, but are subject to opportunity costs such that when one fragment of vision is momentarily achieved another fragment is displaced or further distorted. In short he observes the systematic and rule-governed character of the cramps governing this and that human situation.

This will cause difficulties unless he indulges in systematic intellectual schizophrenia, and cuts off his theological from his sociological activity. The first difficulty is a classic one, so classic as to prevent further discussion here. It is that any observation of the ordered character of human social activity and of the systematic cramps governing that activity leads to a question about freedom and responsibility. Given circumstances *A* and *B*, and given the opportunity costs attendant on course *X* as compared with course *Y*, it begins to look as if the systems of action and interaction are completely determined. And if everything is determined, then moral judgement upon it appears quite inappropriate. However, I do not myself hold a deterministic view, though I do note that every comprehensive system of thinking about society runs into a particular variant of the problem of freedom and determinism. Every system says: these things must be and these things need not be. Indeed, the most potent systems suggest how men may collude creatively with necessity. The only postulate that sociology *qua* sociology clearly requires is the notion of ordered, rule-governed inter-relations. Sociology does not require us to accept that every option is already pre-empted by the antecedent concatenation of circumstances. Indeed, my own view is that options are real just because they are very circumscribed. We can choose pre-cisely because the range of possibilities is constricted.

The second difficulty is also classic in its way, though less continuously exposed to intellectual scrutiny. I have referred to it before in my 'Political Decision and Ethical Comment' (*Theology*, October 1973). It is that any perception of the cramps and costs attendant on action leads to a query about the nature of moral and religious prescriptions. No doubt this query arises from the ordinary, ancient, and everyday observation that we cannot do what we like and that we nearly always achieve something other than what we intended. But the systematic exposure of cramps and costs sharpens the query very consider-ably. If, for example, sociological analysis shows that the conflict of Catholics and Protestants in Ulster is a particular instance in a class of conflicts, so that given the coordinates A to $n \ldots C$ and P are bound to clash, then ecumenical breastbeating becomes a rather otiose activity. Furthermore, if sociological analysis sug-gests that mediators or intermediate conciliatory groups are likely to be impotent or even to exacerbate the situation, then the search for a mediating role becomes morally very problem-atic. The moral problem is not solved nor put on one side by such an analysis, but it is set in sharpened perspective. At any rate, the ordinary liberal and (intermittently) Christian assump-tion that the solution is basically a matter of goodwill is under-mined. The situation may at certain previous junctures have been willed, but it is now determined and goodwill cannot be relied upon to mend it.

No doubt goodwill is required, but the simple willing of the good cannot overcome the structural constraints within which people seek evil. Of course, if everyone were to will the good simultaneously then the structural constraints might be amelio-rated or even abolished, since everyone would simultaneously desire not only peace and harmony but also justice. But one knows on good sociological grounds, let alone on good theological grounds, that an immediate and universal desire for peace and justice is not humanly or statistically likely. Indeed, a structural constraint is precisely the kind of institutional set which buttresses that statistical impossibility. No doubt the mystery of evil is deeper than an institutional set which inclines the will of men towards evil deeds, but the fears and deprivations engendered by institutional arrangements are at least an element in manifestations of 'evil'; and this is unusually clear in Ulster. Evil solidifies; it is more than the mixing of wills.

Contemporary Christians are increasingly aware of how structural constraints engender activities which are morally reprehensible, at least by the normal canons of reprehensibility. There is a variety of ways whereby Christians may confront the problem of structural constraint. One way is to carry on acting charitably in the knowledge that charity and goodwill are not enough. To love one's neighbour will not avert tragedy and crucifixion: so much the Christian religion itself ought to make clear. Another way is to downgrade charitable concern as wrapped in individualistic delusions about the nature of social arrangements and their supposed responsiveness to moral initiative. The new realistic Christian now regards individual initiative as secondary to structural change; and he may even conclude that charity is at best ineffective and at worst positively harmful. (Aid to the Third World for example has often had effects which are economically and morally harmful.) Once the new Christian has grasped his sociology or his Marxism he expresses his radical moral and social discontent in a structural terminology. His prescriptive vocabulary is now composed of analyses of structure and role and maybe of domination, deprivation, and alienation. This new vocabulary is characteristic of the radical section of the middle class, and combines fervent righteousness with the espousal of a semi-deterministic perspective. So sociological sophistication results in a paradoxical combination of a moralistic critique of structures with a depersonalized analysis of how they arise and how they may be dismantled. Indeed, the depersonalized analysis can deteriorate into a contempt for persons as such: Marxist repression has often followed this path. The situation alarms sociologists as well as Christians. The Christians are worried by the query placed against the language of moral exhortation and against the liberal and possibly Christian notion that the increase of persons who live and act in good faith leads to a better society. The sociologists are worried by the way in which the concept of structure can be reified and then incorporated in sets of macro-social mechanisms, so giving rise to fatalism. The sociologists have tried to construct what they call interactional accounts of people in groups which allow for the way men jointly construct their social worlds and exercise initiatives which create as well as reflect the cramps of structure. If these sociologists are right then Christian (or secular) moral exhortation remains a valid way of calling for creative initiatives. In other words if the construction of social reality is a joint enterprise to which all may make some creative contribution, then moral prescriptions and proscriptions are relevant and viable adjuncts of creativity. Morality is not just a film stretched over fatality.

I wish now to move on to the general problem of the referents of religious language, insofar as such language seems to cover the same terrain as sociology at (perhaps) a different level. Let me take three cases of such language since they are partly concerned with the issues of freedom and necessity already mentioned. The three cases are 'original sin', 'the outpouring of the Spirit', and 'the Virgin Birth'.

The three cases are not only concerned with freedom and necessity but in the most general way with the idea of grace. Original sin belongs to our 'nature' and grace is the power to break into the system of nature so as to transform it. We are formed in sin, in a determinate structure of resistance, and transformed by grace. Grace is the theological term for the transformation whereby divine image and distorted reality are brought into closer conjunction. It lies close to the idea of inspiration, that is, the creative flash which alters the pre-existing pattern and reveals a new potency and potentiality. The question is therefore, how do sociological and theological accounts of resistance and potentiality relate to each other?

I take it that original sin can be discussed as if it has some correspondence to, or relation with, the idea of constitutional cramps and resistances. Similarly the work of the Spirit can be discussed in relation to the creative deployment of necessity, while the Virgin Birth at least prima facie concerns new mutations or breakthroughs in determinate systems of necessity. If these possible correspondences are not clear, perhaps they may become so.

The question is as follows. Does the language of original sin really refer to (or overlap with) the notion of inherent cramps, resistances, and limits in the human situation (including, of course, radical concern with the self)? If it does really refer to such cramps, is the specifically theological usage undermined or conversely rendered scientifically respectable? If there is an overlap, what is the nature of the conjunction and disjunction? The notion of 'original sin' and the notion of strict sociological limits to the embodiment of divine images are at least linked by one characteristic: they convey necessity. They are concerned with the ineluctable. But are they concerned with one ineluctable or two ineluctables? Man's 'original sin' is a corporate condition: so how does that corporate condition relate to the sociological perception of limits?

It might relate insofar as highly general 'metaphysical' assumptions act as preliminary orientations to material, without themselves being falsifiable or indeed very useful, apart from their capacity to give an orientation. If man really does push against a colossal and complex structure of resistances, embodied simultaneously in self and society, then a rather pessimistic Christian might be armed with a useful orientation, and one which gave him an initial advantage, albeit (perhaps) an adventitious one. But here we come to an oddity. Such general orientations as original sin or original innocence are not explanatory. Their lack of falsifiability is part of their incapacity to explain. 'Sin' or 'innocence' explain everything and nothing. And lots of theological concepts are like this: basic orientations which provide a generalized image and cannot be set to work to uncover particular cramps, particular limits, particular resistances. The resistances do, of course, contain elements which are very general, but 'original sin' is too general even to disentangle the general elements of resistance from the localized ones.

The notion of 'the Spirit' raises rather different problems, since it is specifically invoked as a quasi-explanatory category. For example, the Christian Church was born (as Jesus was born) by an infusion or effusion of the Spirit. Individual Christians have vocations which are 'callings' of the Spirit. So what does it mean to say that a new religion is brought into being by the Creator Spirit, the Spirit of freedom? What does it mean to say that men and women at sundry times and places are called of the Spirit? Or that the church is infused by and guided by the Spirit? Is this a characterization alongside our social, historical, and psychological characterizations? Is it a form of normative appraisal, an assessment of 'quality'? Is it, for example, like the quality of inspiration which we divine in music or art, but to which we cannot assign a precise causal role? The idea of ecstatic breath entering into and fulfilling human beings is deeply rooted in human language about art and religion, but to what does it refer? Does it refer to the element of freedom in all creation, or to the qualitatively new aspect of a work of art, or to the release and the new perspective which that achievement brings about, or to all these things? Again, this is not just a problem for religion and for religious language but for the relation of scientific descriptions to all language. It would not be so difficult, of course, if theologians restricted themselves to a general defence of the propriety of such language. They could defend the notion that one may use a phrase like the outpouring of the Spirit to cover new, creative, breakthroughs, which lift men from mundane stasis to ex-stasis, that is, to transcendence. In which case the term 'Holy' as applied to 'Spirit' concerns all those instances where the 'Transcendence' embodied a 'wholesome' or genuinely creative and healing possibility, rather than a vision of chaos or evil, not to just those instances for which we have no naturalistic explanation. The trouble is that theologians use the term 'operation of the Spirit' to cover so many doubtful cases. But that can be put down to incautious stupidity, and need not cause us any logical difficulty. It is only necessary to

note again the very general character of the religious description. Whereas 'original sin' covered the general character of
resistance so 'Holy Spirit' designates the general possibility of
creative breakthrough. (There are, of course, specific Marxist
translations for such general terms, and indeed most general
terms have analogues in other vocabularies or play some functionally or substantially equivalent role in those vocabularies.)

But this brings us to a problem posed by one particular
assertion about the Holy Spirit which is fairly central to historic
Christianity. Even generalized references to the action of the
Spirit in the 'empirical' Church create intellectual discomfort in
those who also use the language of sociological description. The
extent of that discomfort depends precisely on how theologians
use their terms, and on what doctrine they hold of the relation
of 'the Spirit' to the empirical Church.

For example, the Wesleyan revival from 1738 onwards may
be characterized as 'a great outpouring of the Spirit'. What does
this mean? Such a characterization could be entirely descriptive
and entirely unexceptionable. Nobody disputes the existence of
extensive 'spiritual' phenomena of a quite dramatic kind leading to changes in life, character, and sensibility. But theological
language is usually normative as well as descriptive: it pinpoints
a happening in order to set it in a context of approval: 'This is
the Lord's doing and it is marvellous in our eyes.' Certain
classes of events are demarcated as representing the divine
activity. Other classes presumably do not represent this activity,
or cannot be given a secure theological imprimatur. The 'spirits'
have to be tested and some tests yield uncertain results.

What, however, is indisputable is the rule-governed character
of all such spiritual phenomena, whether they pass the theologians' tests or not. The lava of the Spirit runs along the lines of
social fault; and the wind of the Spirit blows according to a chart
of high and low pressures. It may be, of course, that the theologian merely wishes to say that in all these 'signs' he obscurely
discerns the Spirit of God, and does not wish to locate exactly
where that Spirit is to be found. It may also be that he suspects
a much more complicated operation of spiritual providence
which occurs under 'signs' far outside the boundaries of

churches and particular religions. He knows it is dangerous to say 'lo here' and 'lo there'. And maybe he also recognizes that in an orderly social universe, as in an orderly universe, the Creator Spirit works within limits, and 'breaks through' according to rules and forms. In which case, the operation of 'the Spirit' may be likened to inspiration in the arts: an act of unveiling, a creative reformulation of pre-existent elements, a fresh fusion, the exploration of a given option . . . If this is how theologians conceive the activity of the Spirit then maybe there is no tension whatsoever between theological and sociological language.

Jesus was born of the Virgin Mary by the action of the Spirit. I choose this assertion because it is not merely important but also likely to arouse embarrassment. Many contemporary Christians are inclined to dismiss the Virgin Birth as myth, as based on misunderstandings of prophecy, and as reflecting views of sexuality they wish to repudiate. Those who think the doctrine physically inconceivable and/or morally reprehensible are also much impressed by the paucity of the historical evidence. So they are not likely to resist a sociological account of the phenomenon. Indeed they may encourage and applaud such an account.

Now a sociological account moves at various levels. I am going to construct an account which shows the sort of hypothesis which characterizes sociology without going into its truth or falsehood. Indeed, sceptics may care to note that such a hypothesis as I now put forward is barely susceptible to verification or falsification even in principle. I mean that although the hypothesis refers to the empirical world it is not clear how it may be falsified or verified. One asks whether it 'fits', whether it is intuitively correct or counter-intuitive, whether it belongs to a generally coherent account of processes in the social world, and so on, but there is no crucial experiment which might establish it or crucial negative fact which might disestablish it. This is true of most important and insightful sociological theories as well as of minor and stupid ones. All the same, hard-nosed empiricism ignores such theories at the price of ignoring many of the things which matter most.

A sociologist may approach the Virgin Birth in many ways, such as, for example, by enquiring what correlation might exist between the mythical conceptions of sexuality and divinity and the roles and structures of society at large. He would assume, initially, some loose though complex correspondence. Doctrines, say sociologists, do not land like meteorites from outer space, but grow organically where they have a supporting, fertile social niche or cranny. The only alternatives to this idea of a (very loose) correspondence of signs and structures are randomness, that is, the anarchic intrusion of the Spirit working with a book of random numbers, or a discernible or mysterious Providence, or innate principles or codes which comprise a fairly economic set and generate internal combinations. (Even these notions are not all straight alternatives.)

At any rate let us, for the sake of argument, assume that signs and structures are loosely related and that the sociologist can make sense of the relations. He seeks an appropriate understandable 'natural' relation or correspondence between sign and structure. Actually there are complex reasons as to why this correspondence may be very loose or occluded, or may express itself in a variety of functionally equivalent forms, but we do not need to explore those reasons here. We do not need to explore them because nothing follows for theology from the assumption of correspondence. God, the theologian may say, reveals himself at sundry times in diverse manners, and he will be seen in one way by a nomadic desert people and in another by a settled agricultural people. The 'names' of God are heard according to a prior resonance within men's social relationships, one with another.

> Adoro Te devote, latens veritas,
> te qui sub his formis vere latitas . . .

So far no problem, and maybe there will be no problem in what follows. Suppose that the Roman Empire, which united many tribes and tongues within a single imperium, set the stage for a universal religion. Suppose too that the monotheism of the Jews based on a covenant relation between Israel and Jehovah, contained a universal possibility. Both these suppositions are a priori plausible. What mutations within the symbol system of Jewry would be necessary to convert a limited covenant relation, rooted in the ethnic exclusiveness of the Jews, into a universal religion?

The biological continuity of the ethnic group would have to be broken and the particular, localized attachments of the family would have to be undermined. A universal faith would have to cut the generational tie and the familial bond. It would have to substitute universal spiritual rebirth for limited continuity. Since the family is based on a canalization of erotic impulses as well as of particular local loyalties, a universal religion would need to redirect the flow of sexual feeling. Local *eros* would have to be converted to Catholic *agape* in that family loyalty became loyalty to the family of God. The reality of brotherly attachment in the biological family would have to be reformed under the sign of universal brotherhood in the family of man.

Now, these sociological pre-conditions of universal faith have obviously been stated with maximum economy and some crudity. There may be a variety of ways in which a symbol system might mutate in order to accommodate them. But it is clear that the figure of the Virgin and the sign of the Virgin Birth fill complementary roles in relation to these pre-conditions. The Virgin Birth signifies a new genesis in the Spirit which breaks out of the biological continuities of the ethnic group. So it complements the idea of being born again by the Spirit of God and thereby choosing the universal community of faith rather than accepting the local community of origin. It also complements the idea of 'the eunuch for the kingdom of heaven's sake' since the eunuch and the Virgin together carry the conception of a universal bond of charity posed against the local bond of familial attachment. At the same time the figure of the Virgin has a potential role in relation to that universal brotherhood, in that the canalized erotic energies may focus themselves on her rather than on this woman or that woman. There is much else that might be said since the Virgin stands as an antetype of the temple prostitute and of sacred sex. But this leads into complicated questions of the relationship of ethical monotheism to female deities and sacred sexuality which need not concern us here.

What does concern us is not the precise plausibility of the hypothesis, but the complications of the type of theorizing. One implication might be that symbols which claimed an ontological or metaphysical status had a real sociological meaning which underlay and undercut the presumed theological meaning. This is reductionism: theological façade merely glosses the underlying sociological reality. Many people are inclined to contrast the metaphysical form with the sociological substance, to reduce poetic image and theological meaning to the basic socio-logic. Thus one highly intelligent and orthodox Catholic student said to me: 'Are you saying that the figure of Our Lady simply functions as a potent symbol of a set of social changes?'

Perhaps I should try to make clearer what sort of hypothesis I have just put forward. It first of all set out certain pre-conditions for the birth of a universal religion. Certain attachments and continuities will have to be broken, and the breakage will have to be carried in a more or less coherent code. I then note that the new Christian code persistently contrasts Spirit with flesh, spiritual rebirth with familial loyalty. I also note that the Virgin Birth is by the Spirit, just as all the sons of God are born of the Spirit. So I have set out a possible meaning for one part of a code which is consonant with the rest of the code and with the general pre-conditions for achieving universality. I have indicated a consonance between a religious image and the sociological requirements of a universal faith. And I have suggested there is an internal consonance within the Christian code between certain key signs: the eunuch, the need for spiritual regeneration, the Virgin Birth.

I have, of course, only touched on a tiny section of the web of signals clustering around the notion of virginity. Varied situations will arouse very varied resonances in that web of signals, so that what at one time carried the concept of breakage may at another time carry a rather different weight of meaning. I am suggesting that one sign and its immediate associated signs lie within the logic of a massive shift from particular to universal.

The sign of the Virgin Birth functions to reinforce the inner coherence of the code, and to reinforce a certain character structure highly compatible with universality, that is, a character structure in which there is a redirection of sexual affect towards every brother and sister in Christ. I have said nothing about origins. At the birth of a religion all kinds of possibilities will be thrown up but only some will be filtered into the core elements of the faith. My whole emphasis has been on function, by which I mean contribution to the broad thrust of a movement, as compared with origin and with long-term consequence.

If I say that a symbol is consonant with others as part of a system which carries a coded message (say) about universality, I do not exclude other kinds of levels of meaning or of 'reality'. Symbols are usually multivalent; and they may 'refer' to a number of levels. In any case if I say that the Virgin Birth codes the signs of universality I am describing how the theological norm of unity is achieved. I am saying how the ontological reality is embodied and how the theological norm is made effective. The embodiment may be partial, the norm may not be fully realized, but that is neither here nor there. I cannot, of course, make any judgement, positive or negative, about ontological reality. Signs mediate sociological requirements, social tendencies, and human aspirations. That at least is clear. Whether they also mediate a deeper, more deeply interfused 'reality' I cannot say. A sociological analysis does not exclude other meanings or exclude other layers or levels of reference. It may, however, help the task of theology by exposing a layer of socio-logic which displays inter-relations and dynamic mutations. If a theologian observes the critical paths travelled by socio-logic he may be helped to locate critical paths in the spheres of theo-logic.

So, what in conclusion? Simply that we have to investigate very carefully the relationship between different languages and between the levels of supposed reality to which they refer. We have, for example, to look very carefully at the relationship between the vocabulary of moral exhortation and of structural analysis. We have, for example, to consider the relation between generalized orientations like original sin, and more particular, grounded forms of analysis. We have to expose the socio-logic informing a symbol systems, and consider what light that can throw on the form and development of the theo-logic. But provided we examine these correspondences and connections with care, and do not reduce one level to another, the result may be mutual enrichment rather than mutual destruction.

5

Comparing Different Maps of the Same Ground

THE primary foci of concern so far in the interchange between sociology and theology have been determinism and relativity. However, neither determinism nor relativity are new problems, and it is not even clear that they are sharpened or seriously altered by sociological analysis. Of course, whoever engages in sociological work will be conscious of the pressure exercised by the problem of more or less strict causality in human affairs, and will be exposed to a persistent practical relativization of his perspective. He will regard norms and ideas as systematically related to a context of time and place, culture and social exigency. He will see how truths which men suppose to be eternal mutate according to the several necessities of modes and styles of social life. But that is, perhaps, just his psychological problem. At the level of philosophy it is difficult to see how his personal difficulty gives rise to a new question for ontology. He simply lives with an acute and troubling version of old questions.

So in what follows I will try to desert the ancient stamping-ground of determinism and relativity, and at least attempt to begin elsewhere. I shall select certain statements from the body of Christian belief and see whether my reflections on them yield anything problematic for theology. I will put on a naïve stare, looking at statements and seeing whether the sociological categories embedded in my mental equipment start to generate oddities, difficulties, problems. It may well be that as I do so the old issues of determinism and relativity will creep back, asserting their usual primacy.

The statements at which I intend to stare are not theological propositions but ordinary working religious sentences. They are respectively from an epistle, a gospel, and a psalm. First, 'If any man be in Christ he is a new creature'. Second, 'That they may all be one'. And third, 'Behold thou hast made my days as a span long and mine age as nothing in respect of thee; and verily every man living is altogether vanity . . . And now, Lord, what is my hope? Truly my hope is even in thee'. I select these working sentences because they are likely to tie in with religious institutions. The first touches on a crucial transition, or shift of religious condition, and therefore will be a leitmotif both in liturgical enactments and personal biography. I will in due course discuss it with particular reference to baptism. The second touches on the bond of solidarity constantly invoked in social and religious language alike. It also has ramifications in the idea of unity as such: the unity of God, of the Trinity, of God and Man, of Christ and the Church, of Christians one with another. The third is an eloquent response to the limits of the human condition, more especially contingency and death. Death and life are the primary counters of religious experience, and provide the ground from which grows a huge tree of symbolism.

If we turn now to the first statement it is first of all necessary to define what it means, or more realistically to hint at what it contains and implies. At one level it is little more than a bare tautology, saying that a man who is in Christ is not as he was previously. At another level it contains in a little space almost the whole of Christian theology. You are not likely to make much sense of such a sentence unless you already know the rest of the doctrines in which it is lodged. However, these doctrines are also themselves dense statements of the same kind, and comprise an arc of intimately related signs and symbols. So all that can be done is to select some points on that arc of cognate signs.

According to Christian faith Christ is the head of the new creation and the first born of many. These are not born by the processes of natural generation but spiritually regenerated, and thereby inducted into a new order of brotherhood, summed in Christ. This new order cancels mere legality and opens up a process of regeneration within the universe itself. Not only is the law of sin reversed within the self but the powers which dominate the universe have received a signal of defeat. So when a man is 'in Christ' he is reborn into a new order where 'the former things are passed away'. To be joined to Christ is to undergo a birth, death, and resurrection of the spirit. The old Adam is supplanted by the new Adam, and this means that all our losses are now to be reversed, including the most severe loss of all, which is death. Christ by dying cancels death, and any one who is 'in Christ' dies with him, sharing in the redemptive triumph of love over frustration and negativity. Of course, this is not to say that all who call themselves Christians grow up into the full stature of the new man. Rather, the benefits of new manhood are open to all men by grace. The tincture of newness is implanted in whoever is open to it.

All this is, of course, fundamental theology and the reader may easily wonder where sociological reflection will begin to take over from theological exposition. But I am, after all, staring naïvely at a tiny sentence, and I have already underlined how the tiniest of sentences contains a taut spring of implication. The smallest atom of religious discourse is a creative and explosive ball. Moreover, I could have begun from any of these tiny micro-statements and traversed the whole arc of meaning. Every point on the arc is integral to the complete cycle of related centres. These centres also subsume each other and thereby provide an analogy of their own meaning. By their own inherent nature they mutually subsume and incorporate, and also point to subsumption and incorporation as fundamental to spiritual relationships. They speak of the logic of relations and exemplify them. And sociology is of course concerned with the logic of relations.

How then does this logic of subsumption and incorporation work out? To be 'in Christ' is to be taken in spiritually and incorporated: 'I yet not I but Christ in me'. There is an I in him, and he is in me. Likewise that I is joined to 'all them that are Christs'. 'He' and 'I' are conjoined with 'they'. This refers to the act of incorporation which constitutes the Church. Christians absorb his body into themselves that their 'sinful bodies may be made clean by his body'. Thus incorporation is also transference: the essential unity covers an essential difference. A transference is also a transition. What was once polluted and alien becomes clean and acceptable. It therefore repeats the sacrifice whereby it has been redeemed. The Christian presents himself sacrificially, receiving the benefits of loving sacrifice, offering them up, and symbolically repeating them in his approach to the divine. So we find that within this thought-world relationships constantly repeat themselves in analogical mirrors. To partake of the benefits of sacrificial love, offered a priori and without condition, you place the sacrifice before God and you remake the sacrifice in yourself as an offering to God. Whereas previously you were 'unworthy to make any sacrifice' you now find that sacrifice is your 'bounden duty and service'. This brings us back to the relationship between transference and transition. You enjoy a change of status, from alien to citizen, from child of wrath to son of God. The term *rite de passage* as used by anthropologists can be applied to the enactments of baptism and the Eucharist quite literally. Those who entertain faith enter upon a passage or journey, and are caught up in a kind of movement. The movement takes them from unworthiness to worthiness, old man to new man, death to life. The journey or passage is a sequence existentially appropriated and symbolically objectified.

Sociology deals in sequence and transition, as well as in subsumption and incorporation. Journeys and joinings are the basic repertoire of the discipline. So also is the difference between in and out: what sociologists call the maintenance of boundaries. Those who join for the journey are different from those who do not. They belong to a different city. The logic of in and out, moving and remaining behind, will generate all kinds of distinctions and boundary markers. Out and in, before and after, will be defined and demarcated by sin and salvation, world and church, new man and old man, glory and shame, pilgrim and sojourner, City of God and City of Man, the Kingdom of heaven and the principalities and powers. The sociologist will see the boundaries of belonging sharply framed in these mighty opposites. Each mighty opposite will express transfers and transits, exclusions and incorporations.

Nothing in the world of thought or of enactment will escape the opposition. If we turn, for example, to baptism, we see how a man shifts from the prior condition of wrath to the subsequent condition of acceptance, conveyed in all the symbolism of crossing. The transition is conveyed by the crossing of water and the sign of the cross made in water. Here the properties of a natural element are deployed to convey multiple meanings. Water is an element through which you cross, in which you are immersed, and by which you become clean. Here we see implicit and explicit one of the great religious sentences: 'in whom, by whom, and through whom'. The little prepositions 'in', 'by', and 'through' characterize the basic structure of spiritual relations. They contain incorporation and transit and mediation. In baptism they link with a triple transition: from enslavement to liberty, from death to life, and from journey to arrival. The water is simultaneously the Red Sea, the Jordan, and the river of death. All involve crossing and transition. Thus sacred history becomes linked to individual history and the isolated individual is set within a vast field of holy images and significant transits. He simultaneously enters the social movement and the movement of history.

All this is ground which the sociologist shares with the theologian. For the sociologist the analysis of symbols and sentences is an essential prolegomenon to understanding how religion works, and for the theologian it is the substance of his discipline. However, the sociologist takes leave of the theologian immediately he considers how religion is woven into the social fabric, i.e. how it relates and adjusts to different types of social formation. So I will take the sentence 'if any man be in Christ he is a new creature' as it relates to baptism and then outline a sociological procedure. This procedure may or may not yield a 'correct' result. I mean that my sociological analysis may not be entirely convincing. But what matters is the approach itself and whether it throws up some characteristic difficulty for the theologian.

When one considers baptism, i.e. the ritual incorporation into the new manhood, one of the major theological issues turns on whether the rite of initiation should be administered to children. The sociologist takes note of this issue and asks the following question: under what social circumstances are Christians likely to perceive this difficulty and to opt for adult baptism? This question cannot be settled by taking all instances of adult baptism and correlating them with a characteristic social environment. Rather one has to construct a piece of plausible social logic and then to see how far the logic is exemplified and contradicted in historical instances. This is a complex and disputable point of methodology into which I cannot go at the present juncture.

Baptism signifies and objectifies the entry into 'newness'. It is not however coextensive with the process of redemption in the individual soul. Rather the rite works as a demarcation point objectifying the point of entry into the company of the redeemed, and signifying who belongs. Now, insofar as Christianity becomes coextensive with a natural community, that is to say with organic and primordial solidarities, the sacrament of baptism will function as entry into that natural community. The 'new creature' remade in the image of Christ will also become, in practice, the 'new creature' who has just arrived in the community. Baptism, as Kierkegaard observed, will be enacted as a Christian version of circumcision. This is not to say the specifically Christian meaning will be obliterated, but it will undergo a partial mutation under the fuctional pressure exercised by the natural community. It will be remade in the image of the organic and primordial relations which obtain in close-knit, solidary societies where religion is woven into the whole social fabric.

However, Christianity is by nature also an aspect of the fundamental process of differentiation, setting spiritual brotherhood against blood ties, and heavenly citizenship against secular belonging. The mighty opposites within which it is framed include this crucial differentiation, and thrust strongly against mere ordinary, automatic membership in a sacralized, natural group. Yet that thrust in part is neutralized by primordial solidarities. The original meaning, if that can be identified, is left stranded in the symbolism, unable to escape the grip of the organic pull. The Church talks as if baptism were a kind of pre-emptive strike for redemption, trying to give a persuasive gloss to a paradox thrust upon it by the social relations in which it is embedded.

No doubt you already observe the multiple problems which attend on the analysis so far. Quite apart from the (perhaps) foolhardy identification of an 'original' meaning I have attributed a theological paradox to a social contradiction. I have suggested that a symbolism of distinctive belonging, rooted in a premature differentiation, is practically subverted by the undertow of an organic social process, and thereby throws up an insoluble problem, Now, I could go further and argue that when that natural pull is slackened, and the individual given space and room *vis-à-vis* social solidarity, then the original symbolic thrust can reassert itself. More than that, it can strengthen the whole individualistic tendency, objectifying a new sense of chosen faith, even though the emphasis is on God's elective choice of the individual. The symbolism of the new creature which is embedded in baptism can now make straightforward sense.[1]

Now, we come to the question as to whether the link posited between infant baptism and organic, solidarity relationships and between adult baptism and a more voluntaristic type of society, bears at all on the status of the doctrines. Does the fact that a contradiction at the level of theologic parallels a condition at the level of sociologic affect the issue as such? And, in spite of assurances to the contrary, are we sliding back towards the old question of relativity?

Let me place this dilemma within a concrete situation. A member of the Church of England on the verge of the 1980s may observe that as the Church slips anchor with the natural community and moves towards the open sea of voluntary asso-

---

[1] I will not go into such questions as to why a voluntaristic Church like Methodism retains infant baptism, and why the Baptist Church does not revert to infant baptism wherever it re-enters the solidary pull of the community, as in the Southern States of the USA. There are mechanisms of conservation which can be cited to explain such awkward instances. However, the instances do indicate why we cannot mechanically correlate types of baptism with types of community.

ciation it begins to reconsider the doctrine and practice of baptism. Such a person would observe that the shift towards denominational status is accompanied by a demand for greater explicit commitment. As belonging ceases to be automatic and becomes open to erosion from various alternatives the criteria governing access to baptism are tightened up. This can be seen as a partial shift to the Baptist position insofar as commitment receives a new emphasis. However, infant baptism remains *in situ* for various reasons, including inertia. The sins of the parents are now visited on the child, since the decision whether or not to baptize turns on their degree of attachment to the Church.

Supposing this sociological analysis were correct, could it have any bearing on how baptism ought to be understood? In asking the question let us recollect that we are considering various ways in which the transition to the 'new man' may be objectified by way of a demarcated entry into the 'household of faith'. We have observed a loose empirical link between organic solidary bonds and infant baptism, and this link can be rephrased as a degree of 'fit'. When the organic community dissolves then automatic belonging by birthright ceases to be 'fitting'.

Here lies the crux, because the empirical 'fit' which we observe from the sociological perspective is translated by some into a sense of what is 'fitting' i.e. appropriate. In the new social situation the transition to the 'new man' is seen as released from the old solidarities, as no longer embedded in the bond of ineluctable belonging. So the proper approach stresses choice.

However, the shift from empirical fit to theological propriety crosses the line between 'is' and 'ought'. It designates an appropriate normative response on the basis of an observed social connection. But this only pushes the normative issue towards the question: 'Why should anybody adjust to the new situation?' Adjustment is not a moral imperative. Indeed, adjustment is often seen as moral capitulation.

At this point the arguments become very complicated, because it is perfectly possible to enquire how far the essence of the transition to the 'new man' may be conveyed by infant baptism in one social situation and by another form of baptism in a different social situation. Controversy is couched in terms of necessary core and expendable variable periphery, and this distinction of core and periphery itself tends to flourish and appeal in the modern situation. Equally characteristic of the modern situation is an argument based on the notion of a Babylonish captivity experienced by the Church either by reason of links to the structure of power, or in this case, by embeddedness in solidary, organic bonds. However, now the captivity is over the distortions which it induced may be thrown off, the truth of original Christianity recovered.

These arguments cannot be pursued further in this paper, since the object has been to stare at the root concept of the 'new man' and then see how this is ritually objectified according to the type of social order. The basic conclusion may, however, be underlined, which is that a 'fit' observed at the empirical level cannot be translated into what is theologically fitting.

We can now consider the second sentence: 'that they all be one'. This too is a statement of incorporation, in which the vertical unity of Father and Son is linked to the horizontal unity of all the sons and daughters of God. It is not necessary to go into the exegesis expounded for the first sentence. Rather, we may turn to the deployment of this statement in the theological justification of ecumenism. The phrase 'that they may all be one' is set to work in an ecumenical context.

Before considering phrase and context we have to note two historical facts. One is that some scholars assure us that Jesus never envisaged a church. Moreover many commentaries do not attribute the phrase to Jesus. The other is that sentences of this kind are not only part of the logic of a theological position but are deployed in a legitimating role. Not only is the phrase a normative injunction to unity but it is also deployed authoritatively. Just as 'thou are Peter' etc., is deployed to legitimate the Pope of Rome so 'that they may all be one' is deployed to bolster the WCC (World Council of Churches) and ecumenism. So we must distinguish carefully between unification as an element in a religious logic and the use of a phrase as an authorita-

tive pronouncement. The latter is of course subject to a philosophical criticism.

The idea of unity is extremely general in its scope and what
follows concerns only its application to the cause of ecumenical
aspiration. One such application might run as follows: the Holy
Spirit cannot be released because of the sin we are in by reason
of our unhappy divisions. This might mean that our unhappy
divisions are sign and proof of the frustration of the Spirit, in
which case it is merely circular. The theologian is pointing to a
particular condition characterizing it as spiritually defective.

However, he may have something else in mind. He may be
saying that disunity is a bar to any renewal of Pentecost. As he
observes the 'deadness' of the contemporary church he may
attribute the advent of rigor mortis to division and lack of full
ecumenical fellowship. Such a statement appears to contain a
hint of explanation as well as mere characterization. He is not
only saying that disunity signifies spiritual frustration but attrib-
uting the frustration to the disunity.

Of course, this may still be another circular statement which
has simply travelled by a larger roundabout. The theologian
challenged by an instance where the spirit apparently moves in
a situation of disunity might say that the Spirit cannot be fully
expressed until disunity is removed. Or he may say that a spiritual movement tolerant of disunity or, worse still, giving rise to
schism, is *ipso facto* not moved by the true spirit of God. If
he does protect his assertion in these ways there is nothing to
be done with him. The glancing empirical reference is in fact
vacuous.

If, on the other hand, the statement is not protected in these
ways we may then adduce our contrary instances. For example
we can point to Methodism and ask whether or not this movement was 'of the Holy Spirit', and if the answer is positive we
can point to the multiple schisms to which it gave rise. Indeed,
we can give lots of similar instances, such as the rise of
Franciscan spirit, which resulted both in heresy and rejuvenation. Of course, we do not put it past a theologian to say God the
Holy Spirit was having to work at that time in a distorted situation and that therefore His activity was also subjected to a

complementary distortion, i.e. heresy, enthusiasm, spiritual excesses. But we have at least shown that in those instances where the Spirit has plainly been at work, at least by the standards of our straw theologian, there also is to be found lively schism and disunity. Spiritual rejuvenation and breakage of fellowship historically often go together. It follows that if our theologian's statement has empirical content then it is inaccurate. The Spirit can work in divisive situations. More than that it even appears to be positively associated with them.

Another move still remains whereby our theologian can wriggle sideways by developing the distinction between the distorted past and the potential in the present. He may concede that in the past the movement of the Spirit has been associated with lively schism, beginning with the division between Christianity and Judaism and the controversy between the followers of Apollos and the followers of Paul. However, in the modern situation, loosely defined, the 'Spirit' is calling us to unity, and He cannot be manifest until unity is in train. Again, this may mean no more than a benediction bestowed on attempts at unity. But it may also be a quasi-empirical statement about the special situation of the modern churches. If so, it lies within some overall view of historical periodization which probably has a metaphysical loading. I mean that a theologian talking about the special characteristics of this present age may be using categories from a philosophy of history. The seeming statement about spiritual movements at the 'present time' is not really an empirical judgement about factors increasingly operative since, say, 1760 or 1860 or even, God save us, since 1960, but a theological apprehension of the current scene, an inspired 'sense' of the new age to which a specific kind of action is uniquely appropriate, i.e. unification.

This 'apprehension' is itself validated by reference to the Spirit and is not susceptible to proof or disproof, verification or falsification. One may, however, observe the criteria by which the new age is marked off and staked out, and these may be a mixture of empirical observation and prophetic judgement. Thus the theologian may say 'We see today that such and such is the case . . .' And then he may interpret this as a 'sign'. The event and its train of consequences is treated as a *Gestalt* which holds together as a comprehensive 'sign'. Once the sign is identified, the theologian argues that we are thereby warned to pursue a particular kind of action, i.e. to be 'led' into unity.

This vocabulary of 'sign', 'age', 'inspiration', and 'leading' is of course specifically theological and is practised by sophisticated theologicans as well as by enthusiastic sectaries. Modernists and ecumenists make free with 'signs' as much as any sectarian, even if their language is less luridly biblical and blatantly eschatological. A liberation theologian discerning the signs of the times in Marxism or student revolt is not less in this particular mode than a sectary surmising he is in the time of the latter rain.

However, the interpretation of signs and the proclamation of ages is not open to empirical test. The Kingdom is at hand. The lame walk and the blind see. Repent and believe the Gospel. These are notes of urgency, divinations and demands, insights and commands. One cannot confute them. It makes no sense to say that as a matter of sober calculation the number of one-time lame now observed to walk has risen above the critical point. No. We are being enjoined to wake from the dead, and the signs which belong to that awakening are anticipatory instances of what resurrection and restoration mean and embody. This proclamation is a demand which simultaneously tells you the nature of the restoration now present or potentially available to you.

Here, of course, we are at the heart of the Gospel itself, and when the ecumenist identifies the Spirit with the cause of unification then we can only appeal to criteria internal to the proclamation itself. We may, for example, ask what in God's name the raising of the dead has to do with the faith and order committee of the World Council of Churches and other organizational entities. We may ask whether, in the original documents, the Spirit is not defined as inherently divisive, so that one shall be taken and one shall be left.

All such arguments, internal to theology, are curiously

flexible in their application. We appeal to a general spiritual 'sign' and draw whatever application suits us—or seems good to the spirit within us. It is, of course, part of the work of a sociologist to observe these flexible applications as they are utilized in religious suasion, whether by Popes or by earnest followers of Seventh Day Adventism or Mr Moon. The flexibility allows room for manœuvre, and any attempt at hardening up such statements interferes with their social efficacy.

For example, that famous justification of tolerance by Gamaliel is often quoted against inquisitorial action. It affirms that 'if this thing be not of God it will come to nought'. However, when the statement is reversed it seems to imply that whatever makes a successful stir in the world is to be regarded as blessed of God. Actually, there are theologians who implicitly hold such a view, but its implications are very unpleasing, even if amended to mean that whatever stays successful over a long period is 'of God'. However, though this statement is used flexibly, it may perhaps be less flexible than most theological forms of suasion, since it is at least formally reversible. Most theological justifications have a much more open texture, the most open of all being the invocation of the Spirit. (Even Series 3 has been justified by the direct operation of the Spirit in the Revision Committee, and that moreover by a diocesan Bishop.)

But to return more directly to our theme: we have looked at glancing empirical statements locked in theological injunctions. Not all empirical statements are so indirect or so bound in to the broader philosophical context. For example, a theologian may say; 'Lack of unity is the principal obstacle to the work of God in England today.' Now this is almost a direct empirical claim. It depends of course on how 'work of God' is defined, but assuming that this refers to a definable extant condition then it is open to falsification. A sociologist may then proceed to show what factors are actually involved, by the normal processes of social scientific reasoning. He may show, for example, that where, as in Scandinavia, the Church has no serious problem of disunity, spiritual life is singularly dormant. He may suggest that it is to such united death that the ecumenical movement seductively invites us.

But it is clear in this instance that the theologian has stepped outside his *opus proprium*. He has made a refutable, falsifiable statement. He is thereby a scientist *malgré lui*. The difference between theological and sociological statements remains, in principle, as unbridgeable as ever.

So let me take a third religious statement which is not at all about multiple incorporations or about unification. It is from the Psalm 39 used in the Burial Service: 'Behold, thou hast made my days as a span long and mine age as nothing in respect of thee. And now Lord what is my hope? Truly my hope is even in thee'. There is very little to be said about such a statement except to notice two characteristics. It conveys the sense of an unavoidable limit, the empirical fact of death. It acknowledges ineluctable frustration and the contingent character of human being. However, it transcends that frustration with 'hope in God'. So within the final social rite of transition, whereby a man is placed with his ancestors, there is reference to another transition. The shift from life to death, socially acknowledged in the burial service, is theologically acknowledged and then placed in the context of another shift, from death to life. There is, if you like, a crossing in two directions; life–death, death–life. The religious statement contains both, acknowledging the universality of death and anticipating the triumph of life. It is simultaneously the language of limits and of transcendence. Nothing a sociologist can say about the social transitions involved in burial can have any bearing either on the undisputed limit represented by death or on the act of faith which denies its finality.

However, our examples may allow us to make some concluding observations about religious language. We noticed how it has to do with incorporation and unification, and how such social acts were rooted in a dense forest of symbols, each entwined with every other. These symbols were 'signs' of transition. They were imperatives which symbolically described relationships. They were also a language of alteration, giving these relationships an altered aspect. The 'elements' in the symbolic language were transubstantiated. Certain relations and certain hopes were organized in a unified symbolic field by the power of signs and images. But nothing a sociologist might tell us about the social reality of the various transitions where they come into play, whether baptism, or eucharist, or death, could conceivably bear on the realities to which signs claim to refer.

6

Does the Sociological Viewpoint Bear on the Theistic Vision?

SOCIOLOGISTS share with those who study cosmology or biology or chemistry a body of methods, of heuristic devices, and of more or less accepted conclusions, some of which may be expressible in generalizations, of greater or less scope. When confronted with the issue of theism, sociologists, in common with colleagues in other disciplines, scan and question their assumptions and conclusions to see whether they forbid or exclude certain possibilities, in this case the existence of God.[1]

Some social and natural scientists may think that certain patterns argue a source of such patterns, or an originating mind or energy, but their material will not talk directly to them, as scientists, of God. If the material confronting us speaks at all of God, it does so by oblique signals, and a great deal depends on how we choose to understand those signals, and how sympathetic we are to supposing they can actually occur. In other words, the discernment of signals depends in part on the receiver as well as on the point of origination. No signal from the material imposes itself on us unequivocally, else we would all register the same message, and nobody could emerge from an open-minded confrontation with the material without registering a signal, and, moreover, one of unmistakable import.

I am merely making an obvious point about the obliqueness, and perhaps even the opacity, of the answers we may receive as we question the subject-matter of our various sciences. As we scan a subject-matter for its pattern of interconnection, its dynamics, and its causal mode, we are directly constrained by what

---

[1] Cf. Lyon, David, *Sociology and the Human Image* (Downer's Grove, Ill.: Inter-University Press, 1981).

is 'out there'. Of course, we have a hermeneutic, or style of interpretation, and a categorial apparatus, but ultimately we are imposed upon by what is 'out there'. We are, if you like, subject to the subject-matter, which is precisely what we mean by objectivity.

This is not the case, however, with this particular and unique issue of what may underlie the whole, or impel it, or set the conditions within which all activity must take place. Concerning that, we are, as I said, never closer than what we take to be plausible and cumulative inference. The direction in which that inference points is never beyond debate, and that direction clearly owes much more to our own background than would be the case with inferences we make in the normal course of science.

The human input into the scientific output has been frequently commented upon, so far as concerns the question of God, and is not seriously disputable. However, it may be proper for a social scientist to emphasize yet again the role of cultural background. He has a special interest in the link between what we bring, socially, to the questioning of material concerning God, and what we take away as reasonable answers.

The human input into our inferences and ejaculations concerning God is most dramatically illustrated in the case of the astronauts. The first man to circumnavigate the moon was an American. As he quested, and as he questioned with wide open eyes the lunar surface below him, his lips framed an answer he already knew, or at least already knew about. He said 'God said, Let there be light, and there was light'. As another cosmonaut, likewise an American, actually adventured towards the surface of our moon, he spoke these words, 'When I consider the heavens, the works of thy fingers, the moon and the stars which thou has ordained, what is man that thou art mindful of him?' The man in the American capsule came equipped with his answer, since his family and culture had provided it for him, along with everything else. We do not know what the Soviet cosmonauts thought, or indeed whether they questioned the material before their eyes in that particular way. Perhaps they barely questioned at all, let alone gave an answer. It is possible that their culture had ceased to give them access to the question.

Yet so far as the Americans were concerned, it was not just a matter of minds culturally sensitized both to query and response. The cultural provision of a question-and-answer book is not the end of the matter. The experience itself, which in this case it is peculiarly appropriate to call a heightened experience, augmented the intensity of the signals received. The answer came back in response to the cosmic question with a new, direct personal authority. It was no longer what was written in the book, repeated like the response in a catechism, without much conviction. The experience was such that the answer had been appropriated, first by a kind of shock of re-cognition, and then by a long assimilation of that shock. Months elapsed before the answer was fully taken in.

As we consider this example, we are not only aware of the contribution of cultural background to the ability of a scientist, or at any rate, a scientifically trained technician, to ask questions and frame answers. The scanning of the material under special circumstances, may alter the tone and the centrality of the question and the extent to which the answer is appropriated and received as bearing authority. The question-and-answer book then, is not inert, but can be lit up with a kind of dynamism, emerging from the experience of a given personal biography.

We are aware of something further. I wrote just now of 'a shock of re-cognition' and I used that tern 're-cognition' intentionally. In ordinary science we engage in discrete cognition. I mean that we are confronted by a limited field of force. There is a sector selected by a particular scientific intention. Within that sector we elucidate, recognize, and maybe reformulate certain patterns. The American astronauts did just that: they discerned this or that pattern or association according to the particular direction of their scientific intention. They observed aspects of their own condition, and they took readings. These observations and readings did not include the ultimate query and question. They stayed within the limits of a particular scientific remit, which defined the kind of engagement which they had with the material, whether it was lunar rocks or their own human bodies. But then they suddenly switched intentions, and opened the Book of Nature to its widest extent to include authorship and the ultimate questions and answers.

This widening involved the whole Book of Nature, and it also involved them in a total response. They were not questioning limited material with a specific scientific intention; they were, *qua* persons, querying the full-orbed horizon, to see whether the universe, taken in by their minds as a whole, spoke back. For some of them it did indeed speak, and as they heard what they took to be a universal and magisterial speech, it was not a matter of discrete cognition, but of global re-cognition. They did not come up close to the material, moon-rock or reacting human body, but stood back. To stand back as a complete human being is to engage in something different from ordinary cognition. It is rather to say, what does 'this sum of things, for ever speaking', say now to me, that I re-cognize. Do all these patterns, rules, dynamisms, modes of causality, principles of development, emit a signal which is not about this or that *modus operandi*, fission or fusion, but about something *inter*fused.

The special act of total attention to the whole, insofar as we are able to grasp it, does not mean that we may not pose the cosmic query to microcosm as well as to macrocosm. Not at all. But this particular kind of query will, at least, also include the response of the whole person to the complete horizon of phenomena. Provided that such a query has been made, then, it may be renewed as the scientist observes even the most minute object. Of course, he may merely *observe* that minute object: what is this mollusc, atom, gene, amoeba? But, providing he has also asked the total question with the whole horizon in view, he moves beyond mere observation of the microcosm. Just as the moon-man stepped back from the material, and asked the largest question in the Book, directing it towards the macrocosm, so we may step back from the microcosm, posing the identical query and discerning, or at least postulating, some ultimate answer. Man, as Pascal observed, is poised between macrocosm and microcosm. The infinitely small and the infinitely great, *les espaces infinis*, lie either side of the middle state of man, and he can put his ultimate query at both ends of the spectrum.

Perhaps I should emphasize that I am not here talking about mysticism. Mysticism is not a form of 'consideration' such as was referred to in that biblical quotation 'When I consider the works of thy hands'. It is rather a form of illumination which does not require any intellectual net to have been thrown over the world, or any complex ratiocination applied to it. The mystical experience does not involve a question about whether or not there is something 'far more deeply interfused'. Mysticism is to be fused. Mystical experience is a condition of being beyond and even apart from even the widest question posed by the intellect. (Whether that condition can embrace society as clearly as it can embrace nature is a complicated issue which I do not intend to address now.)

So far I have suggested a distinction between a specific scientific intention to observe and to make readings or to characterize in relation to a delimited sector of phenomena, and a standing back to see whether something may not be implicated in, or interfused with, the whole. Standing back, as I have stressed, is something we do as human beings located in a culture. However, I want now to develop this preliminary suggestion by considering the specific problems of the sociologist as he stands back from his subject-matter and allows the ultimate question-marks to appear. Thus, the sociologist is no longer concerned with (shall we say) the relationship between different cultural backgrounds and educational achievement or opportunity, but with the 'sum of things' we call 'the social'.

What do I ask myself as I confront that sum? Well, curiously, I do not ask myself the questions which perhaps come most naturally to the natural scientist. I do not ask myself whether society has a theistic origin. Somehow one does not question the beginnings of society with an anxiety about whether God's hand is behind the Big Bang or just inscrutable nothingness. I suppose I could ask a question about the point at which Man became a living soul, which would involve a further worry about the meaning of 'soul', but I do not as a matter of fact bother my head about it. Perhaps that is because I think of man's essential humanity, including his 'soul' as a plastic potential realized by and in social interactions and relations. Life, as Keats said, 'is a vale of soul making', and perhaps he should have said 'social life' rather than simply 'life'. Man is not, and cannot be, in total isolation. The problem of the insertion of a 'soul' at a particular point in remote historical time is as imponderable as the problem of the 'insertion' of a 'soul' in the individual biography, and, for that matter, the emergence of 'reason'. This is not to say that anthropologists and ethologists avoid the issue of the origin of society. But so far as the broad problem of the 'power' beyond that beginning is concerned, it shifts back and back through the epoch of hominids and through the various disputable evolutionary trees, to the issue of 'life' itself.

In the same way the social scientist, asking the ultimate question, does not often tangle with the complex matter of design. Maybe it is mere culpable lack of intellectual curiosity but I have never asked myself, or heard anyone else ask: did God set society up? Perhaps the question is analogous to the astronomer at Mount Palomar asking whether God set the observatory up. The observatory and society are alike humanly constructed. Society is not, of course, put together like an artefact, since it is a flow, an organic continuity, but, nevertheless, we quite properly regard society as a construction. Social life is a continuous creation, without doubt, which we by reason of our human nature, cannot help but engage in. We did not at some point decide to 'contract in' to this process, but we all jointly sustain it. Perhaps the antecedent design lies in the dynamism of the unbelievably complex process whereby our 'nature' emerged as one in which society was sustained by continuous human creation. Maybe, but I must say I have not heard any of my colleagues speculate about that. We are content to understand society as an arena of human designs.

But, you may object, does not God have designs for us? For His people? Yes, He may, but these designs concern destiny not origin, Omega not Alpha. There is, however, a question here, and it concerns the providential ordering of the human narrative. The play is full of our designs (by which I mean our intentions) but is the play in some sense 'authored'? We are the dramatis personae, but is there a playwright? If there is, how free are we to create our own scenes and acts? Shakespeare put the matter very well when Hamlet told Horatio 'There's a divinity that shapes our ends, rough-hew them how we will'. In short, we are faced with a postulated consequence of theism which is twofold: the providential ordering of the human story, and the free choice of humans in making up that story.

Before I look at this twofold consequence of theism I have to stress that it is not precisely theism *in se* which is under scrutiny here. It is a particular religious doctrine about how theism is to be understood in relation to human initiative and the long-term point or direction of the human narrative we call history. I have also to say that there are complex issues bound up in the religious doctrines themselves, which have to do with exactly how providence is to be reconciled with human freedom.

I have further to observe that it is not so much a matter of what sociology has to offer in the way of positive support for this or that doctrine, or interrelated set of doctrines. Just as sociology cannot speak directly about theism as such, so it can only speak very obliquely, if at all, to provide positive support for a religious understanding of phenomena which lie within the social-cum-historical field. Certainly it cannot speak about doctrines which are by their very nature incapable of verifiability or falsifiability. What it has to ask is as follows. Is there anything whatever in this or that particular doctrine, as for example the providential ordering of history, which is in principle susceptible to test, meaning by test the comparative method?

Well, so far as the doctrine of providence is concerned, the question of testability runs into some odd problems, some of them connected with petitionary prayer. Let me illustrate. You will recollect Francis Galton's statistical enquiry as to whether the English monarchs, who are—or were—quite singularly favoured with the petitions of their subjects, both as to their moral and their physical health, showed any special signs of the benefits. The answer I think is in the negative, but in the negative surely for theological rather than sociological or historical reasons. Looking at the longevity and the character of our monarchs from (say) Athelstan onwards, one sees no special signs of additional grace or healthy survival. But how could one possibly know? Neither sociology nor history can conceivably argue that providence intervened to sustain Queen Victoria in a state of saving grace and then further affected her moral condition and, perhaps, by extension the prosperity of her realm. Theologically, however, one can say that the mysterious workings of Providence can hardly be thought to favour monarchs. If the case of monarchs may seem absurd to Americans, the question of Providential intervention with respect to the outcome of wars may not. We speak of countries or civilizations being 'mercifully preserved', as if through tribulations and trials there was a kind of divine protection at work, exercised in the last instance. After the Falklands War the British Government seemed of the opinion that divine assistance had operated well before the last instance, and desired to thank God for it with all due speed. Again, the objection to this is theological, rather than historical, and such an objection must hold that countries are not especially safeguarded by divine favour any more than monarchs, be their cause never so just. The English Church sustained this objection when faced with a request from the government, and although thanks were offered for courage and sacrifice, the theme of the Church was reconciliation.

Of course, the problem is this. If divine providence operates in history, we have no means whatever of singling out the precise action of the finger of God. Setting aside the vulgar supposition that He has favourites among a certain class of potentate or certain kind of country or culture, there seems to be no correlation whatever between the justice of a cause and its outcome, a point made fairly and squarely by the Psalmist when he complained that the wicked flourished as the green bay tree. For that matter, the gospels set the question of mundane rewards for deeds in a wider context: the good and evil tares will continue to grow together until the last and final judgement. The objection is, I repeat, theological. So too is the objection that the more weight we accord to the activity of Providence in the ordering of history, the less can we regard it as an arena of autonomous human action and responsibility. This is not to say that underneath the tumult of wars and contentions, when the captains and the kings depart, there may not be an undertow (or overview, if you prefer) which makes for good, but it is hardly for a sociologist (or historian) to discern it.

The moment we start to declare God's hand, with Toynbee-like hubris, we have broken all the rules which govern our mortal condition. If He has cards up His sleeve then in the nature of God both cards and sleeve are invisible. On the other hand, the arena of human action may have no safety-nets or ground-plan whatever. It could be that we perform our acts on the swings and trapezes, rising and falling, sustained solely by our own skills. The arena, historical and social, to put it another way, stays as morally neutral as physical nature. To God alone 'belong the issues of life and death'. (Certainly so far as Christians are concerned, when God did show His hand in Christ there was no intervention at the crucifixion, and if we speak of the Resurrection, and as a Christian I believe I must, we attest it by faith and cannot look to any normal attestation in history or social science. The Lord did not appear to Pilate.)

That may serve as a useful point at which to introduce the second issue, which is that of human freedom. Supposing that nobody can precisely discern God either in the tempest of nature or in the earthquakes of the social and historical narrative, we may nevertheless understand Him, with some Biblical authority, in the 'still, small voice'. I am not sure what precise interpretation we are to put on that 'still, small voice' as presented in the Bible, but I use it here to introduce and symbolize the inwardness and the visionary promptings of human freedom. I have to note, of course, that the notion of human freedom is only one postulated consequence of theism, and moreover that the doctrine of free will is not necessarily bound up with theism at all. There are varieties of Christianity which see humankind as subject to election in the inscrutable providence of God. About this view I will only emphasize that there is no contradiction between believing firmly in the providential ordering of salvation, and saying also that one cannot know its operation by defining the company of the elect.

But if, for the purposes of this paper, we set aside the complicated matter of theological determinism as it relates to other determinisms, then we are immediately confronted with the problem of human choice in the context of the social sciences, more especially sociology. This involves some attempt to set out a sociological conception of human action.

For sociologists, human actions are both made possible and

constrained by culture. Humanness and the unique gift of speech are potentials only realized by beings as they relate one to another. As human beings relate, signalling by speech and gesture, and also responding to such signals, they build up relatively stable patterns of action, which enable them to anticipate and predict. Without some reasonable anticipations and predictions the whole human enterprise would founder in chaos. Just as physical flight cannot transcend the power of gravity without reliance on invariant aerodynamic properties, so the flight of human intention cannot project itself without stable suppositions as to the governing conditions of human exchange. I do not wish to push such an analogy beyond what it will bear, only to indicate that patterns, physical and social, must be stable, else our projected future will collapse.

That stability means, of course, that society depends on a repertoire of approved means to given ends, sets of admonitions and prohibitions (appropriately sanctioned), and a settled vocabulary of motive. Moreover, these approved means, these admonitions, prohibitions, sanctions, and motives, will be anchored in master symbols of social belonging and legitimate power, which buttress authority, and set the boundaries of the group, and prescribe the hierarchy of status and decision-making.

All that, and more, constitutes what sociologists and anthropologists mean by culture. Quite clearly it is a constraint, since the child, in order to be human and to speak and act humanly, must be inducted into a cultural pattern. He or she will enter into a whole pattern of obligations, to kin, to clansmen, to countrymen, to the society as such, to the signs of its goodness and power, and to those who represent that goodness and power. In this way the unique world-openness and plasticity of human being will be pre-empted by a very particular, distinctive, and constraining cultural pattern.

That may suggest that the choice of the individual will be submerged in the predictabilities of social rituals: rituals of deference and of obeisance, rituals of manners and styles, rituals of work, war, and games, rituals of commitment, awe, and faith. But I would stress again my earlier point, which relates to the way prescribed performance means predictability, and predict-ability allows action. We all of us have to act according to prescribed parts set out in society's dramatis personae in order to speak in our own voice. Moreover, once we refer to our 'own voice', we notice that this too embodies the paradox of freedom and constraint. To speak in our own voice is to be recognizable as speaking characteristically. Cognition in nature depends on repeated or patterned stimuli; recognition in society depends on the consistencies we call 'character'. Character is not the tramline of individuality, but it provides those special markings and modes of being which enable us to recognize a person for what he or she is. So while there are rituals, roles, and charac-ters, we not only 'fit' into the patterns, but exhibit a very distinc-tive 'making', which is our own way of playing all the parts in what sociologists call our 'role-set'.

I should perhaps remind readers at this point of a very general view among sociologists concerning our freedom as humans. Occasionally, of course, they hold that when you have charac-terized all the relevant correlates you have exhaustively ac-counted for a situation or for an action. All such accounts are subject inevitably to the *ceteris paribus* clause, and 'other things' very rarely are 'equal'. But our knowledge of the situation is itself a further variable, or, if you prefer, our reflexive capacity as humans re-orders the situation, though still within certain constraints. We will not and cannot jump out of our social skins, but we will look back along the paths which have led to this point and forward in terms of our purposes, bearing in mind the costs and opportunities already experienced. We not only view: we *re*view.

I referred, amongst the various rituals I cited above, to the particular rites of commitment, awe, and faith. I must conclude with necessary brevity by mentioning the odd fact that the hu-man sciences deal with material which may not only be ques-tioned with regard to certain doctrines sometimes held to follow from theism, but with material which speaks and acts in its own right with regard to belief and unbelief, good and evil, divine guidance and human autonomy, religious adherence or agnostic disassociation.

This leads me back to my beginning where I spoke of astronauts who saw what they saw because their angle of vision had
been socially a given. They asked and received answers according to the philosophical and theological dictionary approved
and authorized for use in their society, or segment of society.
Religion, then, is encapsulated in these patterns of culture, and
itself exhibits the same consistencies, stabilities, and partial
predictabilities, which we described as characteristic of culture.
At the most simple level one knows that a child in Kuwait will
grow up a Muslim, that in Cairo he will be in a predominantly
Islamic culture, but not necessarily a believer. Likewise, one
knows that someone brought up as an Anglican, whether prac-
tising or not, will exemplify a certain style or mode of response
and action. Furthermore, the social expansion or continuation
of these styles and modes is not random, but occurs in accordance with a complex dynamic which is in principle explicable.

Does this whole range of predictability and explicability have
some philosophical implication with regard to faith in itself? I
can only answer in the most summary form. Let me repeat that
it is inherent in the very idea of society as realized in multiple
human exchanges that a child is inducted into a pattern, and that
pattern will include a certain view of the world. The view, however, is not totally fixed, but it is the existence of that 'point of
view' which allows us to focus, exploit, and alter an angle of
vision. To see we must be located, i.e. have a *point* of view; the
alterable sweep of vision must have its angle. I must add that
the degree of alterability in the sweep or focus of a vision also
depends on certain social dynamics which can be specified.
Under some conditions alterability is minimal, under others
it is maximized. One can even specify certain pre-conditions
which might lead, on the average, to a destabilization of vision.
Nevertheless, we do not say of an artist's vision that its quality,
specificity, 'truth', uniqueness, and intensity are invalidated by
the constraints exerted by his social time, place, and biography.
He works within a 'school' and a culture just as *homo reliogiosus*
works within a particular scheme of discipleship and of culture.

By putting the word 'truth' in inverted commas, I set aside a
whole group of problems. I will pick up only one of these.

Religions not only declare a form of faith but in their angle of vision they may overlap the specific angle of sociology. They do so, in particular, with respect to the place they assign to religious faith as incorporating or injecting an unpredictable element into social exchanges and in the extent to which they interpret all social relations according to a face-to-face personalized model. There is thus a sort of proto-sociology lodged in religious doctrines, and insofar as there is such a proto-sociology it is susceptible to a sociological critique. I will simple indicate how the problems arise at the point of overlap without attempting any resolution.

A religion may envisage the action of faith as proceeding outside or beyond the social constraints I have described above. It may, for example, provide an account of conversion which makes it appear as if coming from nowhere and as creating a new biography in total discontinuity from what went before. If, however, we observe actual conversions, that of St Augustine for example, we clearly observe pre-conditions, inhibiting and accelerating circumstances, and we also see that the break-point is not a complete *bouleversement*. There remains a continuous biography and character, active and choosing in a constraining context. We can go further and say that the susceptibility of a given person to sustain conversion to (or inside) a given religion takes place within conditions which will yield sociological rules as to average likelihood of conversion. Religions tend not to phrase their accounts of conversion in this way, but rather to envisage religious change as a *deus ex machina*. The *ex* is overemphasized.

Again, a religion may envisage social processes, e.g. international or governmental relations, in terms of face-to-face dynamics writ large. A religion may envisage social processes in this way because it arises in a matrix of familial relationships and of small groups of disciples which project personal images onto the social world. Protestantism uses such personal images, less because it arises in small groups than because it emphasizes, in some of its forms, the role of the individual *qua* person over against society and other individuals *qua* persons. Whatever the source of such images they are misleading if they are projected onto that aspect of society, highlighted in governmental and international relations, which exhibits system properties. The behaviour of country *A* or party *A* in relation to country *B* or party *B* will exhibit system characteristics only partially reducible to the dynamics of face-to-face relations. There are constraints operative in systems which are relatively absent or differently present in face-to-face immediate relationships. One has only to think of the stylized scenarios acted out between (say) Israel and the Palestinians, or Argentina and Britain, with all their predictable constraints, to see emergent system properties. Yet religion sometimes redescribes these systems in purely personalized terms, and thereby misses or even distorts crucial aspects of social reality. (Marxism, one has to say, is precisely an analysis of macro-system properties which suggest how they may lose their alienated, depersonalized character. Unfortunately, it is sufficiently inaccurate an account of both the properties and the likelihood of repersonalization as to be more trouble than it is worth. Indeed, the dogmatic nature of the way it incorporates itself in social systems leads more often to inhibitions on social scientific enquiry than to positive leads for research.)

A religion may, under the discipline of experience, produce an implicit account of just this difference between face-to-face relations and the resistance offered by system properties. St Augustine, for example, certainly rephrased Christianity to cope with newly experienced realities of power in the late Roman Empire.

So, I have given all too abbreviated an account of some of the relationships which may exist between a theistic vision and the sociological point of view. As I said before, and must now repeat, it is not that sociology can unveil beneath the social guise the lineaments of the invisible and eternal God. Nor can sociology invalidate His presence. Sociology is tentative knowledge not gnosis. All sociology may do is comment critically on such theistic doctrines as may seem, in some of their expressions, to project an image of how society operates. Such an image is a form of proto-sociology, and as such is subject to verifiability and falsifiability. In the main, sociology as a discipline inhibits certain ways in which these images are applied, and suggests formulations which may be less misleading. The precise criticism of a given image hardly proceeds upward to undermine the theistic viewpoint itself.

7

Lawfulness in Sociology:
A Response to Mary Hesse

IN what follows I want to draw out, elucidate, and map the mental pathways of social science, and to do so through an encounter with just one characteristic problem. The larger aim of that encounter is to enquire what kind of lawfulness may be expected to reside in the subject-matter of social science, or alternatively to enquire what kinds of lawfulness that subject-matter properly permits us to impose. Clearly the social scientist engages in a specific form of questioning of social materials, putting them under pressure to elicit a yield or a return. What is the nature of that return and is it 'lawful'?

However, before setting up this questioning and this encounter I need briefly to summarize how social science may be expected to differ from natural science, following for this purpose the formulation of Mary Hesse. In Mary Hesse's view the differences are both of degree and kind. Differences of degree have to do with the extent to which there are objective constraints governing better or worse theories; with the extent of openness or closure in the system under consideration; with the demarcation and clarity of concepts; and with the built-in interpretation of language as distinct from the adumbration of unequivocal propositions.

Differences of kind have to do, firstly, with the presence in natural science of unified and systematic theories deemed progressive in terms of the pragmatic test. They have to do, secondly, with the presence in social science of an ability to extract and elucidate meanings as part and parcel of the subject-matter. In short, the social sciences erect constructions which are fragmentary and discontinuous, and they deal in meanings and in readings of meanings.

These proposed differences of degree and of kind probably attract a fair measure of agreement and they certainly offer a context within which to discuss the kind of lawfulness yielded by scientific pressure on social materials. However, before illustrating that pressure with a characteristic instance three supplementary observations are worth making. One is that not all the operations of social scientists are of the same general kind, a point which might seem to jeopardize the very idea of a characteristic instance. Some kinds of psychology are restricted in principle to just those problems which permit or even demand the deployment of a natural science mode of enquiry. Some kinds of history are restricted to modes of analysis dealing solely with meanings and motives as these make up an 'eventful' narrative. So far as psychology is concerned, it does not seem that this self-conscious restriction yields much by way of a unified and progressive theoretical field. And so far as the concentration on narrative is concerned there exists a penumbra of unarticulated assumptions about regularities, likelihoods, and standard expectations which can be shifted from background to foreground. The important point here, however, is that insofar as these varied restrictive canons are rigorously followed, the operation in question is simply not social science. It may be science and it may be story-telling but it is not social science. Social science has precisely to do with a pressure for some kind of regularity or lawful nature in the universe of cultural meanings. Those historians who just tell stories or those psychologists who deny the relevance of cultural meanings are simply reductionist, though clearly they reduce in very different directions.

The second supplementary observation pendant on Mary Hesse's formulation is that the understandability of the subject-matter is intimately linked to expectability. Meaningfulness is tied in with expectation and prevision, and prevision and expectation turn on some minimal lawfulness in the social world. Events do not just bounce around, but occur in sequences which are all, without exception, explicable. An event is recognizable and organizable as that sort of explicable occurrence, and retrospectively there are no sequences of events of which we can say that they do not make sense. Once we have garnered the relevant circumstances, nothing is beyond expectation and explanation. There is a social order, not only in the sense of ascertainable and semi-continuous structures of social maintenance, but in the unfolding of the social world over time.

This does not imply that we are never surprised, as for example, by the timing and speed of events in Eastern Europe in the latter part of 1989. Nor does it imply that we never need to revise our expectations, including in that our social scientific expectations of the possible role of a single individual such as Mikhail Gorbachev or a pivotal unique event. Prevision is linked to revision. It is just that there are no arbitrary visitations from outer social space.

The third supplementary observation is clearly implied in Mary Hesse's formulation. It is obvious and it is frequently remarked upon. There are no parallels to the existence of quarks in the world of cultural meanings. Maybe there are biological or ecological entities or processes which have unanticipated relevance to (say) our ritual and territorial behaviour and our gestures, but they are also baptized and bathed in the human world of 'meaning'. Maybe there are mechanisms in the arcane spheres of (say) finance and internal monetary relationships best expressed in mathematical formulae, but there is no entity or process not susceptible to intelligent apprehension of a commonsense kind. We apprehend such matters by acts of recognition, not of novel cognition. And that in turn is connected with expectability. What goes on in the stock-market is based on previsions which are revised and revised again with extraordinary rapidity, but all within a framework of utterly ordinary expectations. In other words, the stock-market is lawful, otherwise it could not operate or be operated.

THE SYMBOLS AND SIGNS OF SOCIETIES

At this juncture it is appropriate to introduce a problem characteristic of social sciences which is designed to illustrate the kind of lawfulness to be located in society. The problem selected is taken from the sociology of religion (or more widely the sociology of knowledge and ideology) and it has to do with the way in which societies present themselves to themselves in symbols and signs, in rhetorics of admonition and glorification, and in rites of persistence, continuity, cleansing, and aspiration. According to sociological theory these modes of self-presentation were originally coextensive with religion.

Even when religion took the form of an established but discrete body like the church, the interpenetration of the ecclesiastical body and the body politic for long continued close enough to allow social self-presentation to be projected on the religious channel. Eventually, however, societies became more differentiated and various spheres emerged more or less independent of the church, including the polity. Thereafter, social self-presentation slipped out of the religious channel. It became diffuse, only vaguely transcendental, and in some instances almost wholly secular.

The whole of the above paragraph constitutes a segment of sociological theory which needs to be set out before the problem can itself be stated. However, this major transition, broadly indicated in sociological theory, permits of historical variations of very great significance, present in two nations playing world-historical roles. In particular, Britain did not undergo an unequivocal transition to a differentiated condition, whereas the United States did. Britain started to develop towards a socially differentiated condition, but then retained a church–state format alongside a very broad and attenuated version of the Calvinist idea of the covenant people. The United States on the other hand totally dissolved the church–state format and developed a parallel and equally broad version of the covenant relationship in terms of manifest destiny and similar concepts which today constitute what some sociologists call 'civil religion'.

So how did these two genealogically related states come to differ in this way? Note that this question is still part of a necessary prolegomenon to the statement of the main point at issue. And it is important to emphasize that this prolegomenon will include some very broad historical statements treated as initial starting-points without pushing further back in time to remoter historical causes. Over time the accumulation of happenings produces historical constellations so that a given society exhibits a particular relation of the individual to the corporate, or of the centre to the periphery, or of patronage to merit, or of the co-option of religion to the freedom of religion, and these have to be treated as sociological givens from which certain consequences may be expected to flow.

What then is the basis of the difference between Britain and the USA? In short order, it has to do with an early revolution in Britain which undermined enough of the institutional restraints on modernization to render unnecessary or unlikely the kind of convulsion which shook France and tore apart state and church in mutual enmity. It also has to do with the larger proportion of dissenters in British North America and the steadily increasing range in the colonies of peoples and of churches. Now of course, this type of account needs to be checked against the historical record even though the historical record does not itself 'speak' such an explanation, at least not directly and not in sociological form. (All accounts, historical or contemporary, require to be checked rigorously by whatever forms of inquiry are possible and appropriate, but the group of issues involved in that are not my main present concern.)

Now the actual question to be posed is as follows. Given that the two affiliated societies of Britain and the USA differ as to their church–state relationship and their expression of a diffuse civil religion, how is it that Canada and Australia, both located in terms of history and of sociological criteria between the two, lack either a state church or a civil religion? The Church of England did not become the Church of Australia or Canada. Why? The sense of 'civil religion' which emerged in the new society of the USA did not emerge in the new society of Canada and Australia. Why?

At this juncture, poised to answer these twin questions, it is necessary to interpose some more sociological theory, since it is the theory which generates the questions as well as helping to answer them. True, the questions are reasonable enough on general grounds, but they still take off and acquire form from sociological postulates about the fundamental nature of social order, as well as from assumptions about the likely similarities and differences in the articulation of that order in adjacent societies.

Fundamental sociological theory proposes that societies, at least when they have moved from feudal organization to the nation-state, need an integrating myth as to their origins, character, and destiny, in order to exist, maintain their dynamism, and prosper. The people who make up a collective have simultaneously to receive and to project a portrait of themselves in a national portrait gallery made up of founders, fathers, exemplars, sacrificial heroes, and so on.

In framing a response to the twin questions it makes logical sense to begin with the reason already adduced for the absence of a state–church connection in the USA: the proportion of dissenters, and the range of peoples and churches. Both conditions are present in Australia and in Canada, though to a lesser extent than in the USA. The proportion of English and therefore of Anglicans is lower than in England, though higher than in America. Presumably it is low enough to undermine the possibility of a state church. Furthermore, people from Scotland and Ireland of Presbyterian or Catholic faith who were territorially separated in Britain are mixed in Australia. In Canada people of French background and Catholic faith are territorially concentrated in a bloc which makes the country effectively bi-cultural. Clearly there are levels of overall support for a Protestant state church, and degrees of multiculturalism or biculturalism, which render a state church unrealistic. One could go on to add a further sociological observation with a very wide range of implication, beyond as well as within the cases of Canada and Australia, which is that there exists a critical point where historic, ethnic, linguistic, and religious differences accumulate to the point where not only state churches but overall national integration becomes impossible.

What now of the absence of a civil religion in Australia and Canada? Clearly there are two obvious and relevant differences between them and the USA. The dissenters who made up such a large proportion of the founders of North America carried forward the covenant idea and its millennial overtones from its British origins, whereas the original Canadians and Australians did not. And Canadians and Australians went through no revolutionary trauma of separation from the mother country requiring a crystallization of a new identity. In the case of the Canadians, they were often precisely those people who rejected separation, while in the case of the Australians they were often convicts and therefore not ideally placed to construct a myth of liberation.

There are other relevant considerations worth brief mention. Presumably both Canada and Australia, by remaining semi-dependent on Britain culturally, and economically, and demographically, remained also within the ambit of the British sense of manifest destiny. They were still in tow; and though they constituted large geographical areas their populations were too small for them to play a world-historical role capable of rendering manifest destiny plausible. Their self-projection and identity would have to be composed of other materials.

Such reasons are sufficient, and maybe (as often happens) more than sufficient, to account for the absence both of a state church and of a developed civil religion in Canada and Australia. It is worth noting that, just as historical reasons potentially trail back in a steady regress, so historical singularities, like the expulsion of convicts to Australia, figure in sociological explanations alongside more general considerations. Historical regressions and historical singularities are endemic to sociological understanding.

It is worth noting that sociological explanations addressed in the above manner in two or three instances through the application of comparative method do provide the bases which need to be covered in examining other countries. From the examination of a restricted number of adjacent societies with relatively few differences one proceeds to societies with more extensive differences, adducing precisely such matters as degree of dependence or independence, size, geo-political role, stage of differentiation, range and type of ethnic, religious, and linguistic diversity, and so on. This constitutes the specification of relevant variables in usual scientific manner, even though there are problems to be noted later as to where one variable ends and another begins. Some may be 'hard' with distinct boundaries, like size and diversity of population, some like language and religion are bound up together in a *Gestalt*.

Just to indicate this procedure by way of examples one can ask how Jamaica might compare with Australia and Canada in terms of dependence or independence and in terms of ethnic diversity (including colour); and one can ask how Japan compares with Britain in terms of a monarchical structure re-formed to fit it within the path to modernization. In this way the range of argument and comparison is constantly extended until batteries of types and sub-types of society are constructed and certain crucial combinations of elements emphasized.

Moreover, the power of the original theoretical question about national identity will be sufficient to initiate further probes about its construction in Canada and Australia. If historical rituals and manifest destiny are both absent, what resources are available to create a viable myth for those societies? Could it be the frontier, the land, or mateship? Or are there conditions under which the creation of identity is not of paramount importance. Does the theory itself need to be qualified?

HOW LAWFUL ARE SOCIAL PROCESSES?

All this analytical work is a standard part of sociological procedure, particularly when the question posed deals in whole social systems and thus requires the deployment of a comparative method probing relevant similarities and differences. Certain aspects of this procedure need to be stated or restated before proceeding finally to ask about the degree of lawfulness located in the subject-matter. Clearly the historical element is important in that certain historical patterns are treated as sociological givens or congealed 'conditions' and in that historical specificities, like the sending of convicts to Australia, need to be included in explanations alongside the more general and generalizable sociological elements. So much is quite clear from the above analysis.

What also should be clear is that a sociological explanation can operate powerfully within a given frame, such as that provided by the sociology of religion with regard to questions of collective identity, but they, nevertheless, resist organization into unifying theories such as might bring together (say) crime and education alongside religion. There will be some highly general and abstract frameworks applicable in all areas, and there will be highly significant overlaps between areas, but the frames used for dealing with each area will have their own semi-autonomous conceptual hubs and internal communication systems. (This is what is usually meant by theories of the middle range.)

It is also the case that even within each area of inquiry the shape of the argument is variable according to the angle at which a question is put and the range of enquiry it attempts to cover, in particular the historical scale and scope. Presumably in the natural sciences there is a greater degree of controlled similarity and replication in the shape of the arguments adduced, even when the questions come from difficult angles. To put it another way: the range of viable stories which can be told in response to a question is much greater in social science than in natural science. Within the appropriate rigours of social science there is scope for artistic rearrangement. For example, I can tell a story of the process of secularization focused on the history of European art from (say) 1100 onwards, or on the legitimation of the polity from Filmer in the seventeenth century onwards, or on the church attendance in England from 1760 to 1920. All of these are controlled by evidence, but the selection of examples and the choice of significant and key instances, the periodization, and the kind of connections pursued in adjacent spheres and in relation to more general theories of secularization, depend on the angle of questioning and the power of the intellectual thrust I seek to develop.

It is worth adding here a cautious extension of Mary Hesse's point about the fuzziness of concepts. Certainly the boundaries of concepts like democracy or modernization or the polity are ill-marked. But concepts are also isolated artifically by language when they, in fact, run into each other without any border at all. Ethnicity runs into language, and language into religion and historical memory, and it is often very difficult to treat each as a variable susceptible to a weighting. Rather, they are elements in a situation to be indicated rather than measured. If somebody says that religion is a relatively minor element in ethnic conflict compared (say) to historical memory, it is very difficult to assign firm weightings. Historic memory actually includes religion already—and it depends on language. And yet there is no doubt that these fuzzy interweaving elements constitute texts which when read as wholes and total situations lead on to portentous action. The sociologist is a trained and analytic second reader of texts and situations already read as guides to action.

Most of these differences marking out social science are covered in Mary Hesse's formulations. They do not imply that social science is to be regarded as some kind of inferior activity below the level of proper science and needing to be improved by a deeper understanding of scientific method or even by the recruitment of better minds to the task in hand. It simply has to be accepted that the subject-matter is such and such and therefore sets the agenda for the kind of question which can be put, and the type of procedure which may be followed, and the mode of answer which may be given.

Now, if this is the condition of social science as exposed in a characteristic instance of intellectual endeavour, can it be described as 'law-ful'? Presumably there are different answers to that question which depend on whether lawfulness has to do with exhibiting predictable obedience to very wide ranging laws or has to do simply with exhibiting lawful or law-like character. As to the former there are relatively few such laws extant in social science, and they provide broad orientations to material, some at the level of fundamental notions about the preconditions of social integration and dis-integration, some at the level of wide-ranging processes like differentiation and modernization. Parenthetically, the theory of modernization governing the conditions for the entry into modernity was only glanced at above, since any more extensive coverage would have demanded its integration with the theory of differentiation. Broad theories frequently stay in the background in this way, even though they are actually required for a complete account. At any rate, the important point here is that general orientations are few but essential and provide constant points of explicit or else glancing reference, as indicated in the example just given.

As to the lawful or law-like nature of social occurrence, that has already been touched upon in the initial reflections of this essay with regard to expectability. Few people *ab initio* could have stood in the year 1788 previewing the effects of sending convicts to Australia, and the likely proportions of future emigrants from the different locations and cultures and religions of the British Isles, nor would they have had access to an experience like 'the frontier' or notions like mateship or manifest destiny. These are specific processes and specific notions, with a grain and resonance gained from experience and usage and some degree of inside knowledge. To that extent the circumstances of migration and the key experiences and concepts are all hidden in the womb of time and therefore not expectable. But as time unfolds a myriad decisions are made in Ireland or England or Scotland, in accordance with estimates of circumstances and chances, all of them capable of sustaining an account. And once those decisions have combined to create a given pattern of ethnicity in Australia, and once the frontier or the farm has provided a particular kind of experience, then the collective identity of a nation can also yield an account. A 'situation' may be put together and assembled combining sequences and circumstances, in which are included the different social elements or 'bases' covered above. And that done, the likelihoods and eventualities make entirely law-like sense. There emerges a third reader, who follows the text of the sociological second reader, who in turn followed the text as read by the actors. This text follows in that it makes sequential sense as that which was only to be expected in the circumstances.

CONCLUSION

I would make one last point concerning the implications of the above for the status of religion viewed as a way of understanding the human situation in the world. All that matters turns on whether the law-like nature of the social world as just indicated and exemplified has some fatal implication for the religious viewpoint. Does it matter for the validity of religious understanding that religion is active in the warp and woof of social life in this manner? I would suggest that it does not matter in the slightest. What then of explanations of religion as such, none of which have figured at all in the above analysis. Those, I submit, are simply not part of the sociological enterprise. Explanations of religion, such as those put forward by Marx, Freud, and Durkheim are philosophically based attempts to divert the ontology of religion and show that religion is really generated from and directed to other sources than it claims.[1] Nothing in social science can be adduced for or against these ontological diversions. In that respect Max Weber was truly or any rate exclusively a social scientist in that he had no explanation of religion at all.

[1] To what state the explanation of religion as such is reduced is nicely illustrated in J. Samuel Preus's *Explaining Religion* (London and New Haven, Conn.: Yale University Press, 1987). The book turns, so far as relatively modern theories are concerned, on Durkheim and Freud, neither of whom are taken all that seriously in the social science community with respect to *the* explanation of religion, though they offer important avenues of approach to various aspects of religious phenomena. Marx is effectively ignored, though his theory of religion is not conspicuously worse than theirs. What is not explored is the significant absence of Weber from the ranks of those who offer explanations. A useful recent book is Peter Clarke and Peter Byrne, *Religion Defined and Explained*, where the authors propose *inter alia* a religious understanding of religion. I note incidentally that the argument I put forward here is consonant with the view of John Milbank as expressed in *Theology and Social Theory*.

PART II

Practical Issues

8

The Social Context of Modern Ecclesiology

How does a sociologist *qua* sociologist see 'the Church'? That question may be answered in general and may also be answered with respect to the Church as it exists in the here and now of the modern world. I want to begin by suggesting how a sociologist may see the Church in general, since there may well be certain social conditions and processes which are continuously in operation from the time of the primitive Church to the present. Unless those conditions and processes are set out any focus on the Church today will be shorn of its essential context.

When I come to discuss the Church today, I will juxtapose a sociological view of the Church with a modern ecclesiology as devised by contemporary Christian theologians. The object of presenting such a juxtaposition is partly to see in what way a sociological analysis of what appears to be the case differs from a theological analysis of the 'real' nature and 'proper' destiny of the Church. The juxtaposition is also presented in order to raise the question whether there might be any implications for ecclesiology which follow on from a sociological account. It should be possible to contrast the mode of positive sociology with normative ecclesiology and also to ask how far the one might logically (or indeed existentially) influence the other.

I proceed now to a sociological statement about the nature of the Church in general. Here I draw to some extent on the kind of argument developed in my *The Breaking of the Image*.[1] That argument operates in a dialectical space between primitive eschatological thrust and social counter-thrust. In other words, it would be quite inadequate to give a reductionist account of 'the Church' whereby the foundation documents and primitive

---

[1] Martin, David, *The Breaking of the Image* (Oxford: Blackwell, 1980).

traditions were set aside in favour of social 'functions' such as the expression of certain social conflicts or the maintenance of certain social orders. The reductionist account would be as inadequate in one direction as an account simply based on the self-understanding of the Church would be inadequate in another. The 'Church' enters into all the processes of social maintenance, reproduction, and conflict with a specific character donated by its 'charter'. Whatever else it may share with other organizations in terms of social inevitabilities, such as the definition and maintenance of its own boundaries, the prescription of modes of authority, the relationship to the 'natural' territorial group, and the control of sexuality, it possesses a differentia specifica.

Once we envisage our field of interest as to do with specific eschatological thrust and social counter-thrust, we have to state a crucial rule governing that relationship as follows. *The original 'charter' will undergo distortion, and the degree of that distortion will be related in the most complex manner to the angle of eschatological tension.*

If, for example, a given religion offers a system of prescriptions, including ritual observances and social regulations, which is in principle capable of providing the ordinary social norms of extant societies, the distortion need not be all that great. Naturally, the rules may from time to time be broken. Indeed, under particular constellations of power a rule (say) with respect to the universal equality of the religious brotherhood may be systematically broken. Nevertheless, religion and society may hold together in some sort of natural unity. The religious organization will be so tuned to social 'needs' that it will not require to be differentiated from social organization, in terms of some concept of Church and State. Moreover, the element of force inherent in the internal and external relationships of a society will not acquire moral ambiguity. Thus in Islam religious and social law are not distinct and force is not as such morally ambiguous.

Now, in Christianity, the angle of eschatological tension is considerably greater than it is in Islam. Thus the distortions which it undergoes in achieving some social embodiment within an extant society will be that much the greater. Of course, this can simply be regarded as due to a general lack of social realism and proper detail in the Christian foundation documents. It does not, for example, like Islam, provide guiding norms for the conduct of a 'foreign policy' with respect to other religions.

But that is hardly the end of the matter. Christianity, as originally preached, leans towards interiority and an 'open texture' rather than to exterior observance and a closed system of legal requirements. It conceives of a religious fraternity living by understandings distinct from those which govern civil society: thus Christians are enjoined not to take each other to law or to respond to force with force. These characteristics will be systematically blunted and even reversed insofar as Christianity enters into comprehensive relationships with a society in its totality e.g. a Germanic tribe, the Roman Empire, a nation-state, even an *ethnos* or *millet* under non-Christian rule.

Yet, at the same time, all sorts of consequences may flow from the characteristics just described when social circumstances facilitate their release into the social mainstream. Up to a certain juncture they may be held back or 'held up' in the realm of ritual repetition, symbolic anticipations, and unrealized images, or stored explosively in the sidings of monastic practice. But they are susceptible to partial realizations as circumstances 'select' them as appropriate. Indeed, they constitute a latent pressure in the realm of conceptions and aspirations which, along with other material factors in the social body, make the emergence of such favourable circumstances marginally more likely.

To use a familiar example, interiority as a Christian theme may be picked up from the overall repertoire of Christian doctrine, and may be given a degree of emphasis which not only contradicts other Christian emphases but cuts ruinously into the very possibility of Christian organization and ritual practice. In other words, Protestantism understood as a raising of the level of a religious consciousness in the form of intense interiority may undermine itself and bring about the social revolution involved in the creation of secular space. In a similar manner, the initial differentiation of church and state may pass through a period when it can only be maintained as a distinction in principle and then encounter a conjunction of circumstances, as in the USA, when it is adopted as a central proposition of the constitution. This can be viewed as a secularization of the state. It runs parallel to the way Protestant individualism paves the way for the secularization latent in personal choice. In both these examples, an emphasis lying dormant in the basic reper- toire of a religion persists through a period of massive reversal, in which it remains only implicit, sucked helplessly into external cohesion of organicist social forms. With the coming of the social changes of the late middle ages, it is taken up, activated and made explicit, to the point where it is propounded as the mandatory essence of Christianity itself. At that point, given the new cues provided by fresh social circumstances, other elements in the repertoire are called upon to reopen the eschatological tension on another front.

In short, Christianity (i.e. the Church as it slowly germinates in the womb of society) contains repertoires of images and aspirations which are in various ways at odds with social re- quirements, and which cannot all be realized simultaneously. More than that, there is an element of permanent tension, in that the constitution of society *in se* is resistant to Christianiza- tion. The Christian religion attempts to bring about a unified 'people of God', based on a peaceable fraternity in which all are 'kings and priests' and those who bear rule are the servants of all. This involves an abolition of all barriers: the limitations of 'nations, tribes and tongues', the distinctions between Jew and Gentile, the localism of language, the difference between sacred and profane embodied in the existence of a Temple and of clean and unclean food. This whole geography of division is abolished at the symbolic level by the outpouring of tongues at Pentecost and by the images of spiritual warfare which precede a universal Kingdom of God in which there is 'no temple', no 'middle wall of partition', because 'God is all in all'.

This revolutionary and peaceful fraternity runs up against the fact that those who see themselves as unified must also see those who are not with them as against them, thereby recreating divi- sion. Moreover, humankind achieves a sense of belonging through membership of local 'platoons'. Christianity is sucked into the centripetal energies of the local group, becoming coextensive with it. Inevitably, the natural group is based on hierarchy and force and the bonding provided by the family. All the language of Christianity, rejecting force, reversing hierarchy, and replacing the family of generation with the fraternity of regeneration is then redeployed to support the very things against which it was directed.

Thus the thrust to unity is turned back on itself, reincorporated by society, and the geography of division reappears: temples, priesthoods, the distinction of clean and unclean, partitions, holy lands and sacred places. The clearest evidence for this reversal is provided when the cross becomes the sign of either a religious holy war or the heraldic emblem of a national flag. The sign of reconciliation becomes a sign of man's divided religious and social condition. Perhaps at this point I may be allowed to restate the argument by quoting from *The Breaking of the Image*:

The brotherhood aspires to realize the universal kingdom of God, to bring unity where there was division, peace where there was war and equality where there was false distinction. Holy nations, holy kings, holy priests, holy places and holy lands are all part of the geography of partition and therefore abolished. Relationships of domination are dissolved in the disciplines of love. The inertia of generations is broken by regeneration; the loyalties of the family extend to include all mankind. This is unity and it is coded in images of unity: one God and Father of all, who is in all and through all; one Lord, one faith, one baptism. All nations and tribes and tongues stand before God, Christ represents humanity in the holy place, the middle wall of partition is broken down, the suffering servant is one and the same triumphant King. The faithful wait for the coming of New Jerusalem, in which there shall be no temple because the division of church and world, holy and profance has been overcome. 'Be of good cheer, I have overcome the world'.

This is the aspiration, clearly stated in the New Testament. But what is required of the radical brotherhood? First, the brothers must distinguish themselves from humanity at large, and this means demarcation and separation, that is particularity. Then they must ensure that the life of the brotherhood is distinct from the life of the world. The pull of tribe and family must be rejected and this means control over the natural affections. Agape must counteract Eros. Control means discipleship and discipleship demands discipline. Discipline is rooted in the repetitive rhythms of continuous resocialization and in foci of authority which ensure the maintenance of new standards. The enclave of grace is sustained by rules and the brothers are subordinate 'in love' to fathers superior. A whole hierarchy of spiritual fathers appears parallel to the ordinary structure of paternity and patriarchy. Thus unity has given rise to division and this division is further realized in a complete and comprehensive duality: Church–World, spirit–flesh, body of Christ–body of this death. Without the hope of unity this comprehensive duality could not exist and would relapse into mere inertia, particularity, hierarchy. Division is predicated on unification, just as relativism is predicated on objectivity. Indeed the two problems are related: it is men's pursuit of unity which must express itself in division, just as it is men's pursuit of the one truth which must express itself in awareness of ubiquitous error.[2]

This self-quotation makes clear how the maintenance of fraternity, freedom, and equality must come to depend on fathers-in-god, discipline, and hierarchy.

At this point, we arrive at a crux in the argument. I have given an account of the eschatological tension of Christianity with society at two levels. The first was the level at which a particular emphasis, like interiority, was first distorted and reversed by the pressure of social cohesion and then eventually released in what (for want of a better term) we must call 'exaggerated' form.

The second was the level at which the overall concerted thrust towards unity and perfection encounters an inherent resistance, so that fraternity, peaceability, and equality are re-routed into their opposites. This is not to say that elements of these 'signs of the Kingdom' do not achieve partial realization from time to time, in symbolic reversals of the status quo, in sainthood, in sectarian, utopian, and monastic communities, in movements of social amelioration, and in attempts to establish peace, in institutions for the care of the sick and old; and in the ordinary occasions of charity. But the geography of division remains and is evident in the very existence of the Church itself as a distinct organization. Of course, the basic grammar of 'division' may

---

[2] Martin, David, 125–6. The argument of this chapter is set out *in extenso* in *The Breaking of the Image*.

sustain various transformations under different social-cum-conceptual pressures, but the fundamental fact of division is not abolished. The structure of limits is probed first at this point and than at that, but the condition of limitation cannot itself be transcended. Even the massive probe achieved by Marxism, which attempts to abolish the Church as the main symbol of a divided or 'contradictory' condition and to make God 'all in all' by establishing His illusory transcendence in the ordinary life of humankind, finds itself the prisoner of these limitations. Indeed, the very claim of Marxism to be in process of abolishing 'the division' has strengthened and reinforced the partition at the heart of things.

The crux here is that I have given a sociological account of the fundamental grammar of limits as probed by Christianity, but it is susceptible to varied theological interpretations which enter into the forms of modern ecclesiology. These theological interpretations can be reduced to three, which I now set out schematically.

These three are, first of all, a (revised) traditionalism, second, a meliorist philosophy of history and, third, a version of eschatology which sees the Kingdom as capable of realization on the historical plane. According to the first, the Kingdom is embodied in the Church, in which truth and unity and the potential for perfection unequivocally and authoritatively reside. Outside the Church the Kingdom remains 'in heaven'. It is a Beatific Vision which may be realized intermittently in mystical and saintly experience or which may achieve some localized embodiment in the sacraments of religious communities, but otherwise remains transcendent until the 'end of time'. A variation on this first view restates the ineluctable gap between God and Man's fallen condition, between City of God and City of Man, in terms of a dialectic which will never be at rest and which constantly encounters the structure of limits.

According to the second view, Christianity is an instalment within the system of progressive instalments established by liberalism. Christianity is being constantly retuned and rephrased to meet the new contingencies of the next phase in human advance. The gospels comprise moral prescriptions and perspectives ahead of their time which can be applied along with other progressive insights from various sources to improve the human lot bit by bit. The Fall was not all that catastrophic and goodwill will eventually bring about peace on earth.

According to the third view, the Fall is located only for the time being in systematic structures of social domination and exploitation. The Church is in large measure incorporated in these structures and carries forward the eschatological hope in passive, ritual, expropriated form. The 'promises' apply not to this ecclesial institution within the old order but to the sufferers and the poor, who will inherit that Kingdom of peace, brotherhood, and unity which official Christianity only prefigured. Thus the structure of limits is not permanent: the source of evil has been analytically located and can be rooted out as humankind passes through a 'time of troubles'. Of course, these three interpretations of the same 'tension' are mixed together in concrete instances and it is a rare ecclesiology which embodies one or other of them in a pure form. Clearly for the first, the Church is essential, for the second it is helpful, and for the third it is in process of becoming otiose.

The role of Christ alters accordingly. In the first He is God's Word, the unique incarnation of the Godhead, who reconciles the division in His body as well as through the Church and the sacraments seen as extensions of His body. In the second he is a Leader whose lead was partly picked up by the Churches. In the third He is the liberator who identified a coming Kingdom, and who offers life to all who share in his poverty and suffering.

It is now possible to juxtapose the extant social situation of the contemporary Church (or churches) with modern ecclesiologies, more particularly as those ecclesiologies interpret the fundamental grammar of division. We begin with an 'ideal type' of modern ecclesiology, selecting certain salient features germane to this argument. We then proceed to sociological analysis at two levels, one of which sets out key elements of the contemporary ecclesiastical situation, and suggests what existential links may exist between these features and the approach of modern ecclesiologies, and the other of which sets forward a sociological understanding of limits capable of yielding a critique of modern ecclesiology.

In presenting an account of 'modern ecclesiologies' one is inevitably devising a construct out of certain ecclesiologies which have become popular over recent years. One characteristic of these ecclesiologies has been the deployment of 'organicist' social terminology, notable the 'family', the 'community', and the 'people' in an ambiguous way. A 'family-centred' church may be one which consists mainly of families, or one which by analogy shares the inward-looking bonds of a family. A community-centred church may try to build up the intimate atmosphere and multiple bonds characteristic of communitarian groups, as, for example, 'base communities', or it may try to relate to the wider community at large. Likewise, a 'people' may be a select body 'travelling light' to Zion, or it may take in something of the notion of peoplehood, and also include further political overtones of *the* 'People' i.e. the populace and the *vox populi*. These ambiguous usages may actually reflect a situation where the churches are poised between the status of bodies which protect themselves from external secular corrosion by multiple-bonding, bodies which service a wider constituency, and bodies which have adopted an ecclesiastical version of political populism.

Undoubtedly, these communitarian emphases owe a great deal to a middle-class nostalgia about lost community. They also owe a great deal to the complementary critique of individualism. The notions of individuality, individual achievement, and privacy are regarded as inimical to the creation of community. By a paradox individual self-expression is encouraged and individual achievement is not. The global notion summing up these emphases is 'participation'. This idea, like 'the people of God' borrows political resonance from various ideas like economic democracy, from concepts connected with organicist theories of industrial organization, and from notions of 'consciousness-raising'. All these contributory ideas may be very vague but they do assist in the creation of a positive aura around the word 'participation'. In fact, of course, people have to be taught to participate and when they do so they find their participation is mainly at the symbolic rather than at the practical level.

The ideology of participation aims to lower distinctions between clergy and laity. The *laos* is the Church, and the priesthood is a resource on which it may draw. Thus the priest is no longer a distinctive person occupying a distinctive area but someone on whom the lot (the *cleros*) lights so that he (or she) may act as facilitator for the group. When he (or she) speaks, he does not teach but merely 'shares' his opinions. Again, just as the language of participation was borrowed from a long-standing political ideology favouring *Gemeinschaft*, so the language of sharing, resource, and facilitation is borrowed from social work. Like social workers, priests 'share' without being 'judgemental'. They are in favour of undefined values but do not enunciate them by way of 'judgements'. Inevitably, the Commandments are removed from worship.

This means that the area of 'proclamation' is reduced so far as the little communitarian flock is concerned to variations on therapy. The demythologizing translations of scripture presented by many members of the priesthood are either 'sentiments' or else direct borrowings from the therapeutic style. 'Sentimentality' (in the strict sense of that word as well as the pejorative sense) lies quite close to a therapy which encourages people to find out how they feel, i.e. to appropriate their sentiments.

A pastor exists not to offer a moral template or exemplar but to help them to 'grow'. His role runs parallel to the therapeutic conception of the teacher or parent. Pastor, teacher, and parent do not go so far as to point to any life-way as objectively preferable or better, but leave this open to experimentation. A key word is 'communication', which offers a useful overlap with the idea of 'communicant'. Indeed, there is little in life to do except communicate. In the context of a church, people 'communicate' with one another within the community, and thus the specific role of priest is seemingly otiose, either as teacher or leader in the ritual dance.

At least, this should be the case, but just as the offered 'participation' turns out to be mainly symbolic, so the back-seat role proposed for the priest turns out to be vigorously manipulative. He may downgrade his position by adopting the term 'president', with its useful democratic republican resonance, but he has to ensure that people not tuned to the participatory, communitarian, and anti-individualistic ethos are re-educated. The *laos*, whose contact with the church in modern society is more usually based on tangential contacts rather than multiple bonds, has to be manipulated out of the private self. The result is a covert neo-clericalism propagated under the guise of facilitation.

So this ecclesiology which proposes that a priest be re-moulded in the role of therapeutic facilitator runs into the usual paradox of authority, which is that covert authority based on manipulation is more pervasive than overt authority based on rules. Moreover, it is more personalized. The traditional priest moulded himself within a ritual 'persona', or 'mask', since he did not carry out his priestly duty in his own right. But the modern facilitator, dependent on himself, has to deploy his personality in getting his messages across. He has to come face to face in direct psychic confrontation. Whatever the doubtful validation of the westward position may be in ancient practice, it has the useful modern function of assisting face-to-face relationships between facilitator and those to be facilitated. One may add that in a participatory framework everybody has to work very hard and devote a great deal of time to promoting their viewpoint if the facilitations and the active inner cells are not to mould everything in their own image. The fact that most people in modern society have multiple obligations outside the church means that in practice the facilitator has to deal only with very intermittent opposition. And when that opposition arises he can defend his acts behind the screen provided by the traditional aura of priesthood.

Theoretically these 'screens' have been pulled down. That is as true of the physical space of the church as it is of the social space occupied by priestly roles. The scaling down of the authoritative role is paralleled by the removal of authoritative transcendence in the conception of God, and that means that a church is conceived as a closed circle of immanence, not a pointer towards transcendence. Here, of course, what look like shifts in little local arrangements connect with fundamental theology. An immanentist view of deity, with the authoritative aspects swallowed up by the supportive ones, cannot be at home in a church which is oriented architecturally, directing the eye either eastward or upward. Architects and those who produce theories about the internal furniture of churches co-operate with modern ecclesiology in 'disorienting' traditional understandings. They are propagandists of the circle, which both expresses immanent divinity and the communitarian idea. The gap between humankind and transcendence has been closed: no serious fall intrudes to place distance between man and God. Perspectives must point inwards, steps must be scaled down: no one is to prostrate himself or herself before the holy.

Thus the range of perspective has to be cut down, visually and psychically, allowing neither abasement nor exaltation. Modern liturgies are constructed as expressions of modern ecclesiologies with deliberately flat surfaces. Abasement and exaltation are nowhere to emerge either in the thoughts expressed or the words used to express them. If the invocation of the transcendent should for a moment take hold of words and fill them with incandescent vitality or rhythmic energy, this must be dislocated. Words must be bureaucratically processed until they are flattened out. The bureaucratic focus which undergirds modern ecclesiologies carefully prevents either the visual or the verbal expression of transcendence, and thereby closes off the sense of distance, i.e. the distance which gives man knowledge of being an alien and knowledge of the horizon.

Modern ecclesiology, which is in part a product of international ecclesiastical bureaucracies, evicts the church from the locality, meaning by that the local civic sense and the sense of nationhood. It may embrace the idea of community in the ambiguous sense noted above, but it often rejects the civic role and a role in relation to the global community of the nation. The traditional church was embowered: it stood in a kind of local emplacement linking the universal with the local. It represented a *genius loci*. And it was unashamedly linked with the unavoidable structures of authority in the nation. Modern ecclesiology utilizes the undoubted universalism of Christianity to break free from any sense of emplacement, or national belonging, or social authority. No doubt in the past there were indefensible liasons between religion and chauvinism, religion and legal oppression. But the contemporary dislocation seems to assume that the primal sense of place, of locality and belonging, and respect for the framework of law and authority, are outside the ambit of religion.

In the course of selectively delineating a 'modern ecclesiology' I have already noted certain paradoxes, and perhaps, from time to time, indicated a sociological critique. Overt thrust, as ever, encounters covert counter-thrust, and what is covert is often less easily identified and criticized than what is overt. Two things remain to be done. I have briefly to relate this ecclesiology to a social situation which it both reflects and claims 'prophetically' to correct. I have also to connect my comments on 'closing the gap' made in the course of describing modern ecclesiology with the analysis put forward earlier in the essay about the social geography of division and partition.

The diminution in the role of the ordained priest corresponds to his diminished authority and status in the wider society. He can only cajole rather than command. The authority of the religious professional is now exercised in terms of language and modes of manipulation borrowed from adjacent professions, especially social work. At the same time, the disavowal of authority is contradicted by a bureaucratic concentration of authority within the Church. Bureaucratic authority constantly extends its power, pressurizing dissidents, controlling the bases of religious socialization, eliminating traditional modes of understanding. This coercive power is as yet not fully recognized, partly because it controls the internal lines of communication.

The emphasis on 'community' corresponds to a shrinkage in the constituency of persons influenced by the Church. It would be possible to propose a stricter definition of religious belonging and mould the flock into a tight, resistant, and multiple-bonded 'community'. That is one tendency, and it overlaps with a sense that modern individualism, with its sense of career and its mobility, militates against anything beyond tangential and fleeting contacts with the Church. That analysis is probably correct. It can be combatted by the creation of closed groups, and these can be seen emerging all over the Western world. However, the forms of communitarian ideology propagated by mainstream religion are based on delusions. They do not 'correspond' to any reality.

The dislocation from the civic, from national and legal authority, is an aspect of social differentiation whereby the Church (or the churches) is progressively separated from various sections of society, and becomes a leisure-time pursuit competing with other leisure-time pursuits. Religious organizations are no longer implicated in the hard business of society, and operate vestigially along with other 'expressive' professions in the areas of teaching, therapy, social work, and leisure provision. (It is possible that the urge to embrace 'prophecy', however justified or unjustified in specific instances, derives part of its motivation from a desire to recover a more central social role.)

Underlying these responses to the current social condition of the churches is, however, a utopian sentiment which holds that the fundamental gap between the human condition and transcendence is being closed. The therapeutic approach cannot grasp the difficult dynamism of the political. Nevertheless, the geography of partition is a reflection of humankind's real condition. Disunity is endemic, between man and man, nation and nation, denomination and denomination, religion and religion. The sources of disunity are not incidental, and therefore removable by goodwill, but fundamental. Nor are these sources of disunity capable of elimination by a revolution which ushers in the eschatological kingdom. The partitions code the real world in its fallen condition and the signs of the Kingdom of God coexist with the partitions in creative tension. That tension is of the utmost importance and should be continuously exploited. But to pull down the partitions is only to pretend that the gap has been closed. In fact the 'mystery of God' is not finished.

9

The Limits and Politics of Ecumenism

PERHAPS I may begin with a personal statement, since in what follows I do not want to be misunderstood. I have been initially sympathetic to four revolutions: in educational method, in social work method, in liturgy, and in ecumenical relationships between churches. All four are, in my view, quite closely connected and play into each other. For example, what has happened to liturgy parallels and is reinforced by what has happened to educational method.

However, revolutions have a way of gaining uncontrollable momentum and may eventually destroy precisely those objectives they were intended to bring about. Revolutions can destroy their originators as well as their children. At an early point in the movement of revolution they display maximum potential, attracting many of the best minds and hearts: 'Bliss was it in that dawn to be alive'. But that potential is implicated in a momentum which over-reaches itself and grows destructive. The best slogans of the early phase make easier the worst crimes of the late phase. Indeed, the disguise provided by the best slogans constitutes a covering-note for destructiveness.

All four revolutions just mentioned are, to my mind, now in a difficult phase. For example, educational reform aimed to extend the best in human achievement from the privileged few to everybody. Now it anathematizes anyone who believes there is a best to offer. Once educational reform aimed to expose those key structures, rules, and sequences which were obscured by pedantic detail and rote learning. Now it often denigrates the very idea of structure and offers nothing for the mind to grasp but vague impressions, incapable of cumulative development or of transfer from one context to another. Liturgical change, which aimed at participation by the laity, is in many instances part of a neo-clericalism which resents lay dissatisfaction and deprives lay people of access to the historic continuity of their own cherished traditions.

Likewise, ecumenism. Ecumenism aimed to leap over barriers of prejudice to find what fundamentally unites people. Now it is itself an established viewpoint whose proponents may well be reluctant to listen to anyone who questions their assumptions. Those who put a query against ecumenism are identified and stereotyped as stuck in out-dated polemics, uncharitable, limited, and local, resistant to the ecumenical vocabulary generated in commissions. Not that a sociologist should be surprised or indignant at the way the aspiration towards unity has become a form of propaganda. It is logically and sociologically inevitable that unifiers treat critics as heretics.

In arguing that ecumenism has limits, I have to begin by sketching a sociological view of unification and division. (I stress that I am trying in the main to write as a sociologist and I apologize if I use comparisons which are offensively profane. Nevertheless, I believe that ecclesiastical politics is just like any other form of politics and has to be spoken of in the same manner.)

My first point is that the thrust to unity must itself be a fruitful source of disunity. Unity, after all, has to do both with inclusiveness and with power. The extension of areas of common power must give rise to oppositions and resistances. The urge to the One itself creates the Many.

But that apart, a world religion, even in its beginnings, is not so much a simple unity as a fundamental repertoire of related themes. In the case of Christianity, I happen to believe that these themes are coherent but that they, nevertheless, provide resources to be activated when required by contending groups. Groups in different situations and under varying pressures will seize upon, or be attracted by, this or that thematic element. They will exploit its potentialities and maybe conduct an experiment in seeing how far it can be taken. For example, a group may see how far and for how long one may take the antinomian principle of sinning the more that grace may abound the more. The answer has been—very far and not long.

The forms of social experimentation are legion. You may so accentuate the inwardness of the heart as to destroy forms and formality: you may invent a democratic system of voting in a monastery or commune; you may begin to extrapolate from the priesthood of all believers to undermine all social hierarchies; you may build up a disciplined core of *milites Christi* or covenanted pilgrims to create new celestial cities or to make deserts blossom like the rose. As Bryan Turner recently commented, the notion of binding oneself and the community by a covenant with God is capable of extension to provide the democratic notion of choice in the formation of political units and to social contract theories of the state. At the geographical and the social margins, Christianity has been able to anticipate all kinds of revolutionary changes not yet, and perhaps never, capable of generalization to the total society and to the Church at large. In my view, the radical peace witness acts to inject a powerful idea into the public mind but has mainly to be carried by small separatist groups because it is incapable of generalization to the state as such.

At any rate, this thematic repertoire provides fissionable material waiting for bombardment to explode. Fission is a release of power which occurs on social cue. A nascent group groping for its own self-understanding and definition explores those parts of the repertoire closest to its situation, or indeed to its interests. I am not suggesting there has to be a close fit of idea and interest. There is a free play of logical alternatives in (say) Christology, or sacramental theory which has its own independent fissionable power. Even so rival Christologies often have their social bases. Groups tend over time to select out themes relevant to their situation and these colour, inform, vitalize, and often stabilize their self-understanding. The social velocity of a group gives additional power to a religious ideal and is in turn empowered by it. And that social velocity is usually on a collision course with more static groups, a collision which helps firm up, and may even rigidify new religious motivations. Or, maybe, the social velocity of one mobile group will cross the trajectory of several other mobile groups. They may fragment each other or else solidify their identities by contention.

If very many groups are in contention at once and the social situation is fast, furious, and fluid, as in the English Civil War, the Second Great Awakening, and in contemporary Africa or Latin America, the new religious bodies are most likely to explode and hurl fragments in all directions. Most will fizzle out; some will become tight little capsules of revolutionary ideas; others will take off and expand along novel, even bizarre trajectories. Whether new groups survive or not in the long term depends on how they solve the permanent problems of authority and its transmission, of social and sexual reproduction, of the demarcation of boundaries in doctrine and behaviour, of the balance between adaptability and stability. And these solutions, once they are located, will tend to be wrapped up in a sanctified ball. They will generate protective auras around all their practices which are very difficult to shift. Some of the most radical groups may set up very strong boundaries against infiltrations from the outside world and accept semi-military discipline as a price of survival.

In the sketch just provided of the interplay of religious idea with social cue and circumstance, and with the constraints imposed by long-term survival, I have simply rephrased the general sociological notion that the power of religious take-off requires a social carrier. The group carries the idea; the idea fires the group often driving it to earthly power and glory as well as to destinations beyond our mundane sphere. Set off for the stars and you may end up with Bethlehem Steel, Leverhulme's soap, Hartley's Jam, or Rank's flour and cinemas. Clearly the social carriers are of every possible kind. Rival faiths take off from all the bases of human solidarity and conflict: rival families and villages, status groups, classes, tribes, nations, empires, and the clash of centres with peripheries, authorities with subjects.

Again let me stress the looseness of fit between social carrier and religious motivation. You cannot, for example, say that Methodism has been simply the faith of Cornish tin-miners and fishermen, Grantham grocers, or of farm labourers in the early stages of rural emancipation. Nor can you ignore the way in which religion will smudge as well as express social differences, so that—up to a point—Methodist mine-owners and mineworkers will co-operate and achieve partial equality within the same chapel. At the same time, one recognizes the way the unity of faith may give way in response to the most minute social fissures: rival families may support rival chapels within the same Methodist fishing community.

The essential point remains that the surface of religion will be responding to and mediating all the complex fissures, pressures, and upheavals of human society. It will take on, reflect, create, and be used to support the social face of an empire. It will be pulled into the centripetal force of the emerging nation-state. As archaic hierarchies disintegrate into rival status groups or into classes under the thunderous impulses of industrialization, it will either fragment along roughly parallel lines or—and this happens in most Roman Catholic societies—it will create a social fortress of faith encircling one contending group while the rival group organizes more and more vehemently around some secular banner.

Again, faith may impregnate and be impregnated by the central metropolitan power, acting as an agency of internal colonialization, or—and this is nowadays more likely—it will be aligned with the cultural and linguistic resistance of a threatened periphery. In short, Christian soldiers may march out from powerful centres armed with Bible and sword; but they may also take up encampment in the threatened periphery. Under certain circumstances, faith may exacerbate and prolong the rivalries of centres with peripheries or of one periphery with an adjacent one, as in Northern Ireland. In other circumstances, it will ameliorate imperial pretension, cast doubt on the supposed unity of faith and imperial expansion, and use the Bible to ameliorate the sword. Christian soldiers crushed the Indian Mutiny; Christian priests and ministers have also resisted the identification of faith with imperial glorification or racial domination. They have taken up their social abode in the camp of those marginal groups, in Namibia or Nagaland let us say, to whom they have taken their faith. Indeed, if they did not identify with those groups the message itself would lose much of its resonance.

So, from Charlemagne to Victoria, we have a partial conformity of Christianity to the forces of empire and to the imperial promotion of ecumenism by forcible inclusion. We have the partial conformity of Christianity to the nation-state and its use of ecclesiastical monopoly for national integration and internal colonization. We have the partial conformity of Christianity to status groups and their aggressive denominational embodiments. This gives us the major elements in divided Christendom. The universal Roman Church can be seen as the holy ghost of imperial Rome: the ecclesiastical imperium which catechized and, in a sense, colonized the Germanic tribes. The Byzantine Church was likewise a holy ghost of empire, fighting to control and colonize resistant peripheries. Indeed, many of the non-Byzantine churches compounded with advancing Islam precisely to escape this combined thrust of ecclesiastical and imperial power. The fragments remain in the Middle East to this day.

In the end, the north of Europe threw off colonial status and the nascent nation-states united their ecclesiastical élites and secular élites, church and state, for purposes of national integration. Quite soon after, a *de facto* nationalization of the Roman Church also occurred in much of southern and central Europe: Josephinism or Gallicanism, for example. Moreover, Catholicism as a system of monarchical power united with the expansion of the Iberian states to colonize Latin America on firmly monopolistic principles. Then, as commercial capitalism and then industrialism advanced, both dissolving organic hierarchies in Church and in state, denominations emerged to carry forward complicated and overlapping social mobilizations of areas and classes. These ran very roughly down to the social scale paralleling the downward shift of mobilization, from Calvinism through Methodism to Pentecostalism. Wales is an instance where the religious mobilization of subordinate strata, carried forward by rival groups of Methodists, partly coincided with the mobilization of an ethnic and linguistic identity. Latin America is almost the last instance of ecclesiastical monopoly to begin to collapse in a riot of denominational rivalries, for example in North-East Brazil and Guatemala. These are instances where the end of the alliances of ecclesiastical and secular élites would repay particular study.

In a fully developed sociological analysis it would be necessary to insert here an account of the effects of social differentiation on the fortunes of ecclesiastical élites in their alliances with
and fights against other élites, especially the classic struggle with
the secular liberal élite. Suffice to say here that with the advance
of social differentiation, older ecclesiastical élites begin to lose
their relationship both to key social areas like education and the
organization of welfare, and in some degree also to the integration of nation and local community. That loss can occur by slow
erosion, as in England, with considerable tensions between new
and old élites, as in Germany and Sweden, or by major confrontations, as in France and Italy. At any rate, the net consequence
is that the old religious élites and their constituencies are
marginalized. They are partly cut off from their old social bases
in general élite power, in the central channels of communication, in the old professions, and in the processes of integration in
locality and in nationality. That means that they are no longer
implicated in the application of social force: religious rivalries
are demilitarized. Dissenters are no longer, as they were in
seventeenth-century France, eighteenth-century Britain, and
nineteenth-century Sweden, subject to church–state violence,
suppression, or expulsion.

This is what marginalization means; it allows charity room.
And at the same time, the older Protestant denominations become less vitally connected with particular social strata. In England, for example, after 1920, Nonconformity floated away from
the struggle for civil rights and for recognition which was engaged in by lower middle and upper working groups. Simultaneously Nonconformity lost vitality and relevance. This means
that the older ecclesiastical élites who once participated in the
link of church and state, and the élites of the Protestant denominations, particularly those most liberalized, began to share a
common situation. And that common situation which they
shared in their European one-time strongholds was reinforced
by the common situation already experienced in Africa and
Asia.

The corollaries of the analysis up to this point are, I suggest,
as follows. They begin to set the limits of ecumenism. Let me
say, in a very general way, that as particular social fissures begin

to close up and grow cool, then parallel ecclesiastical differences are also more likely to soften. Thus certain Presbyterian churches in the USA have been in the process of unification because the division between the American North and South is less evident. And certain Lutheran bodies are uniting in part because the ethnic divisions which once underlay them are becoming unrecognizable. Of course, other facilitating circumstaces need to be present: a union is more likely where the churches involved are theologically similar,[1] where they are not so disparate in size that one swallows the other, and where some cherished symbol of identity, like, say, a witness against alcohol or war, will not be endangered. One may also say that class differences will be less obstructive where high status persons of one denomination are in a different area from lower status persons of another denomination.

So far as the analysis is concerned in terms of the Roman Catholic empire, the national churches, and the denominations with their links to particular status groups, I would put forward the following corollaries. First, those who control the destinies of the Roman Catholic empire will act very gingerly in negotiations with those élites of the national state churches which threw off colonial status in the sixteenth century. They, after all, have little motive to give up historic claims in order to accommodate any given national body. To give up what amounts to the divine right of popes would cause a massive crisis of legitimacy and authority throughout Roman Catholicism, even though very large numbers of Roman Catholics quietly disbelieve it. The crisis might play into the re-emergence of national Catholic churches and private option might well become uncontrollable. Moreover, Roman Catholic minorities in countries like England would be placed in an impossible position.

For their part, the existing national churches have little motive once again to cede authority to southern Europe and be reabsorbed in a system roughly ten times as large as themselves. I believe that logically it would require a repudiation of the

---

[1] Of course, there are circumstances when close similarity leads to emphasis on points of difference, as (for example) between the Revd Ian Paisley and Pastor Jack Glass.

reformed element in their past so far as authority is concerned, in spite of the fact that many of the Protestant objections have now been accepted in the Roman Catholic Church of today. No matter how much effort is made to show that recent Roman emphases are almost compatible with Anglican understandings, (at least as understood by some Anglicans) the crux of authority remains. John MacQuarrie's excellent book *Christian Unity and Christian Diversity* founders on this rock; and the recent statement of Cardinal Willibrand's (February 1986) indicates that the rock remains. An empire cannot compromise the keys to its own authority; and a national church cannot repudiate its past. The only possible compromise is one where the national church applies for commonwealth status, acknowledging the papal monarchy symbolically, but rejecting papal claims and Roman discipline. And that, it seems to me, is what people like Father Yarnold and Professor Henry Chadwick are urging.

If the one-time imperial centre cannot, in the end, absorb the national peripheries, can the one-time national centre negotiate successfully with the Protestant denominations? Here the chances are somewhat better. I have already indicated that the ecclesiastical élites of the national churches begin to share a common marginal situation with their sometime denominational rivals. As time goes on, the national character of Anglicanism or Lutheranism will tend to give way to a *de facto* congregationalism. This will be particularly clear where the national church is in diaspora, as is the Anglican Church or the Lutheran Church in the USA, or Australia. There is a further factor of some importance. During the period of establishment, the ecclesiastical and secular élites will have so intermingled that specifically ecclesiastical claims will have lost much of their force. The claims of a national church will go no further than legitimacy, historic continuity, and primacy within a given territory. They will not be ontological and universal claims propounded from a distinctive and separate centre of clerical power.

Even so, those claims to continuity and the tie with the sovereignty, ethos, and history of a whole nation will act as constraints on ecumenical unions, unless these involve the symbolic reabsorptions of bodies like the Methodist Church into the historic continuity. Moreover, it will be far from easy for one national church to treat ecumenically with another national church of a different tradition. The Church of England is unlikely to unite with the Church of Scotland, since the Church of Scotland and its Presbyterian character has been symbolic of the independence of a whole nation. It would not wish to be absorbed into a larger alien whole. Even in diaspora, say in Australia or the USA, there may remain some marginal link between ex-national churches and ethnic identities, though these are undoubtedly attenuated. I gather Scottish identity was not much stressed in the debate over the Uniting Church in Australia.

This brings us to the classical Protestant denominations. These will, over time, have partially lost their relationship to a given embattled social constituency, such as was represented by nineteenth-century Nonconformity. Since they do not make claims to specifically ecclesiastical continuity, they may begin to float with the predilections of their memberships, especially when organized congregationally. They may well become liberalized and lose their hold on distinctive doctrines. That means they are quite likely to unite among themselves, but they are also likely to be wary of union with those bodies which retain specific claims about the forms and symbols of historic continuity, like the Church of England, or with evangelical bodies resistant to liberalization, like the Baptist Church. In short, the optimum chances for ecumenism are among liberalized Methodists and Congregationalists. Presbyterians will be marginally less prone to ecumenical union, partly because they inherit stronger doctrinal structures. Thus, Dr Alan Black has shown how the Uniting Church of Australia, and the United Church of Canada Presbyterians have maintained sizeable continuing churches, at least in certain areas, whereas Methodists have not.

Here we enter a complicated area for any analysis of the limits of ecumenism. Liberalized Methodism may be sympathetic to ecumenism, but among Methodists retaining warmed hearts and, indeed, all those many denominations stressing heartwork and conversion, the situation is more complex. Where hearts are very warm there is often heat, and heat may lead to fission. Pentecostals, who represent the lineal descendants of the religion of the warmed heart, are very inclined to fission. Of course, Biblical fundamentalism assists this process because there can be endless disagreement as to what count as the real fundamentals. At any rate, Pentecostalism is an area of rapid Christian expansion which illustrates the relationship between vitality and schism. As liberal churches decline and unite, or unite and decline, Pentecostal churches split and expand. And in Latin America warm Pentecostal bodies are flung up everywhere as the fissures of social change emerge all over the continent.

Warmed hearts can wax hot over whether or not it is proper to have a choir or robes for the choir, to have an educated ministry or robes for the minister, or to seek a second blessing to complete the first conversion. They can divide over whether to drink alcohol or eat pork. They can split into chapels controlled by rival family lineages or spell-bound by rival charismata. And yet among evangelicals of most kinds there is a grass-roots ecumenism that is indifferent to denominational organization. People come together in great crowds or little cells just to share warmth, certainty, and salvation. I certainly recollect as a child being simultaneously inculcated with a fundamentalist evangelical Methodism and being taken to any church where my parents could recognize what they regarded as 'the gospel'. At one time it was the Methodist Central Hall, Westminster; then it was Richmond Baptist Church; then it was Westminster Congregational Chapel. We fellowshipped with warmed hearts anywhere.

At any rate, the classical Protestant denominations are subject to two kinds of ecumenism. One is based on liberalization and seeks organizational union; the other is fundamentalist and is totally indifferent to organizational union because it goes wherever the gospel is thought to be. That, in itself, is a kind of limit on ecumenism. Those who stress the common experience of conversion are unlikely to be interested in unions with liberals or specially sympathetic to people who link Christian solidarity with organizational mergers. It is enough to say 'Ubi Christus, ibi Ecclesia'.

I have not in my analysis so far touched much on the distinctive concepts of church government. These seem to me to involve some fundamentally incompatible principles. On the one hand, you have in varying degree churches whose appeal is to the organic growth of a tradition and to the inherent character of a hierarchy. You may, if you will, regard these inherent hierarchical distinctions as parallel to an organization of society based on estates. In the modern era these hierarchical principles have been rephrased in democratic form so that priesthood derives from its representative character *vis-à-vis* the whole laity, but the concept of orders is still important. On the other hand, you have in varying degree churches whose appeal is largely or solely to scripture and/or whose structure is viewed as part of the pragmatic division of labour. These churches have evolved in parallel with the growth of democratic political forms. Indeed, these democratic practices were often first tried out within the churches before they were generalized to society at large. Some of these churches of the post-Reformation era have experimented in local autonomy and congregational control; others have favoured a kind of democratic centralism. There are many kinds of combination between pragmatism and appeals to the principles of organization believed to exist in the most primitive layer of Christianity and in the Biblical record. But the principle of a division of functions, which have an inherent character, and which is validated in organic continuity, is to my mind not compatible with principles which tend to this or that extent to stress pragmatic or exclusively biblical forms of organization, and appeal beyond organic continuities and forms to an apostolic succession of the spirit.

I have, of course, omitted the further limits of ecumenism, since the dogmatic para-Christian sects like Jehovah's Witnesses and Mormons are possessed of the plenum of truth. Again, I have not discussed an obvious limitation in that as you move ecumenically towards including (say) Unitarians, you move away from any chance of *rapprochement* with Roman Catholics. It is equally obvious that groups with a special witness to make, like the Quakers, will not want to be absorbed, even though they may be very co-operative.

So much for straightforward corollaries. The rest of what I would want to say can be put in summary form. First, it is not true that Christianity is hindered by its division, except sometimes in what used to be called the mission-field. Where Christianity is most united and monopolistic, the consequences have been either apathy, as in Sweden, or chronic anti-clericalism, as in France. Where Christianity is most pluralistic and most varied, as in the United States, it is also likely to be vibrant. In Africa and Latin America the spread of Christianity goes by schismatic leaps and bounds. Secondly, reunion does not promote recovery. I do not know how far and under precisely what circumstances it is true to argue that ecumenism follows from decline, but the evidence is that numerical decline is not reversed by reunion. The Methodist Church and the United Reformed Church in England have continued to decline after union. In a way unions resemble the mergers of newspapers: they cannot deliver their old readerships to the new loyalty. This is particularly true when two local churches are rationalized to form one.

This introduces a third point, which is that unions are often accompanied by new breakages. Of course, the continuing bodies may be quite small. But even if that is the case, the manipulations required to attain union leave legacies of bitterness. They may also trail the kind of legal disputes over rights to title, property, and schools such as occurred in the Australian Presbyterian Church.

Not only do ecumenical unions generate bitterness, but they can also require a working over of verbal formulae to the point of dishonesty. The rhetoric of unification has to be so inflated that opponents are characterized, not only as strangers to charity and tolerance, but as enemies of the Holy Ghost. Those who retain loyalty to old traditions are surprised to find that what the Holy Ghost said up to yesterday through His spokesmen, He cancels today through his spokespersons. Traditionalists find that things to which they are deeply attached are downgraded, abused, and invalidated, mangled in the machinery of ecumenical politics. Of course, they may also come to recognize similarities between their own practices and the practices of others.

That is all to the good. But people's attachments are to the local and familiar; to childhood memories; to networks of friends; to 'the platoon' in which they were born and nourished. They are not usually all that doctrinal in their loyalties; they increasingly accept a multiplicity of ways to God. Yet they are equally not all that interested in mergers or in formulae proposed by ecclesiastical bureaucracies and their specialized agencies.

What, in general, follows from the kind of analysis I have tentatively put forward? In general, it follows that the sources of division are endemic and the source of unifications specific. I think it also follows that the process of reabsorbtion of the national churches in the universal empire will, in the Pope's words, reach 'a rational limit' imposed by the legitimation required by the central Roman authority. At most, the national churches might acquire a commonwealth status in the Roman empire with a very loose symbolic association to the monarchy. It also follows that those churches whose forms derive from organic traditions which stress inherent hieratical distinctions will find it quite difficult to unite with churches whose governance is based on a pragmatic division of labour or on the models believed to be embodied in the New Testament, or on some combination of the two. It is also not easy to combine apostolic successions based on historic continuity with those based on a discontinuous affinity of the spirit. The point of maximum opportunity for ecumenism arises among liberalized Protestants, particularly when they have floated free of their original anchorages in aggressive or divisive social constituencies. And as I argued, evangelicalism often exploits an ecumenism of the spirit at the same time as it breaks in fragments in response to rival charismata and rival interpretations of scripture.

Even as ecumenical unions occur among the older bodies, especially in diaspora, or in countries where they are minorities, new fissures will open up in response to volcanic social upheavals in Latin America and Africa. As Christianity has declined in Europe and tolerance has increased, so in Africa and Latin America there are huge inundations of pullulating spiritual activity corresponding to differences of spiritual need, whether it be emotional catharsis or healing, and to tribal, regional, and status differences. It is not for sociologists to make speculations about the Holy Ghost, but whatever some theologians may say about His call to union in the old heartlands of Christianity, elsewhere vitality and schism seem to go together. In any case, the pluralism of American Christianity certainly affects ten times as many persons allowing for size of population as the single monopoly enjoyed by the Church in Sweden. No matter that America is the home of ecumenical unions as well as splits: divorcees get married more often than those who stay married. Of course, numbers may not matter: maybe Albanian Christianity can at last be adjudged by one righteous soul, Mother Teresa of Calcutta. Sociologists can only discuss observables.

One suggestion a sociologist may make, however. Our Christian divisions are spoken of as a kind of social sin, and Christians beat their breasts in shame. But divisions can also be seen as a rich variety, exploding from a vital original. Some of that rich variety and experimentation can be, and has been, contained within boundaries set by the Catholic Church. As Macaulay observed, the Catholic Church would probably have made Joanna Southcott the founder of an order. But the rest of the experimentation breaks bounds, and it will go on doing so as long as life remains in the Christian body.

10

Religious Vision and Political Reality

ONE of the major problems for Christians as they contemplate the social and political realm is the extent to which their faith seems to have been converted into its opposite. Faith claims to have 'overcome the world' but in truth the 'world' has absorbed and overcome faith. This reversal is not only sadly observed by Christians but sardonically commented upon by marginal believers and non-believers. Of course the non-believer may rest his sardonic observation of the Church on a variety of philosophic positions, but quite often he—or she—is sufficiently imbued with Christianity to criticize faith for not being true to itself and to the New Testament promise. Indeed, there are many cases where non-belief has been adopted precisely because the Church is regarded as imprisoned by the social chains it claims to break. Part of my object is to show just how and why a liberating Christianity has to be in chains.

So the criticism of the Church is not only self-criticism. It is a complaint from those outside that believers are not sufficiently Christian. The depth of disappointment in Christianity is proportionate to a sense of unfulfilled promise. The critical complaint and disappointment arise at various levels; and the immediate intellectual task is to set these levels out.

One level is very simple and runs as follows. Christians are enjoined by their beliefs to love one another and to do good to all men, but 'especially to those of the household of faith'. But they often do little good to others and from time to time have been notoriously disputatious among themselves. They are, in short, 'no better than they should be'; and everyone knows that 'You can be good without going to Church'. Christians are sensitive to this criticism. In particular those who count themselves among the 'saved' exert themselves strenuously to prove that faith does make a difference. They try very hard to be nice, and to live smiling, helpful, happy, and triumphant lives. Quite likely they engage in social ambulance work for the ill, the aged, the deprived, the depressed, the orphaned, and the outcast.

So the low-level criticism of Christians is in some ways balanced by a low-level acknowledgement that there are certain people, often called 'real' Christians, who 'go about doing good'. Though they envelop themselves in unnecessary paraphernalia, what with praying, worshipping, and reading the Bible, there is some spin-off for the rest of society in their keen embrace of social ambulance work. Churches are tolerable as a channel for the indirect amelioration of social problems.

However, both denigration and admiration at this low level are moralistic and individualistic variations on a more deep-seated theme. Criticism goes beyond the spotty character of Christian moral achievement to include comments at the political level. This more advanced criticism itself comes in two forms. The first simply develops the moralistic, individualistic vein of comment just described to take in the context of political action. It holds that when the Christian adopts various roles in the polis he does not cut a very distinctive figure. His (or her) Christianity is absorbed by the specification of the role rather than being able to transform it.

The disjunction of faith and social performance can be brought out with special poignancy by considering the role of the military chaplain. This is, in the strict sense, a political role, that is, one built in to the central nervous system of power. The chaplain for his part has been commissioned by the Christian community to represent the faith. He is, therefore, doubly commissioned, by Church and by State. As a result he is assimilated to the officer corps, receives salutes, and is expected to obey the military hierarchy without question. The scope of his conscience in social, political, and personal matters is drastically reduced. The chaplain receives the indelible stigmata of a social role and he is subjected to criticism on the ground that he ceases to be distinctively Christian.

The chaplain, as an incumbent of the military role, is often as acutely aware of the problem as the critic. Studies of military chaplains show they often experience tension between their total obedience to man and their proper obedience to God. This tension can be dealt with in various ways which have their analogies among Christians in less exposed social roles. One is for the chaplain to become a 'Woodbine Willie' alongside the serving soldier. Another is to smother Christian sensibilities and try to prove that he can down his pint and risk his life like the next man. Yet another is to reject the role altogether as being too riven by the contrast between priest and military functionary. So here we come to a crux in the argument about the Christian *vis-à-vis* social requirements. He either joins up and experiences unease or opts out. This alternative almost summarizes Christian history.

Societies impregnated by Christianity have often recognized this unease, at least to the point where the clergyman is exempted from military obligation. Most people are expected to obey social imperatives, but an incipient clash between sacred aspiration and profane reality receives a strictly limited recognition in this clerical exemption. Yet this in turn generates its own unease. The representative of the Christian community has at the very least opted out of the fraternal demand for common sacrifice. After all, in a strange way, the army represents an analogue of Christianity by combining fraternity with sacrifice. It offers both a rival loyalty to faith and a close analogue to faith.

The half-believer noting the problem will often be sufficiently imbued with Christianity to comment unfavourably both on the Christian minister who becomes a chaplain and the minister who claims exemption from fraternity and sacrifice. It begins to look as if there really is something in Christianity itself which is a potent source of moral unease and serves to undermine any solution to that unease. Being 'in the world but not of it' is far from easy. Of course, for some the tension can be solved. 'Fear God and Honour the King' is for them a sufficient motto.

If we continue briefly at the level of a moral criticism of roles we find that the Christian politician experiences many of the tensions of Christian chaplaincy. With the chaplain the Christian who enters politics will be regarded as absorbed by the role rather than transforming it. The average moralist-in-the-street says of politicians, Christian and non-Christian alike, that 'they are all the same'. And this loss of distinctiveness will in part arise because parties, like armies, are built on corporate discipline. Too much scope for individual conscience leads to fragmentation, to ineffectiveness and failure. Political discipline will from time to time issue in what looks like amoral obedience to the imperatives of party organization.

The imperatives of politics, like those of armies, are rooted in a principle of limited fraternity. They demand not love for all humankind, or even for those of 'the household of faith', but obedience to the whip. Of course, there is a conscience clause available for use by politicians, secular as well as religious, and this is an echo of the military exemption available to clergymen. That clause can remain operative only so long as it is not pushed too far or used too often.

At the very least the Christian politician may be required to lie for his party just as the chaplain may have to repress any revulsion he feels against orders issued in time of war. To put it succinctly, social life in its political as in its military organization is inherently based on strictly limited fraternities, and these are run according to the needs of canalized conflict or open warfare. The roles of politician and soldier alike demand amoral obedience, the suppression of the whole truth, the propagation of polarized alternatives, the stereotyping of enemies as agents of darkness. They exemplify the principle that it is good that one die for the people, innocent or not, and that one must be reluctant about doing justice once in case one has to do it again.

The Christian may engage in these requirements more or less reluctantly, and with this or that degree of decency, but they are built unavoidably into the role. As I have suggested, they provide occasion for criticizing the conduct of Christians, and create unease and self-examination among those politicians and soldiers who take seriously their convictions. Sometimes tragedy results, as when George Lansbury, Anglican leader of the British Labour Party, was accused by Ernest Bevin of 'hawking his conscience from conference to conference'. Faced with such dilemmas Christians have to work out some *modus vivendi* between feasts of universal love on Sundays and the demands of *realpolitik* on Mondays. Their solutions will reflect the classic answers of the past. Enoch Powell, for example, insists on a strict division of realms. One may decide with Sir Henry Newbolt simply to 'Play up and play the game'. One may, like Jimmy Carter, absorb Reinhold Niebuhr, and take the dialectical agony into one's own soul. One may assimilate a particular form of Christian hope to a version of secular idealism.

Thus far I have focused on the level of roles: what happens when the Christian is involved in a socially prescribed performance within the political sphere, and what kinds of criticism and unease are generated? However, criticism can be developed in a more general way at a further level. This criticism takes off not so much from Christian assimilation to particular social performances, as from the collapse of the whole Church before the realities of social life. The gospel is co-opted by society with what gradually becomes the active collusion of the Church, especially as ecclesiastical and secular élites come to be drawn from the same nurseries. The seat of the Senator and the cathedral of the Bishop abut and even abet one another. In relating to a total society the Church receives the complete stigmata of its social organization into its own body. The stigmata of Christ fade into mainly ritual reminders.

The Church in its foundation documents is, after all, defined as the peaceful fraternity of those under the banner of the cross. When, however, the peaceful fraternity conquers society, and becomes aligned with it even to the extent of becoming the state religion, peace and fraternity are much less evident. Instead of being fraternal the Church reproduces hierarchy and replicates the structure of secular power. Instead of being peaceable the Church is implicated in the violence which maintains the State and in the internecine warfare which characterizes relations between States. It drops pacifism and becomes militarized, apart from certain impotent reservations. Soldiers of Christ leave off the weapons of love and exchange the helmet of salvation for a real shield with a cross on it. Instead of appealing to the voluntary submissions of the heart, the Church may missionize with—or at least alongside—violence. Charlemagne and Pizarro provide obvious examples though the counter-examples of peaceful propagation and protest against violence on the part of missionaries are always present.

The Church, in short, adopts the normal presuppositions of the State to which it is wedded. These include the idea that membership is an ineluctable condition rather than a voluntary decision. People are 'compelled to come in' and the inquisition or some parallel form of social control is the instrument of this compulsion. This means that relations with dissident Christians are also militarized. The State is expected to maintain an ecclesiastical monopoly of the means of grace. (I should say here that the sociological understanding of this situation sees the militarization of relations between Christians and dissidence as rooted in lack of social differentiation. Conversely, as society becomes differentiated and the Church is marginalized the relation between Christians and dissidence become de-militarized, merely part of the rivalry of voluntary associations.)

Clearly these partial and sometimes almost total reversals of the New Testament are part of a tension between the Christian religion and general social requirements as assimilated by the Church. They are commented upon by critical observers as ironic. Indeed, even the Church itself tacitly accepts the irony and continues to express the tension by symbolic gestures towards the lost ideal. The gesture which holds military and political service to be inappropriate for a cleric is a symbolic relic of a profound disjunction between the Christian God and Caesar. The gesture which forbids the Church itself to burn the heretic is a witness to the irony of voluntary love compelling adherence by threat of torture and death. The largest gesture of all is that made by the development of monasteries. This concedes that the Church has, in the main, collapsed before current social imperatives and mostly accepted the low moral aspiration of the average man. So monasticism endeavours to restore the pristine vision in a small enclave of the highly committed. Brotherhood and peace are restored in the wilderness, in the solitary place, away from the force of social pressure and state organization.

So we have noted various kinds of irony in the relationship of faith to society. There is the failure of the average Christian to devote himself to love and service. There is assimilation of Christians to the role performances demanded by the polis, such as soldier and politician, which becomes dramatic when representative Christians, like priests and ministers, become soldiers or politicians. Finally, there is the collapse of the Church itself before the imperatives operative in society taken as a whole. These ironies not only give rise to criticism from non-believers and from believers, but derive directly from the profoundest thrust in the New Testament itself. As I said earlier, criticism of Christianity is typically Christian.

That being so, there arises one further criticism which inverts those already referred to. This criticism begins by stressing the tension between faith and society and the way most Christians fail to bridge the gap between the demands of their faith and what is inherent in their social membership and in social organization as such. But this criticism goes on to argue that the fault lies in the original foundation documents. The Christian ideal is too high, demanding, and hard; the Christian aspiration is unrealistic. Far from the Sermon on the Mount being admirable it is impossible. It has been laid on humanity and the result is guilt or else hypocrisy, or weakness and resentment posing as pacific virtue. Either people are so full of self-hatred that they cannot attain the impossible ideal or they become hypocritical, quietly ignoring the injunctions they claim to accept. On this reading the Church retains all too much of the original message and becomes a machine for manufacturing chronic personal guilt or for engendering chronic irritation with society's necessary social institutions. And insofar as monks set out seriously to follow the ideal they are the worst of parasites, withdrawing from their ordinary social obligations selfishly to cultivate their souls (that is, when they are not being successful landlords and garnering immense wealth). Better to have a good sensible religion like Judaism or Islam where the prescriptions are either perfectly compatible with the demands of ordinary society and/or restricted to ritual requirements which at least do not distract people from normal social obligations.

I have given an account of the clash between religious ideals and political realities. Before I go on to analyse the clash sociologically I have to make one thing clear. In speaking of 'political reality' I do not mean to imply that everything that occurs in society by way of fratricide, inequality, repression, *realpolitik* and so on, arises because it is an essential part of the system. What I do intend to argue is that there are certain very general requirements of social life which are to be observed in all societies (except the smallest) at all times. Before we can make sense of Christianity's revolutionary frustrations we have to analyse the sources of that frustration. We have to elucidate the dynamics which follow when a group tries to 'turn the whole world upside down' by making everybody into brothers and sisters.

Christianity is an attempt to embody the perfect and make the Kingdom of God come on earth as it is in heaven. It is good news to all humankind, but especially to the poor, the weak, and the captives. In the Kingdom of God the mighty will be cast down and those of low degree exalted. There will be no Kings or priests because all are Kings and priests. Everybody will be included in this Kingdom, Jew and Gentile, near and far, greatest and least. The Babel of conflicting loyalties and languages will be silenced and reversed as all humanity breaks into the common speech of the holy spirit at Pentecost. Humankind will be as one in the spirit of love. There will be one God above all, through all, and in all. His Kingdom will be one of peace and it will have no end. And the Kingdom will come as God's Representative proclaims that the present world is under judgement, sets forth the new law of the Kingdom, and embodies the perfect rule of love in his own person. In doing so he himself will encounter the full force of the old order, its violence and its power, and will turn the terrible piercing signs of evil and of death into pledges of love and eternal life. He will meet evil power and the powers of evil in battle armed only with the weapons of love. In this way he will turn a sign of negation into a sign of hope: 'death thou shalt die'.

Christianty will confront the world under the signs of the cross and the common feast. They are the semaphore of sacrifice and loving participation in fraternal unity. And this unity is coded in the New Testament in a whole variety of ways. First, the continuity of generation after generation within the limited covenant of the biological children of Abraham is broken up by the unlimited covenant extended to all who are born again. Christ is the first corner-stone of a new brotherhood, born not of the flesh but by the holy spirit. Second, he breaks down the local loyalty of blood relations and blood brotherhoods. Families and armies dissolve in the unity of those joined in the blood of Christ. Third, the pledges and promises of this unity are constituted by the great feast, the sacramentum or seal, open to all who wish to sit down in the Kingdom of God. Fourth, this involves the abolition of the 'middle wall of partition' between Jew and Gentile, sacred and profane. The coding of division in space is abolished and the Representative Man stands directly before God without mediation. Fifth, this destroys the Temple itself because in the New Jerusalem there will be no need of a distinctive marker of God's presence, since God is 'all in all' and 'the mystery of God is finished'. The Lamb himself is the sole light of the City and delivers the reunited Kingdom up to the Father.

This is the coding carried by Christianity and constantly re-produced and imprinted by the Church, above all in the sign of the cross and the common meal. Both speak of unity in one blood, eternally offered for and to humankind as God's free gift. Christianity incorporates the gift relationship, from God and to God, his sacrifice and ours, as the basis of union and communion and communication.

Now, if Christian signs are read this way, if this Christian semiotic is subjected to this hermeneutic, then the signs immediately encounter the barriers of social logic. The making of the Christian signs arouses enormous tension and this is coded by war in heaven and on earth, the last battle against war and division. To seek unity is automatically to create disunity, since particularity and particular affections are counterposed to universality. The thrust towards unification gathers a contrary and equal thrust to division. Moreover, the passionate search of love in pursuit of unity defines those who remain wrapped up in their own local and limited concerns as unworthy. Judaism in a rather matter-of-fact way accepted the division into Jews and Gentiles, though with intimations of a wider Kingdom. Christianity had a cutting edge sharply dividing even families and the house of Israel into the partisans of unity and those who resisted. The Nestorian Christians in China were cut down precisely because they would convert. This constitutes a social sword and it gives rise to a Jewish criticism of unlimited love and conversion which is largely correct.

And at a more local level this unlimited aspiration has to locate itself in partial systems of power which 'stand in' for universality, and partially expropriate it, like the Roman Empire and its heir the Roman Church. At an even more local level it becomes sedimented in the nation. If you enter the Greek Orthodox Cathedral in Sydney you see the signs of the encounter of Christian aspiration with ethnicity and empire: the Greek national flag and the flag of Byzantium.

Thus, as the Christian code or system of signs in cross and meal is propagated by catechism and canonical scripture, and dramatized in liturgy, it encounters all the difficult elements which sustain normal society, which are founded in the localized blood brotherhood of family and army.

But why? So far as concerns the family it is, in one form or another, a localized tie or union for the sake of reproducing the next generation. The family guarantees physical survival and group reproduction. It is a basis for continuity, the reproductive social cell. In the family inheres the Abrahamic principle whereby the seed of past generations is protected for the future; and it is unavoidable. Some Christian groups like the Shakers have tried to avoid it and have simply died out.

So far as concerns the army (or the warrior band) it is likewise the basic cell of physical survival. The army, like the family, is inherently hierarchical. Officers issue commands and promulgate rules. Soldiers accept discipline and cannot exercise much by way of individual moral choice. They may sacrifice themselves for each other, for laws, for country, for empire, but they must never sacrifice themselves for their enemies.

Here then we see dramatized the warfare between the universal family and the local family, and the clash between the soldiers of Christ and the imperial soldiery. It is Jerusalem in confrontation with Babylon. In the course of this battle the universal ideal inevitably loses and that means that the social geography of partition is restored. The failure of the attempt to overcome the world is coded in areas and in symbols which are bounded, that is, possessed of edges which partition the perfect from the imperfect, the reclaimed from the unredeemed. Instead of the Temple being abolished there appear many temples. Instead of all food being declared good and clean as in St Peter's vision, certain restrictions reappear to symbolize that everything is not yet unified. Instead of one royal priesthood of all believers there are separated priesthoods who are guardians of separated areas. Instead of the Kingdom of God there emerge special holy nations, holy Kings, and holy lands, each hedged about and symbolizing division. Instead of one family under God there is once again the sanctification of the limited family. Instead of the Christian girded with spiritual armour, who has refused the oath of limited allegiance, we have the Christian soldier bearing his cross on a physical shield. The cross itself is now a sign of war not of peace, and it is incorporated in national flags not blazoned as a sign of universal brotherhood. The cross has been converted; it does not convert.

This is not to say that there are no forays into the political realm to try to bring some limited area into subjection to faith and hope. There may be an attempt to establish the peace of the church, to offer sanctuary to fugitives, to outlaw particular weapons, to limit the means and occasions of warfare; but the social logic of local family and political army will have reestablished itself and generated once again the geography of partition.

And the most radical Christian forays into social organization will have to be conducted in small groups, like sects and monasteries, which devise a sharp boundary with the resistant world and whose élite soldiers have to enlist under a hierarchical discipline. They will be vertically and hierarchically partitioned. As they make their forays into the world they will carry radical charges in terms of reforms, but these will have to be built into the group by severe socialization, that is, by a discipline of brothers-in-God by fathers-in-God. The radical charges will be encapsulated in the group as potential explosions of energy: monastic witnesses to the sanctity of work or Quaker witnesses to the primacy of peace. Some of the sharpest incursions into 'the world' will generate the most involved grammar of bound-ary and partition. For example, the Sisters of the Good Shep-herd aimed to rescue prostitutes. The Church considered this one of the most dangerous of expeditions into 'the world'. The task of converting Magdalens into Madonnas would require high walls to be built around the whole enterprise. Even the church inside the convent would need to be divided up into three, even into five partitions, protecting purity in order that the pure might be able to save the impure. The intensity of the battle would be written in a social geography of rigid divisions of time and space. Similarly the vast Cities of God embodied in Baroque monasteries, where all kinds of social experiment oc-curred, were heavily walled in against the unredeemed world.

So, both in the Church and in the radical aims of sect and monastery, we see different modes of affecting the political realm: diffuse reforms in the Church, constantly collapsing in the face of social imperatives, explosive potentialities in the sect and monastery, protected by partitions, but often eventually released into society. The continued existence of the categories 'Church' and 'World' and of 'Flesh' and 'Spirit' would be the most eloquent reminders of a thrust to unity which had been turned back upon itself.

But it is arguable that the tensions symbolized and main-tained by these protective borders are not necessarily uncre-ative. The observation of disjunction between real and visionary is a major motivation for believer and for non-believer alike. The irritant of irony gives rise to potent dissatisfactions, which press against the structure of limits. Of course, every pressure on the structure of limits, and every attempt to unify space, will generate further partitions, a different social geography of divi-sion. Pressure will transform the basic grammar of partition. The attempt to abolish the Church altogether by Marxism and to cut out the symbol of social contradiction which it represents, is just a recent modern attempt to unify space. Recent changes in the Church itself are based on the principle of unifying space by weakening the wall between Church and Society or bringing the People of God to assemble in the House of God around a single focus without partitions and without rails. The reforming partitions are re-formed because of the permanent political nature of society. But the thrust to unity is also a dialectic, held back, but continuously and fruitfully operative.

Perhaps I can summarize. The Church as it is pulled towards the World by the centripetal pressure of hierarchy and social integration, and of local ties of blood, infiltrates visionary images into the everyday accepted reality. First here and then there, these images engender Christian dissatisfaction with the mundane reality and general dissatisfaction with the Church. Only occasionally when tilted at the right angle to society can the Church, or some part of it, release the potential of its ideal images, as in the Philippines and South Africa. Many collaborating circumstances have to be present for that to happen, and so long as the Church retains or forges links with the whole society it will reproduce ambiguities from that society as well as creating them in its own autonomous drives for power. What those collaborating circumstances are can be analysed sociologically, and at least one involves some differentiation of ecclesiastical and social élites.

As the Church tangles ambiguously with social processes it will be wise to deploy its weight at the optimum moment, that is, not throw about such weight as it has all the time and explicitly on one particular side. Even though the circumstances operative at the optimum moment may require an identification with a particular course or side, as in South Africa, pre-independence Rhodesia, and the Philippines, the Church will probably stand back from that identification as circumstances change, fresh divisions appear, and a newly installed regime exercises power more ambiguously and in its own partial interests. In the Philippines, Cardinal Sin has stepped back marginally from the political arena, no doubt with a reserve weight in general available to the new government, but also with a moral reserve also present to be called upon if necessary. (As for the sects and monasteries, I have already indicated how they protect a whole series of experimental deposits of divinity. They provide reservoirs of hope which are channelled into the social mainstream from time to time or maintained as a silent, standing witness to alternative forms and ways of life. The attack mounted on them by the World indicates not only their intermittent corruption and irresponsibility but their capacity permanently to stand for an alternative and spiritual autonomy. The Jehovah's Witnesses at least witnessed for the principle of spiritual autonomy against Soviet as well as Hitlerite tyranny.)

Both compromising Church and rigorist monastery or sect pick up continuing impulses from the sharp angle of eschatological tension set up in the New Testament. If that angle had been less sharp, the warfare of Christian with principalities and powers would have been milder, the tension would have been neither stored nor released, and the continuing irony of the Church would not have been available to create guilt in the Christian or dissatisfaction in the outside critic. Of course, the ideal as embodied in the Sermon on the Mount cannot straightforwardly be realized and, in particular, circumstances can motivate Christians to avoid social responsibilities when they should involve themselves in moral ambiguity. Some will argue that this lack of realism is itself not moral: 'the high that proved too high, the heaven for earth too hard'. But churches exist to raise spires and aspirations, and sects and monasteries exist to protect the dialectic of hope and spiritual autonomy. In this context 'ought' does not depend on the existence of a 'can' because the promulgation of the ideal makes possible in the long-term its partial realization.

11

Religious Comment on Politics

I AM not concerned with some miniature enquiry into the influence of religion on society. I am interested rather in the nature, role, and impact of Christian social comment, particularly of recent years. I want to elucidate certain resistances built into social arrangements and processes which I think Christian social comment likely to encounter and also likely to misunderstand or ignore. However, I will also indicate in summary form how Christian social comment may vary in impact and direction according to different types of situation.

I have to begin by arguing that my problem takes the form it does because of the special nature of Christianity. The Christian religion has a positive relationship to society and embodies affirmations which have social implications, mostly of a very general kind. But it is not a religion, like Buddhism, where the monastery might siphon off the tension between religious ideals and social requirements. Equally it is not a religion like Islam that codifies its claim *vis-à-vis* society in a comprehensive system of law. The Buddhist tension with social requirements can be very high while that of Islam is fairly low. Christians, however, are placed in the special position of accepting society and of wanting the Kingdom of God to come on earth without any extensive legal specification.

Christians lack any blueprint for the right ordering of society. Insofar as a complex system of law is required, it has to be taken from elsewhere and worked up within a Christian framework. Notoriously the new law offered by the New Testament, especially in the Sermon on the Mount, does not constitute a viable social system. Of course, it is always possible to return to the law of the Old Testament, and to legalism, but legalism is precisely what the New Testament claims to supersede.

This open texture of Christianity can be variously viewed from a sociological viewpoint. Talcott Parsons saw Christianity as part of a progressive process of social differentiation whereby the religious sphere and the social system became increasingly distinct. Dr John Hall in a recent article argues on the contrary that Islam presents the most socially advanced of religions precisely because it presents so comprehensive a scheme of social regulation.

At any rate, the new law is vision rather than specification. One solution I have already alluded to, and it is to call in a different system to fill up the gap between the City of God and the City of Man. Another solution is to proclaim an eschatological freedom. We are in the end-time and man may sin the more that grace may abound the more. The external prop of rules is no longer required. In the nature of things this antinomian anarchy will be adopted in times of revolutionary excitement and dissolution, but it cannot last. Yet another solution is to make an heroic attempt to see whether the Sermon on the Mount can be treated as the basis of a new law. This attempt is almost bound to lead to the formation of a small and probably exclusive sect. It will represent a social capsule of Christian revolution and from time to time certain reforms may be picked up from this capsule and applied more generally. A Comenius with his advanced schemes of educational reform was in part a late flowering of sectarian vision; the same is true of the Quaker Ebenezer Howard with his ideas for 'Garden Cities of Tomorrow'.

But more frequent, perhaps, than these various solutions is simply an amnesia about the nature of the Christian documents. This may arise because they are simply not read, as in much of medieval Christendom, or because they are given a particular kind of reading as in much of the history of Protestantism. Obviously I cannot go into the various Protestant readings of the New Testament, but one with which we are familiar complements, perhaps even helps create, the Pelagian apathy of the average sensual Englishman. This reading presents the New Testament as a series of *ad hoc* injunctions to behave well, even to be very, very good. Awkward and explosive charges secreted in the text can be defused and turned into bland exhortation or a manual of proverbial wisdom.

I am inclined to suppose that this kind of *ad hoc*, moralistic reading of the New Testament and of Christianity is likely to exercise a vigorous influence so long as religion and society are in a major way coextensive. This is not to say that religion and society will be folded one into the other without tension. There will be intermittent demands from prophets, saints, and visionaries, who want to give up the security of profession and family. There will be assertions of the freedom of the spiritual arm, which will in part represent revivals of radically religious perspectives and, in part, derive from the temporal interests of ecclesiastical institutions and of the clerical caste. There will be certain discrete but radical extrapolations from the foundation documents which prove difficult to implement: to avoid usury; to embrace sister poverty without reserve; to establish the Peace of God; to outlaw the crossbow.

But in the main, ideal teachings will be applied only to the family, in the form of life-long loyalty, and that only in principle. The most characteristic operation of Christianity will be a vast network of charitable endeavour, especially schools, hospitals, orphanages, and the like. The Church will offer ambulance work in a society which can be sacralized but not saved or transformed.

With the onset of the modern period, however, two crucial developments are to be observed. The first is the vast increase in the scope of personal option, which in particular erodes the force of the rules governing the family. So the limited enclave in which church law about the ideal character of relationships is supposed to operate collapses. The second development is that the Church (or churches) becomes increasingly marginal to the spheres of economics, politics, and even social control. The Church moves out of the structure of semi-necessity governing each of these spheres and can adopt a stance of free-floating comment. This comment will simultaneously involve yet another reading of the foundation documents and some assimilation to the kind of viewpoint found in other marginal strata adjacent to the clergy, i.e. the intelligentsia and the service professions.

This rereading and this alignment with the view of adjacent strata will vary a great deal according to the social situation of the Church (or churches) in different areas of the world. In some places the Church will not be particularly close to any intellectual stratum or service profession: it may be still aligned with a landowning class or, indeed, with an exploited group. Nowadays there are, maybe, certain typical situations. One is where the Church has been loosed from old social alignments with military, legal, political, and other professional castes, and develops a distinctive social dynamic. That is the situation in much of contemporary Europe. Or it may be placed in a missionary situation, where it carries and represents the identity of groups excluded politically or economically, or where it is associated with new élites educated under its aegis.

Clearly, places still exist where the Church remains more 'integral' as, for example, when old social alignments are retained in parts of South America, though this exacts a well-known price in terms of massive alienation among large sections of the population. Again, the Church remains integral where it embodies and represents a frustrated national group: Poles, Lithuanians, or Croats. But in general there is a marginalization in Europe which combines with a missionary situation in many other cultures.

The reading that results combines various elements. There is a partial adoption of political possibilities previously restricted to the Free Churches. *Vis-à-vis* governments and the semi-determinate dynamics of power which govern the political sphere, the traditional churches have acquired the structural position as well as the perspective of the Free Churches. They have done so, however, while still retaining a more collectivist ethos from the organic relationships in which they were previously embedded. Moreover, this new free denominational status has been acquired at the same time as a new free interpretative style has become increasingly available. The old integrated condition, meaning some variety of establishment, or unity with the core institutions of a culture, can be reinterpreted as a Babylonish captivity into which the Church was inducted under Constantine, and from which she is now finally at liberty. This interpretative freedom can, under the impulses available from the New Testament criticism, be developed so as to remint the old symbols, and also to undermine the authoritative character of the previous modes of interpretation. The Christian vocabulary can be given new meanings, congruent with critical political ideologies. The new meanings will be devised in fora like the WCC, where the marginalized Christians of Europe meet with both the new élites and the exploited groups of the Third World.

Now, I would wish to be careful here in that what is argued by those armed with this approach may be as viable as what is argued by any other socially critical pressure group of left or right. Certainly its proponents will have called upon experts to ensure that relevant empirical knowledge can be taken into account. It is not my object to assert that the political positions taken by churches in their role as pressure groups are simply amateur essays in social comment fuelled by the old naïve moralism. My aim is rather to indicate what seem to me the characteristics of much contemporary Christian comment, and, more importantly, to outline what I think are recalcitrant features of social reality. The motto inscribed over my enterprise is 'If way to the better there be, it exacts a full look at the worst'.

Ecclesiastical comment works initially as part of the high level of social rhetoric. At this level speakers of all kinds, secular and religious, simply invoke the great and good words, like liberty, democracy, peace, and progress. The additional contribution of ecclesiastical spokesmen, or to make it wider, of comment with a religious provenance, is in the use of words like loving, sharing, caring, supportive, compassionate, generous, and reconciling. These are not exclusively religious words but they have a natural habitat in the shared discourse of the Church and the service professions. Perhaps it is worth noticing that such words as 'loving' and 'reconciling' have a closer relationship to personal intentions and motives than abstract terms like 'democracy'. All the great and good words, whether abstract or personal, which circulate constantly at this level of social rhetoric, have been worn quite smooth. They are not expected to carry much practical cutting edge, but people are, nevertheless, reassured by their presence. They provide an aura if not substance.

However, there are certain notions which hover ambiguously between the theological and the social vocabulary and their ambiguity can be exploited according to context. One such notion is that of 'sacrifice', and I begin with this example because I do not want to suggest that the exploitation of ambiguity is specially characteristic of the contemporary Church in its present mood. The Christian meaning of the word 'sacrifice' lies pre-eminently in the redemption wrought by the death and passion of Christ. It is extended, however, to cover the sufferings of soldiers and civilians in wartime, and the soldiers' role becomes analogous to the redemptive act of God in Christ. The religious vocabulary shifts ambiguously to legitimate and even to sanctify warfare. Society and God's Israel become metaphorically interchangeable.

A very similar ambiguity is today exploited in relation to 'Christian liberty'. The 'glorious liberty' of the sons of God as expounded in the New Testament has not much to do with political democracy, let alone with 'liberation'. Nevertheless, phrases like 'set us free' can be slid across from the religious context into a vaguely liberationist context. A concept in Christian theology is half-appropriated to validate a particular political position. In a very parallel manner, whole ranges of vocabulary can be reused and reset in an existential, indeed atheist, perspective. Don Cupitt, for example, uses the old words but totally unhinges their direction and reference by using the controlling term 'God' to mean that ethical path which is the object of one's most serious choice.

But there is a further shift which needs examining. It is held that the exemplary acts of God in Christ can be efficacious in social situations. This is in spite of the fact that the death of Christ upon the cross for the redemption of mankind had no political efficacity whatever. The Romans were not reconciled with the Zealots. Jerusalem did not know the things which belonged to her peace and was captured in AD 70 and destroyed in AD 135.

Nevertheless, the role of love at the level of persons, that is between man and God or man and man is transferred to the level of political process. A reconciling agency is posited in social disputes and confrontations which repeats or works analogously to the redemption wrought by Christ. There is thus an optimism of love and reconciliation applied at the level of political process. Now, as I shall indicate below, I do not want to suggest that political processes work according to a completely determinate set of 'system dynamics', or that reconciling gestures are not possible on the part of representative persons or ordinary individuals. But the optimism built into this particular vocabulary does seem to me quite misplaced. Whether reconciliation, even costly reconciliation, 'works' depends largely on specific features of the social context. Many contexts are entirely recalcitrant.

Such optimism is, I believe, part of a general liberal presupposition about harmony reworked by reference to traditional theology. It is also closely linked to a vocabulary about the unity of the Church. The disunity of the Church is conceived as due to culpable sin. Christian disunity and conflict is not seen as socially and existentially inherent, but as due to bad moral management ('our sinful divisions') which is now about to be cleared up by the Holy Spirit. In a paradoxical way the Church has adopted a superficial liberal and enlightened view, about the roots of religious and political conflict and the possibilities of harmony. I say 'paradoxical' because historically this same view identified religion itself as the main source of conflicts, whereas it is now clear that these occur at the system level of political process without any disbenefit of religion whatever.

These presuppositions about conflict, generated in the interstices of liberalism and semi-liberalized Christianity, are matched and supplemented by a conventional 'Book of Wisdom' which contains the commonsense view of travellers on the Clapham omnibus. Where the Church might speak of reconciliation, the people on the bus are inclined to say that really grown men ought to be able to get together and come to some agreement. According to proverbial wisdom, social confrontation derives in great measure from the intransigent wills of leaders. If goodwill is injected into the situation a proper compromise will result. Indeed, 'goodwill' is a concept spanning both the theological realm and this proverbial wisdom. This is the one reason why Christmas can be so inclusive a celebration, mixing faith with humanistic invocations of goodwill. But beyond goodwill there is a further assumption, also rooted in proverbial wisdom: that when the long-term history is taken into account, the moral balance between antagonists is roughly equal. It follows that there is also a policy to be followed where compromise is the proper reflection of that moral balance. However, the existence of such a policy is actually just an act of faith. The peace process in Northern Ireland underlines the point.

Parallel to the individualist presumption concerning goodwill is an emphasis on 'people'. Now, it seems to me that while the Christian reference to people is entirely proper, indeed to be applauded and supported, it is easily distorted into an attitude which would make policy dependent on particular images of people suffering, especially where these can be dramatized (as they now are) on television. Policy whose ultimate concern is 'people' cannot work by extrapolations from dramatized pictures of this or that cost at the personal level. This is a very difficult area for ecclesiastical spokesmen, since it is not easy to maintain a vision where people are of ultimate moment and yet avoid being diverted by dramatized images. The images are true, but they are not enough of the truth to provide a basis for policy. Much suffering cannot be shown in personal pictures.

Parallel with the aspirations to harmony is an emphasis on 'community'. Those who are engaged in the promotion of lasting social bonds can hardly avoid being influenced by communitarian nostalgia. Yet in any situation costs will be considerable in terms of moribund communities. This is not to say that change may be embraced at any price: that would be to justify any pyramid of sacrifice in the name of those who might ultimately benefit. All the same, I think it reasonable to suggest that religious comment is often weakened by communitarian nostalgia just as much as by an individualist presumption. The point must be put very cautiously because the emphasis on people and community includes and emphasizes precisely the social costs of policy which I believe a radically economistic approach ignores at its peril. In other words, I believe that in spite of sentimentality about community there is a hard-headed critique of economism which ought to be pursued. The Church is still embedded in relationships and networks of family and local tradition and understands that people hold to their roots and solidarities and are not movable at will or the call of economic rationality.[1]

The last point I would make about religious comment concerns its level of specificity. Clearly, clergy and Christians generally have to avoid staying safely at the level of the great and good words. Equally they have to speak out in certain situations at the limit where moral ambiguity is much less present than normal. Cardinal Sin, Archbishop Tutu, and Cardinal Glemp have been in such situations. But most situations, taken overall are deeply ambiguous. I do not see that the general situation in France, for example, justifies spokesmen speaking 'in the name of Christ' as to which party should be supported, though the Church retains the right to defend its own specific interests within the polity. Conversely, localized situations and particular issues may be much less ambiguous, and quite rightly attract some ecclesiastical or Christian comment, though I think it may be wise to adopt broad ethical grounds rather than invoking Christianity. That is a matter of judgement. There are parts of France, La Vendée for example, where movements related to Action Catholique have adopted a vigorous role in economic and moral transformations of rural life. But, in any case, many particular issues do not yield a clear ethical judgement: Scottish devolution, for instance, or television in Welsh.

The nuclear debate used to be cited as a prime instance of an issue yielding a moral conclusion and therefore rightly attracting specifically Christian comment. But, although, for example, I did not myself favour Trident, it seems to me that such issues

---

[1] The history of Oldham since the 1960s is a terrible illustration of the way architects and rational planners of urban 'renewal' ignore the roots, needs, and solidarities of people.

are properly poised in terms of 'nicely calculated less or more'. With all the options so dangerous to humanity it is odd that anybody can anathematize other believers in the name of Christ. The whole debate over 'the Bomb' is one where false dramatizations of good and evil, on all sides, actually damage our capacity to take very cool and carefully calculated ethical decisions.

Once we are in a situation of ambiguity then technical questions, notably long-term prediction of outcomes in terms of specialist knowledge, become very important. Notoriously, the predictions may be inadequate, but one must at least seek for knowledge which offers predictions above random. On the whole, Christian comment turns to the immediate human image rather than the long-term consequence. Quite often what is called 'prophecy' consists of demonstrations, tableaux, the invocation of pictures, the use of the name of Christ as a rhetorical reinforcement, the deployment of the big words behind a limited, contingent position. (Of course the attempt to characterize issues as solely technical is just a ruse to prevent Christian incursions into awkward areas.)

When the Church engages in comment it brings specialist knowledge and specific analyses to bear in particular areas, notably peace and colour, but it avoids specificity in relation to central issues where the argument becomes economic and turns on the crucial opportunity costs of e.g. inflation as distinct from unemployment. How much unemployment, for example, is acceptable as a consequence of the monopolistic position of trade unions, over-high real wages, and monetarist policy? Is the economic criterion ever to be applied in pit closures, and if not, then are the long-term consequences for other workers acceptable?[2] Now, any responsible comment cannot stay in the relative safety of large words or calls for unity, but must stake out a technical argument for a given policy, in which all the costs for

---

[2] It is interesting that when the leaders of the NUM made clear to Church leaders that they would not abide by TUC guidelines during the 1984/5 strike the Archbishop of York said it was 'not for us to judge', though disapproval could be taken as implied, and had probably been voiced privately. But, of course, a public judgement would have involved the Church at the nub of a life and death economic and political struggle. The Church prefers not to criticize trades unions.

given groups and values are shouldered and accepted not for the duration of the comment but for the relatively long-term duration inherent in acts of political responsibility. To do this, of course, would bring the Church down to the level of ordinary political action, and might involve it in the constrictions and stereotypical characterizations attendant on all political debate. So, it does not do this, except only in relation to those issues of peace and race I have just mentioned. What the Church does do is to act implicitly as if there are diverse roles available in political debate.

One is the commenting role, which stands back somewhat from specificity, technicality, and party identification. Another is the politically active role for which specificity, technicality, and party identification are necessary. Yet another is the role of the leader of a relatively deprived minority not ever likely to have direct political responsibility, at least in that role. The Revd Jesse Jackson plays precisely this part, which offers him a free rhetoric only trimmed at the edges to the real constraints of political exigency. It is the first and third of these roles which in different circumstances the Church feels able to take up. It can comment, and it can engage in free rhetoric for particular and relatively (or absolutely) deprived minorities. It eschews the role of the direct political activist, except in very special circumstances, e.g. Nicaragua.

Christian commentators do not only rely on a theory of complementary roles in the making of political comment. They are also aware of the different opportunities for comment dependent on context. One cannot say everything at all times. It is obviously the case that a Christian as citizen may speak his mind in the public forum on whatever subject he chooses. It is also clear that a bishop may, while speaking as a citizen, vent a particular opinion, though there are dangers in constant comment or in becoming a focus of controversy in the Church. The real problems arise when a bishop speaks 'in the name of Christ', which easily implies that he speaks for the Church as a body; these problems are accentuated when he speaks in a liturgical context. The liturgical context is seen as one in which the great and good words are embedded in paradigmatic action, and is not to be lightly made use of to pronounce on ambiguous political issues.

I have to make one further comment on the general nature of religious rhetoric before turning to what I believe to be the general objective constraints within which it operates. Religious rhetoric is an expression of a basic grammar written into a society by virtue of its having accepted and slowly absorbed a given religion. I say 'slowly absorbed' because I think the process whereby a culture is stamped with the basic grammar of a religion can take a very long time: centuries. The endless recitations and repetitions of liturgy and homiletics are part of the slow process of writing in the grammar. Certain exemplary pictures and perspectives have to be so reinforced that they form a whole world taken for granted.

This basic grammar or structure of perspectives and pictures is quite tightly organized. This is not to say that it yields a single logical line, but it does give rise to a group of logical lines, expanding organically from the basic root. One line or another will come into view in the course of history as possessing special relevance, according to the thrust of varying circumstances. The circumstances 'select' the relevant branch of religious logic, which then seems to occupy the whole foreground, while the rest of Christianity is mostly recited somnambulistically. The long sleep of liturgy is one in which all the great archetypes are maintained while just one picture escapes from sleep and looms large in consciousness.

I stress this strict but branching grammar because what I am about to say may suggest that religious rhetoric exhibits a shoddy shapelessness. On the contrary, it is an architecture of precise balances in which one fault can widen and undermine a whole structure. A misconstruction at point *A* will ramify through the most distant parts of the theological edifice.

But that said, there is also fantastic scope for variant readings. You have only to think of the myriad implications of a parable. The injunction to make friends with the Mammon of Unrighteousness is a classic focus of varying interpretation; but there is hardly a single story which cannot be pushed in the required direction. The Parable of the Talents can be given a very Protestant reading, with the emphasis on using money and resources with all due diligence. Going out into the highways and byways to compel the wanderers and uninvited to the marriage feast can be deployed so as to justify ecclesiastical coercion. There are always coronation psalms to crown Kings and Magnificats to console the lowly.

Notoriously proverbs come in twos to allow you either to look before you leap or else to act immediately because he who hesitates is lost. The religious sign is both *A* and not *A*, so that the cross stands simultaneously for the non-violent martyr and the Christian crusader. Indeed, the religious sign, like the political sign, is often most powerful when alive with dynamic contradiction. Few people notice the contradictions within the sign. They receive only the sense of the 'field' within which the sign operates. The cross is 'in the field', and that is enough. Prophets and priests, like politicians, have licence to contradict themselves, because so much of their diction consists of signs and pictures. Like Walt Whitman they can say:

> Do I contradict myself?
> Very well then, I contradict myself,
> (I am large, I contain multitudes).

Indeed, you will never pull in the multitudes unless you do contradict yourself.

I mentioned the importance of establishing the correct 'field'. Religious and political vocabularies have to be so deployed as to convince listeners that a speech is authentically 'in line'. This reference back sets the speaker in the correct genealogy and is much more important than logic and consistency. The messenger always cites his credentials and does so by the invocation of correct words and the pronouncement of statutory curses. A great deal of what a religious or political commentator does consists in proper verbal stationing. Every picture has to be 'framed' in all senses of the word 'framed'.

Now, how does this flexible medium of comment and vision engage with the permanent conditions and contingent limits of social reality? Well, in one way it refuses to engage. We, as we absorb the sermon and the political speech, segregate it from what we know about the world, that knowledge which we have either by tangible experience or professional expertise. The statements are bracketed, partly for safety, and often because their purchase in the world we deal with 'out there' is so small. This indeed is itself one of the prime conditions of social life. At one moment in one context we accept a world of rhetorical devising. At another time we operate according to the understood limitations and requirements of mundane existence. We understand perfectly well that the sermon or political prophecy must be disengaged from the world in order for it and the world to survive. The rhetorical vessels and their fluid contents have to be put in a specially segregated area, roped off from ordinary secular space. That is the first and great condition of the real world: the understood segregation of comment from facts.

What then of these facts, belonging to the semi-determinate world of system dynamics? Put in that way it may seem that we are speaking of reality which can be expounded only in sociological theory. But we are also speaking of a world which we know by commonsense. We have a preliminary and pre-theoretical sense of what the constants and the constraints are. Name any sphere of human action, like the operation of the stock-market, and we have a commonsensical apprehension as to how it has to be worked. I want to use that apprehension to build up a few statements about conditions, constraints, predictabilities, and limits. Each situation, whether it be the market or a union negotiation, or a diplomatic exchange, generates its typical script which we know almost by heart. That well-known script requires only a touch of theory to give us our general conditions.

The most general condition is that indicated and manifested by the existence of the script itself. In everyday terms we know that scripts are, as we say, 'all too predictable'. A script emerges from aggregate behaviour. Each contributor to a situation is unique but the overall consequence will be the set script for that situation. A contributor may even withdraw and refuse to say his set piece, but the play of social dynamics will then proceed without him. Political choice is not individual choice writ large, but something operative within very strict margins. This is not to say that certain conditions may not be specified where the individual contribution is much greater than normal. A Lenin or a Woodrow Wilson makes a difference. Without Margaret Thatcher the train of semi-determined scripts accompanying the course of the Falklands War might not have been set off.

The next most general condition is the narrowing of options, boxing actors into a corner. That is not quite the way to put it, since if strictly true, options would in time disappear altogether. But there is, in a given situation, a steady narrowing down of choice and closing off of options. The commentator or sermonizer will speak in terms of what would have been possible if such and such had not already taken place, but each sequence of choices solidifies into a trajectory. You can see this most clearly in the sequence which precedes a war. A relatively open system has a specific, pre-existing tendency to closure, which sucks decisions forward faster and faster towards the vortex of the whirlpool. Many industrial situations have narrowed and narrowed over time until the script becomes totally formulaic. People are inducted into roles with formulae attached and can no longer even imagine a slightly different performance. The logic of society consists in considerable measure of these 'locks' which are specially resistant to speeches and sermons. In ordinary talk we recognize these locks when we refer to 'knee-jerk reactions' and 'vicious spirals'.

Take the existence of a party and the constraints inherent in party organization as a prime case of system dynamics and 'locks'. A party is itself a kind of lock: the lock of antagonistic horns which cannot disengage. There is a paradox in this, which is that nothing can happen without these constricting rival solidarities. The general social condition illustrated here is that the limited solidarities and their stock rivalries are necessary. The constrictions they generate form the pre-conditions of any creative political action. Thus the individual who constantly consults conscience in his adhesion to party and in his political decisions is abnormal. He even sometimes makes relatively moral outcomes more difficult to achieve. The point has to be very carefully stated. The process itself tends to grind conscience out of existence and to promote the amoral playing of set games. A characteristic instance was provided by those American foreign policy experts who infiltrated Albanians into Hoxha's Albania, knowing they would be killed, but accepting no moral responsibility. That is a profound *déformation professionelle*. But the individual conscience as it is conceived and expressed by moral commentary and by sermonizing is unreal. The moral vantage-point seized by the sermon is a false one.

The real constraint of political adherence and the morality inherent in it can be formulated more humanely perhaps by setting out the situation of the individual participant in a system of aggregate political behaviour. The politician has made an initial judgement that the goals and policies of a party are closer, though perhaps only marginally closer, to his conception of the social good than other parties. Once he joins that party he must obey a set of group imperatives at least partly rooted in the brute need to survive. Thus, he must accept the leadership in crucial matters, and refrain from dissociating himself from policy except in extreme circumstances and in matters understood to be decisions of conscience alone. All this amounts to a severe circumscription on his acts and expressions of opinion. He cannot speak the truth freely. Beyond that he has to contend in public that crucial differences turn on the election of his party and he has to present other parties in stereotypes and caricatures. The failures of those other parties must be attributed to their policies not to events and circumstances beyond their control. Above all, within his own party he will experience a strong impulsion to exert pressure against all those who, in any way, ignore these constraints. He knows that survival depends on solidarity, and solidarity on threat and obloquy. Fear is the bond of fraternity as much as faith or love.

These constraining conditions of political association operate both above and below the level of the party, say at the level of nations and trade unions. The differences of level may be blurred, since a party may define itself as coextensive with a future revolutionary nation, combining the loyalties of a whole society with those of a millennial political sect. Or a party may see itself as the idealized historic core of the nation. A trade union may, of course, be assimilated to such parties and display the same holistic loyalties. It may also, by virtue of the ecology of certain industries, become almost coextensive with the solidarity of a complete community, and this in turn may overlap a regional loyalty: miners in South Wales have traditionally cherished communal and regional solidarities as well as union loyalties. But analytically, one can suggest there are variations in the constraints operative as between unions and nations, below and above the level of party.

A union or trade association exists mainly for the advancement of the interests of its members, though it may also control standards of performance and entry, and define a professional ethic. The role of such an association is governed by the logic of leverage. If it can police entry and demand a closed shop, that increases leverage: power breeds power. If it can cause rapid distress or disrupt an essential function, that likewise is a source of power, sometimes so clear and obvious that it need hardly be exercised. Of course, those who lead such associations and unions will appeal to more general notions than their own limited interests, and may well invoke the interests of a whole class even as they pursue policies which will impoverish or put out of employment other members of that class. Historically, the solidarity of classes has rarely been more than the contingent and fleeting overlap of sectional interests. The concept of fairness deployed in negotiations will depend on the strength of the association or union. If it is very strong there is less need to deploy general concepts of fairness. And so on. The logic of leverage includes a use of fear and force parallel to that which sustains the fraternity of parties, above all else the weapon of excommunication. It includes the appeal to ancient solidarities built up in previous situations, which may be deployed whatever the character of contemporary disputes. And there is, of course, a necessary appeal to potent myths and martyrologies.

At the level of nations, all the constraints which operate in trade associations and the party are reinforced. The solidarity and the fraternity of nations is not incidentally holistic but inherently holistic. Membership of the nation involves and expresses the very fact of social existence itself, not just the aspect of political action or economic interest. Nationality subsumes these and transcends them with an all-embracing claim. It is possible to be apolitical; you can sometimes avoid joining a union; to be stateless is to be bereft of social existence as such. Meanings are mediated through the nation's language, and the past through its charter myths, stories, and selective history. National service is rarely regarded as optional and obedience in that service is defined as a duty correlative to citizen rights.

The deployment of themes and motives with an all-inclusive and religious weight and resonance is matched by a quite stark acknowledgement of the notion of national interest, above all in international disputes. Sometimes this will be loaded with an additional freight of political Messianism, whereby the national interest is made coextensive with a doctrine of universal human liberation, as in Russia and America. Indeed, a nation can sometimes summon up the fearful and ultimate fraternities of the millennial sect: such a nation has a mythology which organizes all life with the depth and range of membership in the Jehovah's Witnesses. (Parenthetically, when this happens a war is launched between the millennial national society and the millennial sect very much more ferocious than the intermittent war between secular élites and ecclesiastical élites.)

To the constraints of national fraternity and national interest, even at their most minimal, must be added the conditions of international political bargaining and exchange. These are most clear in wartime but never cease to operate. Such relationships are congeries of force, though cross-national fraternities can build up if the logic of alliances stays constant sufficiently long for co-operation to yield ties of friendship, particularly among peoples with similar material, political, religious, and historic culture. This will push interested rivalries below the level of naked conflict to the level, for example, of Britain's war against France in the First World War and America's war against Britain in the Second.

Those who play the key roles in articulating these fields of international force act within a small range of options. They attend to a logic which will bend the internationalism of universal religions or universal schemes of political liberation. National interest will triumph over Islamic unity. Wars between communist states will be even more ferocious than ordinary wars because national interest will represent itself as the true guardian of the universal hope. A Richelieu will pursue the national interest of France, not the international interest of Catholicism. The Vatican is a special case, but the logic of geopolitics is followed without remission as Irish and Ukrainian Catholics at different times have discovered. And this logic means attention to the average tendencies of international actors, i.e. the almost determinate script, generated by the net effect of average tendencies rooted in the checks, balances, and imbalances of power.

How then does the grammar and rhetoric of religion relate to these constraints? Clearly, I cannot discuss here the application of the fundamental grammar of religion, since it provides a taken-for-granted medium of everything said even when it has undergone major secular metamorphoses. My book on *The Breaking of the Image* (1980) was concerned with that problem. But something can be said about the fluid rhetoric of religion by way of a sketch of typical situations. Most of what I have said hitherto has had something of an Anglo-American provenance, even though I have referred in passing to very different situations where the Church is related to Third World minorities or élites or exploited groups or to whole repressed nations, like Poland, Lithuania, and Croatia. Let me then conclude with a topology of situations and the way Christian rhetoric may relate to them.

There is, first of all, the situation in the North European Protestant world, where the Church has been very extensively marginalized. It is clear that the Church feels that its services as a source of social legitimation are more dispensable than they were, and it will only give full transcendental insurance and assurance to the nation when the issue is survival, as in all-out war. Otherwise it will characteristically express reservations about the justice of particular wars and the means by which they are prosecuted. As for internal conflicts it will distance itself both from radical right and radical left and take up positions in the politics of welfare. It will align itself with the characteristic emphases of the service professions, of which it is now one among many. Ecclesiastical comment will emphasize broad issues of urban decay, race, and peace, eschew detailed economic arguments, and avoid most direct economic conflicts. This comment will be heard respectfully, and occasionally (as in relation to the Nationality Bill) it will be heeded. Mostly it will be just noted but otherwise ignored or dismissed as naïve. I should add that in my opinion Protestant influence on society works more at the level of cultural motifs and moral cultures rather than through ecclesiastical comment.

In North America, the situation is different. Whereas in Scandinavia and Britain churches have been gently floated down a central tide of semi-secularity at the level of communications (e.g. the BBC) and state institutions, in America there is a genuine pluralism which enables massive areas of conservative religiosity, Protestant and Roman Catholic, to retain vitality. Thus apart from the liberalized mainstream Protestant denominations, like Methodism, which pursue the same left-centre comment found in Northern Europe, there are massive religious pressure groups capable of maintaining themselves indefinitely, by an all-embracing institutional life and especially by the use of private ownership of modern communications. The Moral Majority, so called, has to be listened to, at least at election times. Moreover, the Roman Catholic Church can elaborate what Cardinal Bernardin recently called a consistent and comprehensive moral position, on such matters as abortion, nuclear war, and (in the near future) economic policy. No doubt the American electorate concerns itself mainly with domestic issues of employment and the rate of inflation, but the liberal Protestant, conservative Protestant, and Roman Catholic sectors can operate as fairly effective pressure groups, and genuinely influence opinion. Of course, this will run into certain barriers, notably the separation of church and state, but it is interesting that Cuomo and Geraldine Ferraro felt obliged to defend the distinction between what they accept personally as Roman Catholics and what they proposed as public policy. They had to stake out their political role *vis-à-vis* their obedience to ecclesiastical pronouncements such as those of Archbishop O'Connor.

In Catholic Europe, there is a combination of the marginalization which has occurred in Protestant Europe with more integral relationships. Roman Catholic Europe has been wracked by a more prolonged and bitter war between ecclesiastical and secular élites than elsewhere. To the extent that the ecclesiastical élites have been partially marginalized, they have to maintain their base in the process of socialization, and this has given rise to renewed tension over schools, in France, Spain, Italy and, above all, Malta. The Church remains integral enough in many sectors, either to express their traditionalism or to take a part in their development which may well lead away from traditionalism. Thus it has been an integral and indeed rather radical element in the shifting economic and moral transformations of the French countryside. But there has been a war within Catholicism itself, for control of the extensive social and inclusive networks with which the Church in Europe tries to maintain itself. Thus in Dutch Catholicism, which established a very extensive network of cultural defence, there has been a social schism between critical elements, associated with the 'knowledge class' and the traditional social sectors. The network lost cohesion and gained criticality. Political comment grew and church practice declined.

The overall result of this situation has been a partial withdrawal in most countries from identification with the older *intégriste* position or the more recent Christian Democratic position, and the emergence of varying degrees of radicalization. Given that the Church does retain some of its old command of an inclusive social network, its voice has some impact. Obviously this impact is enormously increased where the identification of the Church with repressed nationality means that it can be 'integral' in the old sense and also engage in radical criticism. In Poland, Christian symbols stood for national survival and were closely linked to the struggle for representative institutions. Indeed, the Church almost profits by the demolition of these institutions, since it then becomes the residual legatee of popular aspiration. Were representative institutions to emerge they would gradually channel more secular impulses, and might even rival the Church, though the fund of goodwill towards the

Church and respect for its pronouncements could not easily be dissipated.

There is no way easily to summarize the Central and South American situations, though these provide the main theatres for an influential liberation theology. In several countries, like Brazil and Chile, the Catholic Church has both remained integral and been partially separated from secular élites, and can thus channel popular discontents and radical criticisms. However, it is not the only religious force: both countries have experienced massive Protestant inundations, and Brazil in particular is affected by widespread cults like Umbanda and Spiritism. In other countries, like Venezuela, it was never really integral and was effectively subjugated in struggles with radical liberals. Thus it is weak, as well as divided between a majority who broadly support and are happy to 'ornament' the state, and a growing minority who are engaged in popular movements. The political impact of the Church is almost nil. In yet other countries, like Argentina, there remain substantial elements of the *integrista* Catholicism. In parts of Central America, as is well known, the Church is estranged from the ruling group, and sides with a rebel movement. In Nicaragua it had a delicate task, in that the Sandinista government is engaged in very extensive resocialization, especially of the young, and the specific role of the Church in the future is not clear. In places like El Salvador and the Philippines, the Church has been a massive constraint on dictatorial power.

The remaining situations must be summarized even more briefly. In parts of Africa the Church gradually became identified either with exploited and repressed groups, as in Namibia, or with the new élites, who had been mostly equipped by Christian education. This position allowed the Church to channel anti-colonial protest and also to retain enough moral capital to challenge the aggrandizements of the new élites, as in Zimbabwe and Uganda. In other areas of Africa, the Church may represent a territorially based section of the population over against an Islamic government, as in Southern Sudan, or have connections with particular sectors within a wider federation, as

Catholicism had with the autonomist aspirations of Biafra. In parts of Asia, like Japan and India, the Church is likely to be inserted into relatively educated and 'progressive' sections of the population and make a political contribution consonant with that social position. And in the kind of conditions existing in South Korea it may be major focus of social criticism.

Clearly, there is a vast range of situations in which ecclesiastical or religious comment may be heard, and these are funnelled, focused, and affected in a very complex way by the Vatican and bodies like the World Council of Churches. Most of my comments on the political language of the Churches were concerned with the relatively marginal situation of Churches in north-western Europe. A much more extensive analysis would be needed to embrace all the relevant situations, from Poland to El Salvador, from Namibia to South Korea.[3]

---

[3] The issue here is the extent to which secularization also involves privatization. For a lucid and powerful rebuttal of the privatization thesis see Casanova, José, *Public Religions in the Modern World* (Chicago: University of Chicago Press, 1994); see also Beyer, Peter, *Religion and Globalization* (London: Sage, 1994).

12

The Peace Sentiment: Old and New

THIS chapter is not concerned with a particular group, but with a theme which was prevalent in the milieux drawn upon by the current wave of new religions. That theme was peace. However, this desire for peace was in some ways continuous with the older versions of pacifism (some of them sectarian, and some based on the individual conscience), and in other ways discontinuous. Lots of features in the older versions were reproduced by the newer ones, but transmogrified, ordered in fresh combinations, given a different thrust and tone. The social context of the 1960s realized new potentialities in older themes. So this chapter has to begin by setting out the original thematic material before contrasting this with the mutations which that material underwent in the crucible of the 1960s from which new religions emerged. This original material is analysed in some detail precisely because this is the context, the 'resource', from which crucial attitudes and ideas were taken and developed. The emphasis throughout is on Anglo-American culture, since that is where the peace sentiment has been most widely diffused. The last section is concerned solely with what such mutations might imply about the society in which they occurred.

THE KINDS OF PACIFISM

The classic manifestations of pacifism were of two principal kinds. One was Christian and sectarian, based on a principled withdrawal from the institutions of overt coercion whether within nations or between them. This Christian, sectarian withdrawal had to build up a very distinctive and enclosed pattern of socialization, such as obtained amongst the Mennonites and the

Quakers. This was necessary to maintain the integrity of social withdrawal, especially against state interference and/or the corrosive power of national enthusiasm. The second classic manifestation of pacifism was rooted in the autonomy of the individual conscience. It might be based on a secular liberal principle, appealing to a Kantian moral imperative, or else on the typical stance of the free churches. So far as a religious variant was concerned, it lacked the comprehensive social backing provided by enclosed sectarian socialization and leaned rather on the general respect for personal conscience generated by evangelical Christianity. Perhaps this particular response occurred most where evangelical religion had undergone some partial liberalization. But whether secular or religious it rested on a conception of sensitive ethical autonomy nurtured in a vigorous self-discipline. It was high-minded and controlled.

However, there was a third variant of pacifism which existed alongside Christian sectarianism and religious or secular high-mindedness. This comprised a semi-anarchic hedonism, for which all constraint, whether exercised by the state or by the self, was inimical. The free self was the source of creation and delight, whereas the centralized authority of state or of the strong ego was repressive and destructive. Such a viewpoint could accept neither the discipline of high-minded conscientiousness nor the total long-term environment provided by the sect. Rather it depended on a broad, sensuous *rapprochement* with the world based on and induced by 'permissive' socialization. In the course of such socialization the hard elements of social life, external coercion and self-control, were carefully avoided or kept at a distance by adults, and by a welfare state which provided indulgent protection.

Protected in this way the hedonistic ego is free to construct perspectives from which hierarchy, discipline, and compulsion are absent. It can construct a responsive world where wish is—almost—law. Within such perspectives one may, perhaps, desire to build up a *gemeinschaftlich* community, but it will not usually require the taking of vows or obedience to rules because harmony and peace can be established naturally. Such peaceable communities may be joined by the children of pleasure at will and left at will. They need not assume any long-term commitment which can constrain and restrict their future options. A communitarian 'kick' is just one temporary expedient among others. Inevitably in such a milieu there is no place for the concept of an ineluctable national loyalty and of military formations demanding absolute obedience. The psyche does not submerge itself for the sake of a 'generalized other' embodied in a national group, or admit subordination to an institution. Unchosen loyalty and invariant obedience are anathema.

This third variant of pacifism was precursor to the modern situation. This is not to say that all or most of the new religions adopted this generalized rejection of hierarchy and coercion. Indeed, some of the religious groupings were formed in reaction against just this slackened loyalty to the collective and loosened focus on achievement and discipline. It is simply that a particular version of the peace sentiment was diffused in the broad milieux out of which members of new religious groupings were drawn. It characterized the pool of broad orientations, ready for transmutation into the several varieties of overt commitment found in such bodies as, say, the Hare Krishna or the Unification Church or the Children of God.

One should not suppose that these orientations, characterizing the new peace sentiment and diffused at large in the recruiting sectors of the new religions, were totally distinct from the attitudes informing the older pacifism. As I come now to describe these older attitudes, it will be clear that many of them were vigorously revived. At least there were enough plausible resuscitations of the classical approaches to convince some traditional pacifists that they had acquired new allies. The difference lay, however, in new conceptions of self and citizenship. Outside their specific rejection of war, the Quaker or Mennonite sectarians, and indeed the liberal or Christian devotees of conscience, were reliable, and self-consistent over time, both as people and as citizens. The new generation was not reliable in the same way, and might shift rapidly through any number of psychic colourings which could even include the momentary espousal of exemplary violence.

What the peace sentiment within the perspective of new religions drew most from the liberal and sectarian utopias was pervasive suspicion and the denunciatory style. The older liberal suspected the diplomats and secret diplomacy, the armaments manufacturers, and the military interest. So too did the most recent generation, focusing its suspicions on the military-industrial complex with almost paranoid zeal. Old and new displayed a common capacity to oscillate between impossible optimism and total pessimism, simultaneously welcoming the New Age and announcing the Apocalypse. Both saw so much empirically wrong in 'the World' and so much potentially right. All the varieties of pacifism espoused a mutated version of the Christian concept of the World in which the forces of evil (or the 'system') are concentrated, and which stands over against the kingdom of the innocent and the good. The binary view of good versus evil bound together classical pacifism and the more modern rejection of war.

The above analysis has been concerned with a major mutation of the peace sentiment. It has relied on a contrast between a classic sectarian withdrawal as found in, say, the Mennonites or the lonely Protestant or the Kantian conscience, and the diffuse hedonism of today, which finds certain kinds of group loyalty and social demand unacceptable. This hedonism arises, as has been argued, in the broad pool within which new religions fish for converts. It thus belongs to the assumptions which govern the context of new religions, even though certain of the new religions may be in sharp reaction against those assumptions.

Nevertheless, the protest against automatic memberships and ineluctable loyalties, against all hierarchy and the impersonal dynamics of coercion, within states and between them, is a central part of the milieu where the new epiphanies make their showing. By that, I mean that where the sense of selfhood is governed by the empire of desire and the principle of personal happiness, one cannot conceive of loyalty to the demands of the state or to the commands of the sergeant-major as overriding. Young people in certain milieux just happen to belong to a particular country and do not accord any sanctity to its demands upon them. They have never felt that they had to do anything, certainly not to obey military discipline, merely because the

twists and turns of foreign policy might from time to time require shows of military strength in Cyprus or Kenya, in Korea or
Vietnam.

THE GENERAL LOGIC OF PACIFISM: OLD STYLE

Clearly there are problems in setting out any general, principled
objection to war. A Quaker who respects the divine spark in
every human being differs from a Jehovah's Witness who rejects
all secular wars and awaits Armageddon. Neither a Quaker nor
a Witness has very much in common with a Marxist who es-
pouses revolutionary defeatism until such time as he can openly
and violently pursue the class struggle. One way round this
diversity is to set out the implications of an attitude to the state
and to national loyalty which eschews violence. Thus one may
attempt to set out a minimal logic of the pacifist approach
together with certain extensions which frequently follow. This
logic will be distinct from the revolutionary defeatism of a
Marxist or the apocalyptic attitude of a Witness. It will also be
distinct from the attitude of those who hold that some particular
war is ill-advised or evil, yet nevertheless make such a judgement within the presuppositions of 'normal' politics. Those who
would reject a particular intervention, say, in Saudi Arabia, but
who nevertheless work by the checks and balances of ordinary
foreign policy do not share the logic of pacifism.

What then follows from a principled rejection of inter-state
violence and what kind of perspective does that imply in relation to national loyalty? The first and pre-eminent consequence
is a rejection of tribalism. Perhaps it is wrong to speak of 'consequence' because the rejection of violence and of tribalism are
conjoined together at the core of the pacifist approach.

Clearly there is here an extraordinary challenge to sovereignty, whether by reference back to New Testament norms and
Biblical authority, as was usually the case in Christian pacifism,
or by an appeal to a universal membership in Humanity over
and above local attachments and national demands for solidarity with fellow citizens.

From the viewpoint of the state, the nub of the challenge turns around the rejection of the magistrate's command to 'serve in the wars' (to quote from Article 37 in the Anglican Book of Common Prayer). A nation is a tribe writ large, which demands that all within its boundaries defend its unity, honour, integrity, and interests. The duties and privileges of the subject are articulated within the nation. He finds and receives his primary social place according to national laws and customs. To step outside national membership is to assert a personal judgement lacking social root and local sanction. This is why the psychic shift in acknowledging a higher loyalty to humanity is so profound. Both the demands of the state and the social foci of belonging militate against it. You have rejected the ultimate claims of the state and its laws, and resisted the pressures of local solidarity.

The objector must consolidate his stance against this huge contrary pull of centripetal social force. Except in a very few countries, like contemporary Britain, he is required to submit to national service. That involves a discipline of arms and accepting that enemies are defined by state decision. Choice of weapons and style of hostility are not up for nice, individual scrutiny. Armies are run on the conditioned reflex of automatic obedience, not on the conditional reflections of autonomous conscience. This means that the objector must work out a response both to the contingent local character of national loyalty and to the arbitrary, total nature of discipline.

The demands of the pacifist conscience require that no exceptions can be made for wars of self-defence, and that no place exists for the Augustinian concept of the just war. This means that a foreign policy based on tactical considerations and convenient military strikes becomes impossible. Likewise, a state would have to jettison alliances, since these are based on international groupings of power and the threat of force. It would be impossible to threaten force and never to use it. For the pacifist true to his own logic, any pressure beyond moral suasion is inadmissible, however commendable the objective. The only possible form of foreign policy becomes moral appeal and broad dramatic gestures symbolizing peaceability. Foreign relations are converted into a form of moral theatre.

The appeals and gestures of moral theatre may perhaps be accredited with redemptive potential, depending on whether the redemptive agent is able to carry out the gesture with a perfect heart. Here, there lurks, perhaps, a hidden eschatology, since a gesture must have once-for-all efficacy. Policy cannot possibly consist of a series of gestures, especially since the failure of the first gesture may mean that you are no longer at liberty to make the second. If your enemy does not quickly accept your peaceful, wide open arms, he may tie your arms behind your back.

There is another difficulty at this juncture which has psychological correlates. The difficulty relates to how a pacifist may expect moral gestures to emanate from social structures which he sees as deeply dyed in systematic evil. The psychology on which this expectation is based combines intense optimism with intense pessimism. If the nation-state is deeply implicated in alliances and threats, bluffs and feints, lies and subterfuges, it is hardly likely to achieve a reformed character overnight, let alone a redemptive role. Cynicism can hardly be bedfellow to hope, though this is precisely the logic and the psychology of the pacifist position. One has to combine a sad knowledge of what the state actually does, with fantastic expectation as to what it may potentially do.

On the whole pacifists incline to an optimistic view, since a fully fledged pessimism reduces pacifist witness to useless protest and the pain of obscure, unnoticed crucifixions. Perhaps it would be more true to say that the pacifist develops a mind in two compartments. One compartment deals with ordinary, mundane political transactions as depicted in daily newspapers, about which he becomes more and more cynical. He supposes that foreign policy is a noisome charade, played out by consummate hypocrites. Every item concerning malpractice at the foreign office is treasured as evidence of the secret plots in which diplomats are always engaged. The other compartment, however, opens onto a quite different view. The pacifist sees a profound peaceability deep down in things, that only awaits release to spring to life and power. Whatever states may do and statesmen may pretend, in Man as Man there abides a yearning to unite with all men everywhere. Man is innocent; social organization (and/or ignorance) is to blame. In God or in Human Nature there lurks the untapped yet all-powerful remedy.

It then becomes necessary to identify which aspect of social organization is the key to evil, or whether indeed social organization is maleficent as such. The process of identifying the cancerous centre or core is not characteristic of all pacifists. Some are content with a general negative characterization of the state and the organization of force. Others, particularly those who believe that pacifism is a practical contribution to a better life, tend to identify the one sole source of malignancy. Once found it is rarely let go again. The real cause of war then becomes the activities of armaments manufacturers, or the needs of capital seeking outlets, or the psychic spiral of mutual fear, or the instinct of dominion over others, or the inculcation of a sado-masochist psychology. It is in this context that the pacifist may turn to the Marxist arsenal of concepts, since the Marxist analysis is specially useful for justifying deep pessimism about the present with hope about the future. The pacifist dialectic of pessimism and optimism can find sustenance in the Marxist analysis, providing, however, one does not accept the necessity of class war. The pacifist swing to the left often comes to stop just where the Marxist analysis demands struggle and even violent revolution. Many pacifist consciences were exercised by left-wing demands to support the Republicans in Spain.

When the pacifist encounters the dilemma posed by the Marxist he is pushed towards an extreme doctrine of the relation of ends to means. This doctrine holds that what is morally wrong can never be politically right, or that the end never justifies the means. This view cannot be held solely with respect to the external relationships of states, but must necessarily be extended to the whole activity of law-making and law enforcement. Thus it would be improper even to make an example of a criminal or a naughty child *pour encourager les autres*. Indeed, the very activity of law enforcement becomes morally questionable. Sometimes this extreme and implausible conclusion may be avoided by proposing a distinction between non-violent acts of legal suasion and acts of violent law enforcement. Alternatively, it may be held that law within states is based on a moral consensus which precludes the kind of war of 'all against all' characteristic of fighting between states. Or again it may be argued that the police use the minimum persuasion necessary for compliance and that this suasion is aimed at identifiable individuals, not against some social mass, indiscriminately defined as the enemy. There are various ways of weakening the analogy between internal force and external war, so as to allow the former and preclude the latter. All the same it remains true that a pacifist will feel the pull of the anarchist position. He will lay stress on popular capacity for peaceful compliance without resort to external incentives or threats. Thus, the optimism generated by his broad view of foreign relations is transferred to internal relations. A pacifist will rely on the force of a moral appeal and seek out what William James called the moral equivalent of war in all the social relations in which he engages.

However, should it seem that people or groups remain recalcitrant and continuously resist moral appeals, then the pacifist has to save his optimism by claiming that people only resist because of their unhappy circumstances or because they are not accorded social justice. Thus the pacifist repeats an intellectual tactic developed in the field of external relations, which is to deploy a quasi-Marxist analysis of internal disputes. People are not activated by an inherent greed nor are they naturally disposed to power and the corruptions of power. They are, all of them, honourable men. Only the dishonourable disposition of society makes them appear dishonourable. Institutions have corrupted their natural goodness.

However, this itself generates a difficulty since the pacifist now feels a hostility towards all those who support the current disposition of goods and rewards. He is caught between discerning the divine spark in all men and suspecting that the divine spark has been dampened or been blown out in the case of capitalists, military men, propagandists—and their dupes. Men must follow the highest when they see it but a wretched claque has closed their eyes. If the majority goes morally blind, and loses the natural gift of sight, then the real villains have subverted it by propaganda.

With a little twist this view may degenerate into a conspiracy theory of history. In any case, there remains the difficult question as to whether the revolution in social circumstances will come from men's changed hearts, or will be brought about by structural upheaval. At this point pacifists divide. If structural upheaval could occur in the course of a peaceful and natural social evolution, then the structural mode might be preferred. But it is well known that the midwives of revolution are equipped with pincers for reluctant births, and may resort to Caesarian operations. Thus with the onset of any revolutionary crisis the pacifist will draw progressively back, or if you prefer, he will regress to the true reactionary logic of his beliefs.

Of course, in delineating such options and tendencies, I am presuming a modern context. Nevertheless, the broad logic tends to be similar across different periods, even though the content and the precise formulations and vocabulary differ. A pacifist in the past would have expected the Kingdom of God to occur by a transcendent intervention aside from and beyond his own efforts. He would, in short, have adopted an eschatological hope. This would be associated with the combination of high optimism and profound pessimism already described. Those who were entrapped in the present aeon had been handed over to the power of the Evil One. But precisely when that power was most rampant and abominable, redemption would be nigh. Whether the Evil One is the Devil or a socialization subverted by the military-industrial complex, the structure of belief is broadly parallel.

Moreover, the logic of social withdrawal is similar in very different periods. Once a pacifist (in either the twentieth or the sixteenth century) perceives himself enmeshed in relations shot through with violence, then he will wish to withdraw from them. In the sixteenth century the only way to withdraw was to join a sect in which some enclave of a new and better society already existed. For the sixteenth-century believer, this enclave might be conceived as God's Elect, a little flock already saved out of the realm of darkness, awaiting the moment of deliverance. For the twentieth-century believer the enclave may be an embryonic anticipation of a new way which is soon to become universal. That will be the fullness, but this is the taste. The twentieth century offers more scope than the sixteenth for establishing embryonic communities which establish in miniature what will soon be realized universally. Indeed, ever since the eighteenth century some pacifists have been able to set up communities where violence is eschewed, the law abrogated, and brotherly love alone allowed to be the binding force of society. It is difficult to be a pacifist on one's own, integrally involved in the regime of violence and law. The solution is found in the sect or the utopian community.

Within such communities the logic of non-violence will take various forms. It may, for example, be extended to include animal as well as human life. The brute creation was no more established for the abattoir than was the human creation. Here the symbol of blood may come to play an important role. War involves the shedding of blood. Blood constitutes the sign around which the supreme evil is concentrated. Therefore, all activities which call for the shedding of blood are to be condemned, and red meat itself becomes a symbol of raw violence. Hence the varied connections between a pacifist position and vegetarianism.

In articles 37 and 39 of the Prayer Book directed against Anabaptists, the controverted issues included capital punishment and the taking of oaths as a solemnity according ultimate respect to the law. So far as capital punishment is concerned, a pacifist will almost always be opposed to it. In capital punishment the state arrogates to itself the right to take an individual life and this is only marginally different from the right to take collective life. The justice of the court may be more discriminating than the justice of the pre-emptive strike against some 'enemy city', but the right of the state to execute 'judgement' is present in both cases. The pacifist will be disposed to say: 'To the Lord alone belong the issues of life and death.' He will tend to adopt reformatory rather than retributory theories of justice. He will also, by extension, suspect or condemn corporal punishment, a position which in the modern period he will illustrate with arguments drawn from the psychology of aggression and sado-masochism. In the extreme case, the pacifist is opposed to all violence against children, animals, criminals, and other states and he thus participates in the generally progressive sector. (The reverse does not apply: members of the Royal Society for the Prevention of Cruelty to Animals are mostly not pacifists.)

There are certain consequences which bear on the pacifist perspective which follow from the overall impact of all the distinctive attitudes discussed above. Clearly people who hold such an ensemble of attitudes are going to form quite a small minority and arouse the kind of hostility which defines them as cranks. The urge to consistency which leads to a total rejection of all violence, and even of police forces, feeds this definition. There is then set in motion a spiral of mutual reinforcement whereby crankiness is attributed to pacifists and the attribution helps to create or reinforce such crankiness as may in fact exist. Pacifists respond with an impaired sense of their own normality and come to value abnormality as an index of virtue. They suspect the wider society of desire to persecute. Those in positions of power are regarded as founts of misinformation and the generality of mankind are defined as dupes of propaganda. Since propaganda is always operative to some extent, there is plenty of evidence to reinforce the plausible view that nothing emanating from 'worldly' sources is true, particularly if it reinforces the war-spirit. Thus pacifists in the Second World War were very reluctant to credit the elimination of the Jews, equating such information with the atrocity stories circulated about the Germans after the invasion of Belgium in 1914. Inevitably, all these processes are accentuated by war-time. The sympathy felt for pacifists by some ordinary denizens of the world tends to evaporate. They, after all, have had to submit to conscription, and the objector is defined as a shirker or a coward. A rather generalized scepticism about the state and its purposes becomes converted into a sense of shared deprivation and mutual comradeship. The pacifist is soon regarded as an outsider and a defector.

This means, that pacifists try to cite instances of 'realized eschatology' which contradict the normal view that war is some kind of institutional necessity. Pacifist lore teems with examples of groups or countries who rejected the weapon of violence and were the better off for doing so. Thus, a kind of sugared utilitarianism results. On the one hand sacrifice is the way to redemption, but on the other hand the willingness to be sacrificed may mean that the cup will pass away. Not only is pacifism certainly right, but also probably advantageous and useful. The utilitarian argument from the greatest happiness principle sorts rather ill with the Kantian objection based on the intrinsic wrong of taking life or offering violence. Those who (like Bertrand Russell) deploy this kind of utilitarian argument can become protagonists of *realpolitik* should their estimate of the utilitarian calculus tip in the non-pacifist direction. Russell recommended pacifism in 1937 and dropping the Bomb in 1947. At any rate, the pacifist, confronted by the war-spirit animating the vast majority of his fellows, is inclined to idealize some other country as exemplifying a more moral approach to international relations. India played this role for a period and so also have Sweden, Switzerland, and Denmark. This idealization of countries other than one's own finds its Marxist analogue in the way members of the non-pacifist left persistently point to some new utopia, as, for example, 'Soviet Russia, a New Civilisation' or China, or Cuba, or, nowadays, Albania. The 'True Land' has to be created in the eschatological imagination if it cannot be demonstrated in reality. Pilgrimages are made to the True Land and excited accounts given of how much better things are ordered elsewhere. This knowledge of better things elsewhere feeds the superiority felt by Marxist and pacifist alike towards the unenlightened mass. The 'People', idealized by Marxists and pacifists, then become an imaginary point of reference contradicted by every instance of how most people actually behave. The feeling of sharing the Messianic secret amply compensates the feeling of being inferior or cold-shouldered by the wider society. Indeed, the sense of superiority and the sense of persecution can mutually feed each other.

THE OLD LOGIC OF PACIFISM:
A RESOURCE FOR THE 1960S

To what extent, however, does such a group of attitudes link with the phenomena of new religions and inform some part of their outlook on society? How did elements in the syndrome just outlined mutate under the pressures and dissolutions of the 1960s? How did the Campaign for Nuclear Disarmament and the liberal Student Christian Movement, both of which provided friendly environments for pacifism, feed into and *dissolve within* the psychic revolutions of that period? (I merely note in passing that the genocidal potentialities of modern weapons often accentuate the tendency described although they may also breed apathy by making individual protest appear useless.)

Here after all we have a distinct sector of the progressive climate which loses a certain distinctiveness of outline, and solidity or specificity of content, under the dissolutions of the 1960s. Once it had been a position (though linked by congruity and affinity to all kinds of progressive attitudes), and then somehow this position started to free-float as an element in a wider universe. Pacifism lost the suffix 'ism' and began to bob about, suddenly salient with banners inscribed 'Make Love Not War', and, equally suddenly, lost in the ensemble of attitudes—or even submerged in waves of exemplary violence. Along with the Campaign for Nuclear Disarmament and the Student Christian Movement it slid into a melting-pot. The Peace Movement of the 1960s was not coherent in its sources, its ideology, or its psychic base.

The fire beneath the melting-pot was individualism, but an individualism of an odd kind because it had constant resort to structural understandings of man's parlous state, and persistently erupted in 'mass demonstrations'. The atomized psychic reality appealed to the concept of a patterned, malignant social base; the whirling, individual atoms fused in masses and then diffused in a hundred grouplets and in sheer personal anarchy. And this made sense because these individual atoms were set free enough from constraints actually to notice structures (industrial or military) when they ran into them. The attempt to live 'according to nature' had gone just far enough for the structure of society to seem as unnatural as it was glaring and obvious. Only personal exploration or loosely formed grouplets, dissolvable at will, or mass, temporary aggregations of shared fury and/or love, conformed to the state of nature. In such an atmosphere not only was loyalty to the state incomprehensible, but loyalty to any particular named organization with a stated creed or written-in attitude. The edge or boundary round such an organization, especially when large-scale, had to be rubbed out. Hence the near-dissolution of CND, and the practical demise of SCM as it declared itself 'open' to the world. Hence, also, the tight little groups, political or religious, which were eventually left as hard distillations within and after the Great Dissolution.

So the pacifism which coloured the post-1950s outlook was a free-floating element, loosely connected with intermittent searches for community and with a general slackening of national loyalties. The mobile exploration of the self undercut both a principled adherence to the Protestant conscience and a disciplined attachment to national loyalty. Every loyalty beyond the experience of the individual, except maybe to Mankind in general, was experienced as alien, even indeed as a consequence of machine politics and bureaucratic governance. To young people, reared on doctrines of self-exploration and on adjustment to purely personal environments, the demands of the nation appeared to have no persuasive power. Membership in the nation was a genetic accident, at best the nexus of certain utilitarian reciprocities: taxes paid for welfare services rendered.

Since neither national membership nor personal discipline exercised an appeal, young people were cast adrift from the ancient anchors of the state and the settled psyche. Their pacifism underwent a mutation into something more diffuse than traditional pacifism. It was part of the background, an unemphasized item in the repertoire of attitudes, and would only become active when challenged by some demand, particularly some dangerous demand based on the calculations and pressures of international politics. The impress of socialization no longer bit deep enough for young people to sacrifice themselves to the contingent twists and turns inherent in international affairs. On the contrary, any national service demanded in the course of such political pressures aroused intense resentment towards both service and nation. This, of course, leaves aside whether or not such demands were more or less ethically justifiable. In other words, even had the Vietnam War been more justifiable than it was, the base of automatic loyalty was no longer present. One incidental implication of this is that the more tender-minded and democratic a state is, the less it can rely on its membership in the contingent matters of foreign policy. A democratic, individualistic nation conducts affairs in the semi-amoral arena of foreign politics, weakened by the effect of its hedonistic mode of socialization, and facing grim adversaries whose whole effort emphasizes automatic obedience and national fervour in the cause of totalitarian discipline.

That wider consequence apart, the pacifism of the post-1950s was not so much a principled objection to war as a state of mind which found national loyalty, and especially obedience until death in the cause of policy, just incomprehensible. Young people revolted against such concepts of loyalty and obedience with intermittent rituals emphasizing 'Love Not War'. They made a kind of ritual war on conventional society in the cause of love.

But there was no counter-collective to which the majority of them adhered, such as a Hutterite community or a utopian experiment or a Mennonite sect. Some did, of course, seek out some peaceful bond of loving community. Most dipped into intermittent community as a partial baptism *en route* to other experiences and other kinds of chrism. They dabbled in liminal *communitas*. But they belonged to no single group, and they travelled along loose networks in the interstices of the agencies of work and government. Their broad psychic tendencies fostered loyalty neither to nation nor to any specific group but only a mobile participation in loose, overlapping nets of relationship. Ensconced in this way pacifism was not a matter of principle with a logic of its own, but an item in a wider, implicit, psychological set. War and the military constituted an unthinkable intrusion, a visitation from *realpolitik* without a shadow of justification.

When the outer limits of this 'unrealistic' set became uncovered and visible, or when the psychic travelling and the constant cycle of dissolution became intolerable, there had to be a scramble for new bases of stability within which the distracted soul might re-form. If a base had previously been laid down in the earliest years, then that might be re-utilized in modified form to sustain and support the re-formation. Not under the old name perhaps, though lots reverted to or discovered a neo-fundamentalism, but by way of a new cultic stabilization.

WHAT DOES THIS SAY ABOUT THE SOCIAL CONTEXT?

What do such mutations imply about the societies in which they occur? Can we read back messages about the overall context which harbours and produces them?

First of all, something may be said about the social impress on the psyche with respect to the style of personal identification. Every society must stamp an impress on the mind, insofar as nobody can avoid culture and still realize their human potential. This stamp has, over the centuries of nationalism, included a sharp edge or margin distinguishing native from alien. To be 'a national' was something crucial to the sense of belonging and it was built into the sense of identity. It was, so to say, a psychological identity card. Along with the identity card or identity disc went a near-automatic loyalty which could be called upon. Identity and loyalty were almost consubstantial. People might not be all that happy to take up soldiering, and would hardly welcome the press-gang, but they did not easily conceive how they might be divested of exclusive identity and loyalty. Yet this is precisely what has now started to occur in certain western liberal societies.

Alongside this partial undermining of identity and of automatic loyalty has gone a parallel tendency to dismantle all disciplines based on automatic responses. Psychic fluidity is not compatible with standing rigidly in rows immediately responsive to the word of command. The change is plainly observable in many spheres: school, church, and public assembly. In school, for example, rows are broken up, formal assemblies are discouraged, *esprit de corps* is devalued, and old-fashioned drill converted to physical education. Individualism militates against militarism, and against the ancillary disciplines which provide it with a base.

One may or may not regret such shifts with respect to identity, loyalty, and discipline. Probably few will feel sorry that the state can no longer rely on 'Your Country Needs You'. But there are other implications about the moral sensibility characterizing some contemporary western liberal societies. This psychology may embody a hedonism which resists any sense of cost or paradox. Good things are accepted very easily as part of the natural order, and their lack is treated with incredulity and horror. Frustration cannot be borne and rapidly issues in a sense of being ill done by. Moreover, in the fluid groupings based on loose, cultural affinities, so much has to be personally negotiated that alienation and a sense of chaos ensue. The individual becomes a nervous octopus constantly sensing out his environment for markers, points of stability, indicators of direction. The defensive margins of selfhood become susceptible to marauding explorations. The objective outer world also dissolves at the inquisitive touch of personal exploration. The lineaments of the 'out there' (God, Society, and even physical constraints) collapse as the individual loses the markers which mediate meaning and provide his sense of 'the given'. The cultural images which might mediate meaning revolve or dissolve too rapidly for secure linkages between the self and the environment to be formed. This results, amongst other things, in the shared sense of a collective historical trajectory and lineage being corroded. History, as a donation given by the collective past, with markers and pointers for a future, loses its power. The idea of a classical, objective form ceases to be understood, whether as liturgy or poetic tradition or mode of government.

Such a situation generates certain kinds of explanations which either transmit the sense of disquietude in simple, easily swallowed capsules or else provide deliverances, also easily swallowed. This is not to claim that everything that lives demands a *Weltanschauung*, but it is to say that those nurtured in a world without sharp edges are likely to push at their environment for a solidity which will give them definition. Many, perhaps the vast majority, acquire tags which serve as interim guides to chaos. These tags are not worked up into coherent systems of ideas, but provide the materials for conversational ping-pong. They are expendable wisdom about male and female, job or career prospects, the over-world of politics, the nature of opinion itself. Everything tends to be reduced to opinion. The idea of a strict either/or becomes unintelligible, as does the idea of a demanding religion, and the idea of qualitative distinctions. Of course, in some sectors, quality and discipline impose themselves as they do in sport and music, but much of existence is handed over to mere preference and opinion. Faith is a 'religious preference'; a variable liking for Shakespeare or Beethoven is just one subjective option among others.

Within these softened centres of liberalized society, there may emerge a very different reaction which seeks for edges and distinctions, which looks for comprehensive truths and explanations. In the past pacifism would have been one component in such explanations. It would have been woven into the fabric of a sectarian faith or else at the very least implicated, in the overall *Blick* of old-fashioned liberalism. Of course, pacifism can still arise in this way and become incorporated in a rigorous, or at least well-defined, dissentient viewpoint. But more frequently, pacifism now arises in the sector which lacks social and psychic definition, or historical trajectory and purpose. It has a kaleidoscopic life, mixing first with this element and then with that, temporarily tipping over into aggression and as quickly righting itself again. It cannot give an account of itself, nor can it pass itself on except by contagion.

A society which exists over such incidental agglomerations of sentiment and feeling, finds the cultural content of education and socialization difficult to determine. It can, of course, emit just the contagious signals which arise from the collective calculus of immediate desires, but these do not provide solid psychic fare, shared meaning and being, a common symbolism connecting past and future, a language for mobilization. Furthermore, the necessities, costs, and paradoxes of politics, especially of international politics, remain as unavoidable as ever. A population released from automatic loyalties and unequipped with a sense of political and social necessity is ripe for disillusion. It is the raw material of a crisis of legitimation. Legitimation in such populations turns immediately on the ability to meet desires and expectations, and has no positive, defined emplacement on which it may rest. It is perhaps arguable that this is just as it should be, but it means that societies which exemplify the desired situation are placed at risk; or else they must engender new obfuscations about their true nature in order to survive.

The point can, in conclusion, be put even more sharply. The survival of collectivities, such as tribes and nations, depends on a structure of decision and foreign policy which is resistant to moralization, without necessarily being totally amoral. The structure can be given an intellectual defence, but in order to work it requires a vigorous impress on the psychic substance of its membership. This impress is not provided by the hedonistic calculus of self-expression, and no viable foreign policy can possibly ever be erected on the net resultant of such a calculus. Thus, not only is legitimation placed at risk, but survival itself. Technical superiority is thereby made into the main defence option, and vacillation becomes the ground of policy.

PART III

Addresses to Clergy and to Teachers of Sociology

13

A Socio-Theological Critique of Collective National Guilt

> Crimes are committed by individuals. There is no such thing as collective guilt.
>
> Lord Weidenfeld, Newsnight, 18 November 1995

IT often happens that what claims to be Christian thinking is secular high-mindedness glossed by a Christian vocabulary. That is conspicuously the case with regard to the current move in the upper echelons of the mainstream churches to promote apologies between nations based on the notion of collective historical guilt. There are those who think that it would make sense and be politically helpful for representative national figures to come together, maybe in some holy place, and there express contrition and seek forgiveness for past historical wrongs. An example of this type of thinking would be provided by Brian Frost's *The Politics of Peace* (1991). Mr Frost is an Anglican and a Methodist who ran the 'Forgiveness and Politics Study Group' of the (then) British Council of Churches and is one of the activists promoting projects for international apologies.

I suspect that most people encountering such proposals would think them beneficent or at worst irrelevant. But even if they are merely irrelevant I believe they trail moral implications that are offensive and represent a serious distortion of Christianity. I will suggest that their use of a Christian vocabulary obscures conceptual borrowings from the presuppositions of nationalism. Of course, it comes as no surprise that Christianity can be partially fused with nationalism. What does come as a surprise is that moves purportedly designed to attack nationalism should be so rooted in the opposing ideology.

Before going any further, I had better make clear what I am not arguing. I am certainly not arguing that religion is entirely an individual or private matter with no implications for politics and incapable of contributing to public debate. Nor am I for a moment suggesting that moral criteria have no relevance to international politics. After all, the Christian religion in particular turns around the Victim who suffered violence in His confrontation with the polis. My contention is rather that the profound categories of classical Christianity have been rearranged and abused to subserve a version of secular high-mindedness dependent on a category—that is the nation —which is alien to Christianity. The subtlest heresies occur where one of the fundamental building-blocks of theology is out of alignment. A misalignment at base undermines the integrity of the whole edifice.

I will put the core of my objections to these proposals, as follows. They involve an illegitimate transfer of the moral criteria which may properly govern face-to-face relations between an identifiable malefactor and an identifiable victim to the opaque realm of large-scale collective behaviour. Once this transfer is effected the distinction between innocent and culpable is blurred. Of course, it often happens that culpability is blurred but in this case it is blurred specifically by being attributed to every member of a social category. The category is the nation and I work out the argument below in those terms. But it can also be ethnicity, or colour, or gender, or religion. The point is that the category, whatever it may be, is ascribed and involuntary.

This attribution to a social category not only blurs the distinction between innocent and culpable so essential to all justice, but implies the automatic transfer of guilt from one generation to another through membership in the nation, the ethnic group, or whatever. It is, therefore, a grotesque abuse of the category of original sin, which is likewise involuntary but only in relation to the universal category of humanity. That is why it raises no issue of innocence over against culpability. Certainly, original sin inheres in a collective membership, but it is a membership we all share in 'Adam'. It also passes automatically from generation to generation. But again that passage across generations is not unjust because it concerns the universal fracture of the divine image we all inherit without exception.

The injustice and the moral outrage involved in the imputation of collective guilt through membership in ascribed categories and its transfer from generation to generation can be conveyed in dramatic illustration. If the ascribed category is nationality, i.e. citizenship, then the girl being born at this very moment in democratic Germany must shoulder responsibility for the deeds of some citizens of Nazi Germany over half a century ago. Equally, a black child born in a Bristol suburb of Afro-Caribbean parents cannot avoid acquiring responsibility for 'British' involvement in the slave trade. If that logic holds, then presumably a black child born in a West African tribe whose seventeenth- or eighteenth-century rulers sold their subjects to the slave traders also incurs guilt and responsibility.

I cannot believe that anybody can seriously contemplate such consequences without moral revulsion. But let us take the second and third of the instances just offered and see what would be required in order to evade them. With regard to the guilt and responsibility imputed to the black British boy in Bristol it would have to be argued that he was exonerated on grounds of colour, whereas the white boy next door was culpable either on grounds of colour or else because he was genuinely part of British culture in a way the black boy was not. In my view such evasions are just as morally intolerable as the original imputation of innocence and guilt in terms of citizenship. They should be repudiated.

With regard to the guilt and responsibility imputed to the black boy in the West African tribe that conclusion could be evaded by showing that in West Africa there was no continuity of government or political unit or even territory over time. But what does such an evasion in turn imply? It could imply that the innocence or the guilt of populations depends on whether they have been so unlucky as to live in a social environment where territory and government have been stable and continuous. Alternatively, it might be argued it is not populations as such which acquire guilt but governments or ruling classes which can be shown to have some kind of continuity with past governments or ruling classes. If the latter evasion is adopted then some historical questions of a rare complexity are opened up.

For example are the Howards of today, who provide an aristocratic leadership of the Catholic community, implicated on account of class affiliation in the deaths of the Catholic martyrs some few hundred years ago? Does John Major, as British Prime Minister and representative of a recent brand of populist neo-liberalism (as well as son of a circus performer) incur the transferred guilt of (*a*) Lloyd George with respect to the black and tans, (*b*) the behaviour of the Anglo-Irish aristocracy in the eighteenth century, (*c*) James II at the battle of the Boyne, (*d*) Oliver Cromwell at Drogheda, and (*e*) the Norman-French aristocracy who set up the Pale in Ireland in the first place? If that all sounds absurd, it is no more so than what is suggested about corporate responsibility. If John Major should turn out to be tainted by Lloyd-George, the Welsh liberal, but not by the Norman-French, one would certainly ask by what criteria continuity is or is not retained.

I interpolate a clarification. So far as I personally am concerned I am perfectly free to judge a past action as morally wrong. Of course, I have to examine the complexities of the situation, the alternative courses realistically available, the likely consequences and costs of those alternatives, and the standards of the time. The same is true of a representative person such as the Queen. In principle she may pass an adverse moral judgement on the land apportionment in New Zealand which followed the Treaty of Waitangi in 1840. She has, as it happens, expressed that judgement publicly, though it cannot be an act of contrition. Happily some partial legal remedy is also available. But cases involving legal remedy are quite limited in number, because so few cases are clear-cut and the original contracting parties rapidly cease to be the only parties involved. As the case of Northern Ireland amply demonstrates very little of history can be morally unwound without exacerbating the tally of injustice.[1]

---

[1] It seems to me that the Queen's action in relation to the Treaty of Waitangi is, in principle, the same as Chancellor Kohl's repudiation of the acts of Germans under the Nazi regime with respect to the holocaust. Symbolic gestures of this kind

In short, most of the expansions, plantations, and migrations of the past cannot be undone. For one thing all claims to be the original native population themselves rest on previous migrations, displacements, and expropriations. Furthermore, peoples mix and cannot be sorted out. One has, therefore, to say that recent arrivals quite quickly acquire rights indistinguishable from previous generations of the native born. They by no means stay in permanent moral discredit in relation to them. In practical terms this means that nobody dreams of sending the descendants of the Aztecs back to northern Mexico in order to compensate the Toltecs, and nobody expects to repatriate all the inhabitants of North America back to their original countries, or the Irish Celts back to the Russian steppes. Any attempt to sort out sheep and goats in this way would, in fact, amount to racism.

How, then, does this bear on the question of forgiveness between nations? It bears on it because the moral accounting of some theologians really does depend on ideas of collective moral agency based on a historically continuous corporation identified in terms of 'the nation'. However, my principal object is not to deconstruct 'the nation'. I need only to point out that the myth of romantic nationalism underpinning this concept of the nation was constructed by the efforts of poets, historians, and political theorists not much more than a century or two ago. The criteria of 'native' and of the proper boundary of the nation are all contentious. Above all, *the* story of *the* nation in *the* national territory is a historiographical construction aimed as much at legitimating the present as at accurately rendering the

are appreciated. In such cases there are relatively few intervening factors and relatively few third parties and there is a simple moral asymmetry of a very grave kind to be recognized together with consequences for the living susceptible to reparation. As indicated in the main text, such situations are quite rare and cannot involve the notions either of collective guilt automatically incurred by membership in the nation, or collective guilt transferred across the generations. If I were asked a question about Nelson Mandela's symbolic gesture of forgiveness to the white community, I would understand it as making sense in relation to those who in any way morally colluded with the premises on which the apartheid regime was based. Though such people would be numerous they could not be defined in terms of colour. Moreover, Nelson Mandela has retained in principle the distinction between innocent and culpable to the extent that those guilty of crimes are to be charged and tried. They are not, of course, all those who are guilty.

past. What was a series of conquests and expropriations, one superimposed on another, is smoothed out in a continuing story of 'our' people based on the contiguity of geography rather than the continuity of history. Kings Arthur, Alfred, and William the Conqueror are opposed narratives welded into one. It makes as much and as little sense for me to claim continuity with Arthur as it does for contemporary Turks to claim—as they do—continuity with Homer and Herodotus because they lived in Asia Minor. All these narratives once deconstructed fall into ruin, and it is precisely such narratives that supply a premiss for a theological moral accountancy based on collective guilt transferred over generations.

It is, of course, true that the 'we' we call the nation does share intersecting cultural genealogies of a given character which do over time build up and reflect a sense of common membership, and have come to constitute a group of recognizable psychological profiles. We consume these genealogies and absorb these profiles as part of our constant construction and reconstruction of ourselves as contrasted with others. This is how we recognize ourselves and others in the past, so that accounts of *the* British by Henry Adams and Henry James, and of *the* Americans by Fanny Trollope and Charles Dickens, retain some verisimilitude. We do inherit overlapping communities of memory, reinforced by the solidarities of common experience like war, even if these memories are rearranged and in part invented. And since our identities are built up in this way we become creatures of the past, real and invented, as well as free agents facing on to the future. Our pasts do flow along distinctive channels into our presents and it would be perfectly reasonable for us to be alert to untoward possibilities latent in our inheritances. That goes without saying. But that does not involve retrospective responsibility or contrition or place us either as nations or individuals on an international stock-exchange of moral credits and debits. We are all equal before God in terms of His grace and our response to it. (So we might as well stick to the General Confession in the Book of Common Prayer.)

A major problem inherent in this whole controversy has more to do with how we use language than with ideology. We converse, we communicate publicly, and we even write history in terms of loose, broad categories and collective nouns. We speak of the black experience and we speak of Britain's role in the Middle East or British policy at Versailles. It is this use of broad categories and collective nouns which lends spurious plausibility to the kinds of proposal criticized here. Atrocities are not committed by *the* Bosnian Serbs. That is the way some Bosnian Serbs talk about the atrocities committed by *the* Croats, and it is precisely that social and linguistic premiss which leads to eternal feuding and indiscriminate revenge.

Such disastrous shorthands may or may not be linked to ideas of corporate responsibility, but they are retained in use because precision would be intolerably roundabout. Nevertheless, the result is that parts are regularly confused with wholes and individuals are regularly taken to represent the character imputed to the whole. Moreover, it is the persistence of collective nouns over time which helps shore up the notion of continuous collective moral agency persisting over time. When a country like Rhodesia changes its name to Zimbabwe we recognize the discontinuity. But when, like France, it does not, we fail to recognize a very similar discontinuity as if, for example, the government of General de Gaulle could be held responsible for Vichy and the government of General Pétain.

I offer an illustration from precisely the kind of historical wrong for which some theologians would demand expiation: the opium wars prosecuted by Britain and France against China in the mid-nineteenth century. A historian writing about these wars might refer to British policy and even say that 'Britain' was responsible for certain acts.

But presumably in actual practice it was some section of the Foreign Office which thought there was an advantage to be gained by the opium wars, perhaps for the nation, more likely for some sectional commercial interest. In no way was the nation as such involved, and no blame can conceivably be attached to anyone now living. Nor can we reasonably expect contemporary British governments to shoulder blame for this slice of history, let alone express regret to the present Chinese government and/or people. The malefactors and sufferers are all dead and no legal remedy is available such as is available through the revision of the Treaty of Waitangi. The principle is clear: those who did not perpetuate a wrong cannot express contrition to those who have suffered no wrong, and that holds whether we are talking of British citizens or British government. And if, incidentally, guilt were supposed to inhere in British citizenship one might ask whether the Irish evaded the obliquy when they left the United Kingdom, leaving blame on the shoulders of the other three nations including, of course, Chinese migrants. As for those Britons who have Irish grandparents born in the Republic their moral status defies imagination.

TWO ILLUSTRATIONS

That completes the exposition and I now offer a couple of illustrations which I use to generate some reinforcing comment. One is drawn from liturgy to show how political prayers can trail unacceptable implications, and the other is drawn from an article by the theologian Paul Oestreicher to draw out the looseness of this kind of political rhetoric.

The liturgical illustration concerns the prayers used at a session of Christian leaders in the North of England, chaired by Anglican and Roman Catholic dignitaries. These prayers were in a three-part sequence, the first invoking ecclesiastical genealogies—'We are the Children of Rome, Canterbury etc.'; the second invoking cultural 'credits'—'We are the Children of Bach, Beethoven, Chopin etc.'; and the third invoking cultural stains 'We are the Children of Auschwitz etc.'. After this third prayer we were asked to say 'Kyrie Eleison'—'Lord have mercy upon us', clearly implying that 'we' in some pan-European sense bore a responsibility with regard to such crimes for which we might properly ask God's mercy.

Clearly the problem begins with the second item in the sequence where we assembled 'our' cultural credits or genealogies or whatever else it was we were informing God about. The strong impression given is that these prayers balanced credits against debits, sources of pride against reasons for shame. It is, of course, true that Bach, Beethoven, and Chopin are in a general way part of European culture, but do I as an Englishman and member of the EC give thanks for them? Is an Israeli or a Japanese or a Pennsylvania German excluded from giving thanks for them? Supposing we had declared ourselves 'Children of Shakespeare', would I as an Englishman offer special thanks by comparison with an American, or an Indian, or a Caribbean, or indeed anybody anywhere? Clearly the implications of cultural self-accreditation in terms of national or European citizenship are distinctly odd.

That being so, is it not even odder to express contrition for Auschwitz in terms of European citizenship or some entity such as 'Christian Europe'? All kinds of questions spring to mind. Should 'we' be contrite about the Katyn massacre, which though it took place on European soil was perpetrated by Russians? Are American and Caribbean Christians excluded from responsibility for what happens in (so-called) Christian Europe? It so happens that a black British citizen was present at these prayers, born in the Caribbean and representing the Pentecostal Church. I wondered whether he, too, was expected to say Kyrie Eleison and if so on what basis? Had he acquired transmitted guilt along with his British and EC passport? Was he guilty simply by being a Christian? That seems a bit unfair, somehow. Was he exonerated on account of being black, and if so is guilt colour-conscious? Might I as a child of Anglo-American revivalism half escape as being virtually mid-Atlantic?

My second illustration is taken from an article by Paul Oestreicher in the *Church Times* for 6 August 1995. Canon Oestreicher begins by recommending we love and forgive our enemies. Naturally I find no difficulty with that, particularly as I am not a victim and have no enemies to speak of. But then Canon Oestreicher extends the idea of forgiving enemies to the quite different idea of expressing contrition and offering forgiveness for corporate guilt. This idea has, he says, become a major theme among Christians, and he goes on to list some notable wrongs, such as the Irish potato famine, Hiroshima, Dresden, the Treaty of Waitangi, British concentration camps in the Boer War, and the Japanese invasions of China and

Korea. Canon Oestreicher calls on us to choose between a corporate amnesia which buries the past and taking up 'our' responsibility for the sins of our fathers and mothers. (I note that the Canon's political correctness now blames my mother as well as my father for the Irish potato famine. I also note that he uses the loose broad categories I earlier complained of by referring to 'Japanese cruelty'.)

The trouble is that when we work out the implications of this rotating international ritual of contrition and forgiveness we arrive at some astonishing scenarios. As we all start listing our corporate sins (with no historical cut-off point that I can see) we should presumably all repair to a venue designated by the United Nations. Once there we begin what is in essence a secular version of the Last Judgement. In other words, just as the Christian categories of the individual and of man generically have been converted into the category of the nation so the Last Judgement has been fast-forwarded out of eternity into secular time. Moreover, the divine Victim who is also the Judge is now a whole series of corporate victims who apply not to the mercies of God but to a judgement of history operated by historians.

Clearly the universal day of collective atonements offers a bonanza to a whole class of appointed historians and conciliators, since one clearly has to make sure that all wrongs are properly revealed and their causes correctly identified. Nor will the selective list of standard crimes offered by Canon Oestreicher be remotely adequate to the demands of comprehensive justice. We must bring to book the Chinese dynasties, the Moghuls, the Incas, the Campbells, the political descendants of Vlad the Impaler, Tamerlane the Great, and Selim the Sot, the Albanians who massacred Greeks, the Greeks who expelled Muslim Cretans, the great-great-great-grandchildren of the Barbary Corsairs, and so on and on. This will be the Great Assize of all human infamy since the beginning of time. Given the likelihood of disputes considering the range of malpractice to be unveiled, the degree of responsibility incurred by various parties, the relevance of extenuating circumstances such as provocation, a committee could be appointed chaired by Professors Scruton and Hobsbawm, assisted by panels of approved victims nominated *inter alia* by Louis Farrakhan, several Kurdish factions, and the Armenian Liberation Front. At the end of it all each of the High Forgiving Parties would bow solemnly to each other, receive and give absolution and regard themselves as quits. And we could then start up all over again.

Before passing on I need to put down a marker concerning my own position. Contrition and forgiveness only make sense between persons or in relation to God, and they can only concern acts in which one is personally implicated through one's own deliberate fault or culpable negligence. Contrition and forgiveness may sometimes alter relations between persons even when only one party is so minded, and they must by definition do so when parties are mutually involved. But forgiveness between collectivities makes no sense and also makes no difference. The dynamic of redemption is not a moral technique to secure the better conduct of geo-politics. In the realm of international relations nothing is likely to follow from gestures of forgiveness, even if they are noticed in the media, which is unlikely. To think otherwise is secular optimism glossed by Christianity.

A Scenario

What has been said so far can be summed up in a scenario off the beaten track of standard liberal exempla, which are generally drawn from a tiny group of modern ex-imperial democracies with longish histories as nations. What, however, might be the moral balance-sheet between the governments and/or peoples of Sicily and Libya? How might one work out a tariff of contrition for Sicily to be offered to the Libyan dictatorship?

Sicily is an autonomous region of Italy, and from about 1911 to roughly 1941 Italy occupied Libya. The first question is: are the Sicilian people who were joined to Italy in recent times, and now have autonomy, responsible for the colonial ambitions of Italy, more particularly in its period of Fascist government? The second question is: how do we trace the genealogy of Sicilian moral responsibility prior to Italian unification back through the Kingdom of the Two Sicilies and the Bourbons to the Normans and the Muslim Aghlabids based in North Africa? If it does not extend back in this way what determines the cut-off point— geographical location in Sicily? ethnicity? religion? regime? type of regime? or what?

NIEBUHR REVISITED

A great deal of this muddle could have been avoided if the theology of Reinhold Niebuhr had been properly understood and permanently absorbed, particularly as set out in *Moral Man in Immoral Society* (1932). So, in a brief aside, I now need to rework Niebuhr in order to reinstate the difference between the moral dynamic of face-to-face relationships and relationships between collectivities. Let me now illustrate how a political role differs significantly from a personal role.

I begin with the order to a British submarine to sink the *General Belgrano* in the Falklands War of 1982. I happen to think this order morally unjustified and it may well be that the chain of decision can be traced to Mrs Thatcher and/or a small group of advisers. It could be that Mrs Thatcher herself came to view the order as unjustified, and said so, but that would be purely personal and of no great political significance.

The point is that war-time decisions are vested in small power élites and there is an extended chain between major decisions and minute implementations. There is, therefore, a dispersal of moral responsibility. In the particular case of the *General Belgrano* the decision was made in a complex political and military situation where those concerned had to take rapid decisions by the minute. It is, therefore, difficult to arrive at some moral accountancy and, moreover, any such accountancy would have to extend to the total situation.

Presumably, the prime objective of our theologians has to be moral justice to all parties, not just a specific judgement of one person's role. Justice would involve a moral assessment of all the actions on either side, reaching back from the immediate to the more distant past. Once that assessment is attempted, it becomes difficult to see how the chain of apology and contrition is to be set in motion. Who should apologize to whom for what? Perhaps General Galtieri should apologize to Mrs Thatcher and she in turn to the parents of the drowned Argentinians. It is not clear how the cybernetic spiral of actions and reactions is to be unwound. Anyone who has heard the mutual recriminations of spouses can imagine how complex the issues must be once nations are involved.

All this is to say nothing of problems connected with the disavowal of Royal Navy servicemen or contemporary political considerations which might inhibit or render counter-productive any attempt to unwind the moral and causal weave of that war. What is clear, however, is the non-involvement of *the* British as such in bringing about a state of war. It was not we as citizens who were the authors of the acts which gave rise to war.

Let me take another example. Similar problems would arise were one to propose an apology and contrition from *the* United Nations for failing to secure designated safe havens in Bosnia. It seems 'the' British preferred humanitarian responses to the overall situation, and so did the wrong thing for the right reason, just as 'the' Americans in advocating military intervention did the right thing for rather doubtful reasons. Should, then, the British apologize for failing to kill more Serbs and the Americans for killing a largish number of them? As preliminary en-quiries indicate, there is no way of apportioning blame within the complex resonating web of actions and reactions between the Secretary General of the UN, the various governments, and the commanders in the field. We do suspect that direct respon-sibility lies with General Mladic, and if so that is where justice should be meted out.

The discussion above has already hinted that the possibility of apology depends on the nature of one's political role. Apologies by archbishops are as easy as they are meaningless because they are not political players. Thus the Cardinal-Archbishop of Armagh may express regret for the deeds of the IRA which have nothing to do with him, but since the members of the IRA express no regret it is not clear what his personal regrets can signify.

It is axiomatic that all the players in the political dance proper must at some juncture be extremely economical with the truth. Consummate and principled hypocrisy is a *sine qua non* of political virtue in many situations. And that includes the refusal to break ranks and concede any more than is absolutely necessary. Those who break ranks are repudiated and those who concede more than is necessary offer propaganda opportunities to the opposing side. Each side has to pursue a policy of maximization in which survival depends on the maintenance of credit with one's own supporters, with the public, and with the international community.

In short, corporate action works by semi-predictable game-plans whose rules are understood between the various conflicting parties, and not by moral gestures. The survival of corporate bodies turns on solidarities and minimal unities which bind members together *vis-à-vis* opponents. Each individual has, therefore, to be under a discipline that inhibits moral spontaneities, and this discipline constrains leaders as well as followers.

That applies in inter-party conflicts as well as international conflicts. In political debate in the House of Commons, for example, it is simply not an option for the leader of the Labour Party, however Christian he may be personally, to forgive the Conservative Party or to express contrition about the behaviour of his own party. Individual action *is* different from corporate action and that is why the Lord's Prayer does not apply across the floor of the House. Politicians are not there to forgive each other their trespasses or even to pay over-precise attention to the prohibition against false witness.

A CHRISTIAN POSITION?

Before looking at what Christianity might actually say, it is worth asking a question about the Bible, since Canon Oestreicher mainly justifies his position by reference to the Hebrew Scripture, though he also refers to that curious hybrid Judaeo-Christianity. His argument is that the Bible treats cities and nations as corporate moral personalities and that God calls on them to repent as such. He adds that at the beginning of the parable of the sheep and the goats (Matthew 24: 30) Christ refers to 'the nations' gathered before the Son of Man. But Oestreicher neglects to mention that the actual separation of the sheep from the goats is definitely not in terms of nationality.

Presumably these Old Testament notions are open to rational critique among all non-fundamentalists. If, for example, God orders Achan to be stoned for the deeds of his family we dismiss the notion as primitive and unjust. The same applies to the divinely inspired collective elimination of the Amalekites. We certainly do not promote such notions of corporate blame as the proper basis for contemporary law. Moreover, the story of God's mercy to Sodom and Gomorrah on account of the minority of just persons has very different implications. And even if peoples are called upon to repent before God this seems rather different from being adjured on account of their bad behaviour to other nations. Unless my copies of the Bible are uniquely defective, I do not recollect prophecies commanding the Israelites to apologize for ethnically cleansing the Amalekites or for bringing indiscriminate plagues upon the Egyptians.

It is true that in his gospel St John does blame 'the people of the Jews' for various actions, but we can only assume this is an example of the linguistic convention already mentioned where a collective noun does duty for a group of individuals of a given ethnic group. Nevertheless, the history of anti-Semitism shows just how dangerous such misleading locutions can be. Jews do not carry forward collective moral responsibility over time.

As for Christianity it is one of those radical developments of Judaism which struggles to be free of this corporate, indeed biological, membership and stresses judgements based either in terms of personal responsibility or on grounds of our incorporation 'in Adam', i.e. our status as human beings. Jesus is on the one hand genealogically rooted in Israel but he is also the Son of Man, born not of the will of men but of the Spirit. He creates a universal fraternity based on the redemption of persons converted out of every kind of secular identification. That is precisely the point of Peter's confrontation with and conversion of

Cornelius the Roman in the Book of the Acts, chapters 10 and 11. (That there is a profound Jewish critique of this by Franz Rosenzweig is not much to the point here.)

The Christian understanding of forgiveness has to do with our separation from God in a radical self-love and a self-interest which ignores the claims of others or exploits them for self-aggrandizement. This is sin and it inheres both in our corporate human constitution and in our individual brokenness. Though we are made in the image of God that image is universally defaced, and we have ourselves through our own deliberate fault personally defaced it.

The consequences of defacement are to be viewed in the scarred visage of Christ, who by meeting enmity with love turned it to love's advantage. He absorbed our brokenness in the brokenness of his body, and so met the cost of reconciliation. Love's expense created the overflowing treasury of grace, from which we draw on a fiduciary basis, that is—solely by faith and trust. Nevertheless, we endeavour to respond to grace by ourselves leaning on grace in the power of the Spirit—to find ways of forgiving as we have been forgiven and to ensure the spread of peace and justice.

This dynamic of redemption saves us, both communally and individually. As a redeemed community we gather in family solidarity around the table, sharing the fruits of the common earth, bread and wine. These symbolically carry the freight of a shared redemption, since they represent both the broken body of sacrifice and our incorporation in reconciliation, wholeness, and resurrected life. The same dynamic also saves us individually, by entering into our bodies and by washing us in the waters of baptism, ferrying us from darkness to light and from corruption to incorruption. Thereafter it becomes a duty, so far as may be, to institute the rule of the kingdom of heaven in the ordinary affairs of the City of Man. At the heart of this City of Man is now a recognition of disfigurement through the sign of the cross, and there are also elements of partial mutuality and self-giving which faintly reflect the glory of the Eternal City.

However—and this is the crux—the dynamic of redemption, coded in an enacted symbolism of breakage and restoration—

the Eucharist—which actually constitutes the Church, encounters a structural resistance inherent in collective action. The ravages of this resistance are reproduced simultaneously in the body of the Church and the body of society and have to be countered by an everyday practical wisdom not itself written in to the foundation charter of heaven's kingdom. That is because a foundation charter has to exhibit the fundamental images of sharing in the feast, including the outcast and uninvited, raising up the fallen, seeking the lost, restoring the sick, reconciling enemies and honouring the image of God in all his creatures and creation. Those images indicate the standard and the goal, whereas it is left to practical wisdom to explore how far neighbourliness and caring can be built into the social fabric.

That exploration may involve some very varied and even paradoxical choices. Those choices emerge as the dynamism of redemption encounters the dynamism of our collective nature, represented by enmity, violence, and the subordination of some people for the advantage of others. Politics can be the expression of an attempt to circumvent through the energies of practical reason these inbuilt resistances, fragmentations, and subversions. But there can be no once-for-all redemption of the political, and that is as true today as it was two thousand years ago. The dynamism of redemption cannot be transferred to the political problem except at the margin. The collective has its own social nature which allows it to build in some elements of morality and vision. That does not mean, however, that it constitutes a morally responsible (and, therefore, redeemable) corporate agency over time. If that were so we would all be plunged for ever into irredeemable guilt.

In sum, the mistake of Christian utopianism is to conceive the polis as just such a corporate agent. That mistake represents an abuse of faith because it attempts simple transfers from the sphere of redemption to the sphere of politics. These transfers themselves damage redemption, turning it into a simplistic programme, which mirrors secular categories and which shifts the last judgement from the realm of eschatology into a historical possibility. It hands justice over to historians and politicians. Christianity then becomes a mode of secular self-righteousness and denunciation, bypassing the careful assessment of different means of amelioration. Should Christianity be fully secularized in the form of a once-for-all attempt to set up the kingdom on earth, either by exemplary violence, or by exemplary non-violence, the problem is compounded. Neither has proved efficacious and the attempt collapses in confusions and ambiguities. It follows that it is impossible to read off political policies from the charter of the kingdom, though the potential presence of the kingdom and the judgement it represents remain the constant point of reference. The kingdom remains an iconography of compassion and warning.

The problem may be that Christianity has been partially released from the task of doubling for social authority. In carrying out that task it reinforced repressive consciousness as well as decent orderliness and critical moral imagination. The contemporary release should allow Christianity a freedom to be itself, using the open texture and differentiated character of modern society. However, a partially footloose clerical intelligentsia has misconstrued this opportunity and reorganized Christian categories so as to transfer guilt and expiation to the sphere of the polis, leaving personal existence forlorn and untended. People are urged to take responsibility for sins they could not have committed and to treat these sins for which they are responsible as the externally imposed overflow of social structures. Thus, whereas in classical theology it is God who is the divine Victim and bears the weight of sin in grace and love, in the new theology it is we who are the victims. But given the nature of society we are fated to bear that with resentment and without expiation. That, indeed, is an abuse—not of religion—but of Christianity.

A Meditation on Secular Process and Notes towards a Theological Response

INTRODUCTION

I SUSPECT that we are close to an end-time for the kind of relation between Church and Society that has obtained in Europe for over a millennium. That does not mean wiping the slate clean but finding the right balance between disentanglement and retention. In what follows I speak of how the vines of faith can be entwined around deteriorating social frames. I also suggest that disentanglement entails unique costs in Europe, because that is where the church has been most deeply embedded and where the secular impulse was first generated, both from within faith as well as poised against it. I am going to argue that the European situation, especially ours here in the UK, is only one of several possible outcomes of the encounter of faith with modernity. In particular I ask just why the United States should have had so very different an experience.

A sociologist has to ask for a minor trade in indulgences. Because sociology deals in the true—or at any rate the fairly plausible—rather than the novel, it has to report and respect the obvious. Again, because sociology cannot control its variables experimentally it has to include informed speculation, and that usually includes a personal angle. Worse still, what it offers does not sound like that extraordinarily elusive entity, 'the real world'. In truth, sociology is a particular kind of ascetic reflection which for special purposes often filters out the colour and the real-life initiatives of human beings. So what follows needs to be treated as an exercise in socio-logic and as a way of establishing connections by comparison. All mapping is reduction, abstraction, and identification. As for any reference to the heavenly city, it will have to come later. Theology too, like any other queen, waits till the rest of the company has been properly assembled.

I have just suggested that the essence of social reflection is controlled comparison: between different cultures at the same time, and at different times in the same culture. Comparison unlocks connectedness. In taking my focus as mainstream religion in Britain I begin by making sideways comparisons with neighbouring cultures, especially western Europe and the United States. Then I move on to shifts within our own culture over time, especially the growth of problematic kinds of individualism.

A SOCIO-PHYSICAL MAP OF EUROPEAN RELIGION

We now ascend in an imaginary satellite, high above western Europe, and observe the way its religious geography relates to the ordinary geography of human settlement and to the contours of plain and mountain. Cast your eyes down and observe a vast northern plain and a teeming population, mostly towards the Atlantic seaboard. This is the epicentre of secularity on our distracted globe. Supposing now we hatch in degrees of religiosity and secularity in shades of black and white. We find there are two main secular concentrations.

The first, which is virtually bleached, extends across all the north—Poland and Lithuania excepted—from Birmingham through Amsterdam, Hamburg, Copenhagen, and Berlin to Tallinn and Helsinki. The external indicators for this area are astonishingly stable and uniform: an average Sunday attendance in the national churches of 2–3 per cent and something less than one person in six engaged in religious activity. If you wanted evidence of the rule-governed nature of the social universe this would be it.

The second area, less bleached but only faintly grey, radiates out from the Paris Basin up to Brussels and has fringes pointing south. These two areas should be the focus of our analytic eye.

But we need to allow into the periphery of our vision some darker (that is more religious) surrounds lying at some distance from the prime centres of secularity. These darker areas either reflect the physical geography of circumambient highlands and islands or they are discernible cultural islands in confrontation with their local secular capital. Sociologists would put a linking needle through both, using the polar concepts of centre and periphery. You have cultural peripheries of different shapes and sizes resisting the radiation of the secular capital: and at the same time you have the highlands, islands, and peninsulas. These provide shelter for peripheries which are physical nests of religious counter-culture.

Let me illustrate those two principles. First shade in a little more darkly the highlands and islands of the north in an arc taking in Ireland, Wales, Scotland, highland Norway and Sweden, and the Finnish lakes. Then shade in medium dark the Alpine hub stretching out in each direction: Alsace, southern Germany, western Austria, Croatia and Slovenia, the Veneto, and so on. You will need some whitish patches of course for places like Basel and Geneva. Then shade in medium dark the Spanish peninsula behind its mountains, especially the north, and the Italian peninsula.

That is the socio-physical map of religion. But I have suggested it overlaps a map of cultural islands, some of which are in physical nests, some not. But whether they nestle behind physical protection or not, they mostly stand in historic opposition to what is now a secular capital. Quite often they are supported by a distinctive language and, of course, a distinctive historic myth. You need add in only one other element, which is that religious identity firms up and intensifies at a historic border with another confession or country.

This can be illustrated by examples. The hinterland of Bergen is sheltered by mountains. It defends a distinctive language and religiosity and resists secular Oslo. The peninsula of Brittany defends a distinctive language and faith against secular Paris; likewise the Basques defend their faith, language, and land against what they call 'atheist' Madrid. Flemish-speaking Flanders defends itself against French-speaking Brussels. Catholic western Austria resists secular and sometime socialist Vienna. Croatia offers a very nice illustration of what it is to stand at a border of languages, religions, and empires; and, of course, it offered resistance both to Orthodox Belgrade and to communist Belgrade. Alsace also stands at a linguistic, imperial, and confessional frontier. And, perhaps surprisingly, Catholic Germany has also seen itself as a threatened border area: first against Protestant and secular Berlin and then against the pressure of the border with the communist east. In all these nests, large and small, history and memory lie semi-intact. Even the British Isles fit in to the pattern. The centre and south and south east are part of the secular mainland but religion increases with each move north and west. The influence of religion is more palpable towards the peninsulas of Wessex and Wales (especially North Wales), and towards the Scottish peninsula (especially the highlands and islands). It finally acquires maximum influence in the ultimate island of Ireland. And there, of course, lies the border of the great confessions, as well as a border of ethnic groups and historic myths.

However, that geography is already almost history, except at the north-west extreme of Ireland and the south-east extreme of Croatia, Serbia, and Bosnia, where it is all too contemporary. We need now to alter the colourings to convey the changes since the 1960s. First, slightly increase the bleaching across the northern plains from Birmingham to Tallinn and (rather more dramatically) begin to bleach the secular heart of France. The European secular centres strengthen. Then lighten the islands of resistance, just a little at the edge of Europe in Ireland, very dramatically near the centre in Catholic southern Holland and somewhere midway between these two in Flanders and Brittany and Scotland. Next, somewhat decrease the dark hatching of the Spanish and Italian peninsulas. The implication is obvious: Europe is becoming unified by radiation out from its secular centre, and by a radiation out from the local secular capitals of London, Amsterdam, Brussels, and Paris to their local peripheries.

Other, equally dramatic, changes have occurred. Three borders are coming down or are down already: the external border with the communist atheist east; the internal border between contentious Catholicism and contentious secular Enlightenment; and the historic border of Protestant with Catholic Europe. They are all connected, of course: Catholicism loses cohesion and loses its enlightened and communist adversaries at the same time. France, in particular, is no longer racked by the struggle raging from 1790 to 1905 and even up to 1960. As for the weakening of the Protestant–Catholic frontier it takes many forms, although the fundamental reality is that Catholicism is becoming individualized, or, if you like, Protestantized, especially in France and Holland. In Switzerland, for example, the difference between the confessions is being reduced to a residual identity, a totemic adherence, which merely inhibits intermarriage. Individualization means that mass attendance is losing its obligatory character: Catholics in Glasgow suddenly felt no special obligation to go to church. Very significantly the rate of reproduction in Catholic southern Europe has now dropped below the rate in Protestant northern Europe, and in some areas is below replacement. Though the Pope seeks to reassert ecclesiastical authority, the magisterium has little social purchase. John Paul II is only a totem. And so in a foreseeable future the authoritative magisterium of the Catholic Church should follow communist autocracy into history and the result will be psychological fall-out. By comparison the independent Church of England paid its dues to modernity on time and with a modicum of good grace.

EXTENDING COMPARISON TO NORTH AMERICA

Here we come to a slight crisis in the thrust of the argument. Basically I want to focus on the group of northern national churches, especially the Church of England, but I need first to take my observation satellite much higher to bring in the Atlantic and the United States. It is not enough to make cross-cultural comparisons within western Europe because we are all exposed to cultural radiation from the great Republic beyond the western seas. We in England are doubly exposed because we share virtually the same language and, give or take a few exuberant oddities, virtually the same religion. What originates in the USA arrives in England. In most respects we are an island which has been towed out half-way to Boston, Mass. but equipped with a channel tunnel to Europe at least a thousand miles long.

But here lies a problem. Historically the British (and the Dutch) invented pluralism and religious competition and exported them to North America. The British were religious exporters before they became religious importers. Once the English and Scots and Irish colonists had (in 1775–83) expelled the London government through a Civil War in the British empire there was a persistent burgeoning of religious competition and vitality for a century and a half. To this day American religion remains on a very high plateau, even after the impact of the baby-boom generation and the Sixties. It follows that modernity and religion are not, as such, incompatible. In Dallas and Atlanta faith and rational technology go together. The spires intersperse the banks. If Lutherans stay in Scandinavia with its onion domes and organs they relapse into dull indifference. Transfer them to the American Midwest and they are all alive as members of the Missouri Synod.

It is a puzzle and throws into high relief the oddity of England. Throughout much of the nineteenth century, says Callum Brown, Britain shared in the competitive religious vitality of America. But then it fell back into the pattern which now affects the whole of northern Europe and is extending itself throughout the European Community. I shall now proceed to suggest that it did so because it shares with the rest of Europe the crucial distinguishing feature of an established, ex-monopoly church, rooted in territory and intertwined with the élites and with their power and social style.

Why is America so different? There are various possibilities. You can conclude that the Holy Spirit in His (or Her) wisdom prefers saving Americans, especially in Arkansas, Texas, and the Deep South. The Spirit bloweth where it listeth but it listeth most of all in places like Little Rock and Dallas. Some people do hold that view, though it is perhaps not entirely a sociological accident that most of them live in places like Little Rock and

Dallas. Indeed there are actually statistics compiled by southern Baptists listing the proportion of US citizens going to hell state by state.

But if we stay with sociology we have to locate the significant transatlantic differences, the differentiating factors. Of course the world wars affected Europe and North America differently. An absolutely major difference is that on this side of the Atlantic there have been religious establishments which have exercised a partial monopoly and which have been intertwined with the social hierarchy, with national history, and above all with the land and the locality. Clergy in established churches have often seen themselves as civil servants manning service stations where needed, not as entrepreneurs running a voluntary organization which has to find a market niche to survive and to pay its way. In the United States things are otherwise, for better for worse. But we cannot leave the American puzzle there.

The American case stimulates the most important question of all, which should frame the whole of this discussion and fully justifies a brief excursion from the main line of argument. Is Europe the vision of the secular future? Is Sweden the destiny of the ex-Protestant world, and France the destiny of the ex-Catholic world and are they both together the destiny of the whole world? If so we would have a powerful secularization theory substantiated by a massive convergence. Or, is the United States just one of several divergent outcomes, or even maybe itself a likely pattern for the future? My own studies of Latin America over the last seven years suggest it may be switching from a European religious future to a North American one. We have already seen how Britain reverted to Europe, but Latin America may be doing the reverse and going the American way. It is sufficient for now to note that in Europe the vines of faith are being slowly disentangled from slowly collapsing social frameworks. Would there—could there—be a rechurching of Europe? Certainly that is the view of the distinguished American sociologist Rodney Stark. Social space is undoubtedly being cleared. Either there will be a vacuum—something that has never happened before—or religious nature fills the vacuum. If the latter is the case then the light dusting of

Pentecostal churches from Bristol to Kiev could be a portent. Likewise the burgeoning Baptist community of Romania.

ESTABLISHED CHURCHES, DUMB CERTAINTIES, AND LAND

We return now to that northern European tier where religion encounters its chilliest environment. In England and in Scandinavia we still have the outer frame, the external façade if you prefer, of an established church providing markers of land and locality, symbolizing a continuity and storing a mythic history. Its sacred places are the cairns set up by the ancestors inviting the ancient Biblical question 'What mean these stones?' They still offer the ceremonies of place and time, especially at the breaking points of human existence, and above all as the receptors of the bodies of the dead. The bells of Sheffield and Liverpool tolled the number of the dead after the tragedy in the football stadium at Hillsborough, and Southward Cathedral brimmed to overflowing with those who came to mourn sons and daughters lost in the sinking in the Thames of the pleasure-steamer *The Marchioness*. The civic sense and the deep respect for civility can still find a location before the shrines of a national church.

This can be seen all over the northern rim of Europe, from England to Finland. Guildford Cathedral received the hostages from Iraq. In Finland each September Helsinki declares itself an open city and tens of thousands pass in to the vast forum in front of the cathedral steps. They stroll, eat, buy, and play music. Then as darkness settles in, the dome is caught in startling bursts of light, Finlandia is played with its yearning hymn-like cadences, and in the church a continuous St Thomas mass is celebrated for all those myriad doubters who usually stay silent in the outer court. On such an occasion you can hear a nation communing with itself. In Oslo when the King died the centre of the city was a sea of candlelight in a mute expression of corporate grief. It is as if icons and ceremonies in sacred places can convey a knowledge of frailty and mystery which stays resolutely dumb when faced with more explicit affirmations. In many parts of the north this dumb knowledge is suffused with a brooding sense of care for the land and for the natural world; for many people the church remains a bower settled in a landscape. That, however, is only part of the story of church and nation.

We all know there are other places where this sense of church and nation is less beneficent, more threatened, more threatening, more militant. Throughout Eastern Europe the repressions of the last half century have wedded ethnicity and religion together. And where rival ethnic groups have confronted each other at disputed borders religion has become a badge of mutual hatred and a motive for national mobilization: in Bosnia, in Cyprus, in Armenia. In western Europe its last redoubt is in Ulster. In such places religion becomes partly assimilated to the unending feud of neighbour with neighbour, to the history of hate, and to the blood tie of the clan. But in England and in Scandinavia, and indeed much more widely, even our own more sheltered (and therefore milder) versions of all that are receding into folk memory. We are, perhaps, inured to the sculptured arsenal of Westminster Abbey. But when you are confronted in a Finnish church by the statue of General Mannerheim, leader of the whites against the reds in the patriotic war, you once again are obliged to recollect a history of aggression and assertion and threats to existence which forge, for better and for worse, the morally ambiguous unity of people and church. Fifty years of piping peace in Britain have left all that crumbling and emotionally remote. The mythic histories which sustained it are recited less and less, and new generations of clergy and even teachers no longer know how to pick up the flying echoes. Pacific jamborees at Glastonbury or modern pilgrimages to Iona cannot mean what Kosovo means to Serbs or our Lady of Czestochova to the Poles. The music of Greensleeves may evoke the rural idyll and the green and pleasant land, but for the rest Kipling was right: all our pomps of yesterday are gone and our navies have almost melted away.

Of course, there are re-mobilizations of identity in western Europe but these flows of feeling mainly tell us how high the tide once was. Europe itself has no overarching myth, unless you count occasional performances of the Ninth Symphony or the opening fanfare of Charpentier's Te Deum in 'Jeux sans Frontières'.

A book that gives some idea of the world we have lost is Linda Colley's *Britons*.[1] She shows how the Protestant religion turned peasants into patriots and brought England, Scotland, and Wales into a common national and imperial project. The project was fired up by rivalry with Catholic France: hence Waterloo Station and Trafalgar Square. Nowadays that rivalry is reduced to lamb and fish, and as for the continued union of the Kingdom it is hardly something we may presume.

We, for our part, walk around our parish churches, ignoring the imperial history on the tablets. But Remembrance Day does briefly interpose the query: just how accessible are these inscriptions, what mean these stories, how many now embrace these conceptions of national duty, or link sacrifice in war with the Lord's atonement for sin? The tides of blood recede. And we know that suddenly even the solidity of the monarchy looks exposed, especially the Protestant monarchy. Probably it will survive. But the idea of a Protestant Defender of the Faith—*the* Faith—is unlikely to figure very largely in its future, and some people plainly feel the royal family mirrors our modern 'family values' all too closely for comfort.

In any case the Church of England itself faces in so many directions that it would not know which loyalties to mobilize if it wished. It stands at a junction of the USA, the old and new Commonwealth, and Europe. The affiliation of evangelicals is with the fundamentally Protestant culture of the USA, and of the Anglo-Catholics with European Catholicism, while the majority of Anglicans live in Africa. As for the liberal leadership in the church it is firmly multicultural at home and would probably embrace European Social Catholicism and M Delors and his successors, provided it could at the same time avoid the embrace of John Paul II.

There is a question here of the identity of the Church of England—though not of Anglicanism—and it is as uneasy as the

---

[1] Colley, Linda, *Britons—Forging the Nation 1707–1837* (London: Random House, 1994).

identity of England itself and the springs of English self-esteem and cohesion. It cannot straightforwardly be put down to the existence of a multicultural society, because (religiously at least) England includes a mere 4 per cent of non-Christians.[2] The changes are more deep-seated. They belong precisely to those gently collapsing frames around which the vines of faith are twined. If one wanted a profound index of changes one would cite the falling figures for baptism. After all one of the social supports of baptism, apart from superstition, was the idea that Christening initiated a child into the English community as such. English people did not have forenames; they had Christian names. Nowadays, however, liturgists write baptismal services all about entry into the Pilgrim People of God through the waters of death and regeneration. No doubt the social meanings and the theological meanings were always at odds, but now we see them part and go their separate ways. Theology grows uncomfortably explicit, liturgists devise appropriate symbolisms, priests ask awkward questions about commitment and eligibility, and society loses its ceremonies of entry. Another tide recedes.

COMPARISONS OVER TIME: THE MAJOR SHIFTS

We come now to the second principal part of the argument, where we in the main shift to changes over time rather than comparisons across cultures. In particular we consider the most corrosive agent of religious bonding, which is the continuous expansion of individualism at the centres of our western European society. Like so much else which causes creative trouble for Christianity it is in part implied and nourished by Christianity itself, but there it is held in check within corporate disciplines and normative governance. The church constantly digs its own grave.

By definition individualism spawns infinite variety, but I am following many others in identifying two versions: expressive

---

[2] For careful and reliable discussions of this whole range of issues cf. Davie, Grace, *Religion in Britain since 1945* (Oxford: Blackwell, 1994).

individualism, having to do with the expression of the self, and acquisitive individualism, where acquiring the goods predominates over achieving the good. These are hardly novelties but in what I have called the 'centre' or 'core areas' of European society they are options almost universally exploited and endlessly encouraged. Since I cannot possibly refer to all their religious implications I touch only on two of them: the 'self-religions' which openly embody a fragmentation of the religious impulse, and evangelicalism which includes some of the elements of both kinds of individualism but corrals and checks them by incorporation.

Briefly I have to deploy some sociology and use its shorthand. In particular I need to deploy the ideas of mobility and differentiation. The context of individualism is provided by mobility, that is by movement in all its forms: moving about, shifting social location and social roles, being in instant communication through modern media. And the context of individualism is also provided by differentiation, which means the separating out of social spheres. According to a standard sociological theory (of which I happen to be critical) these processes consign the church progressively to the personal realm, the social margins, and the private sphere.

Mobility is self-explanatory and merely means that people move not only between generations but often several times in a single lifetime, that they can change their social status, that they receive communications on a global scale, that they travel and have novel experiences, that they are aware of a constant acceleration of social change. This leads to a variable and multi-faceted presentation of the self in different spheres of activity and to a mobile social face. It also means that you cannot expect to be reinforced in your views and beliefs by constantly meeting the like-minded, and thus that believers in particular are conscious of being a minority unless they choose to restrict their contacts. Young people in particular have come to experience a fluid environment. Their cultural generations have become shorter than their biological generations and they find their principal point of reference in their peers. Of course, society has never been static, but the current rate of mobility is higher than at any previous time. It means that minorities are fragmented by external influences and that peripheries are drawn into the cultural radiation of metropolitan centres unless protected by prejudice and the conditions of the ghetto.

All this means that institutions embodying continuity are subject to greater strains than ever before. It is not so much a problem specifically for religious institutions, as for all institutions which carry forward cultural continuity and for all agencies of socialization including the state itself, as well as the family, the schools, and the universities. Social reproduction and the maintenance of identity and tradition are rendered problematic and tradition is forced to become self-conscious by labelling itself 'traditionalist'. In particular the transmission of authoritative role-models from man to woman, parent to child, craftsman to apprentice, teacher to pupil, religious leader to lay person, is rendered problematic, particularly where relationships of subordination have been undermined as they certainly have in relation to women and the young. Even the very idea of a role-model or a moral and professional exemplar is jeopardized. Morality is conceived less in terms of evaluation and discipleship and more in terms of optimal life-styles or life-stances. For some people such shifts even have implications for any religious vocabulary which embodies metaphors of fatherhood or of political authority, for example kingship.

Differentiation is not quite so self-explanatory; I used it as a key element in my own *General Theory of Secularization* because it is one of the most universal of social processes.[3] Broadly, it refers to the process by which social spheres and intellectual activities are released from ecclesiastical tutelage and from theological modes of thought. What was once assembled around the hub of the church—teaching, healing, leisure, administration—as well as law and the patronage of the arts—separates out into numerous autonomous spheres under the control of their own professional experts. Moreover, in those spheres where the church still remains chiefly active, such as therapy or moral counselling or social assistance or rites of

---

[3] Martin, David, *A General Theory of Secularization* (Oxford: Blackwell, 1978).

passage, there emerge secular equivalents such as the social worker, the psychiatrist, the counsellor, the registrar.

These developments occur, of course, over time, in particular the last four centuries, but especially the last two and a half centuries since the Industrial Revolution and the last two or three decades of an accelerating technological revolution. Fastening now on this time-dimension we can identify the pre-industrial, the industrial, and post-industrial (or post-modern).

'Had we but world enough and time' I could deal here with how the Industrial Revolution tore apart the social fabric in which the church was embedded; how the social constituency of the church then became tilted towards groups still embedded in that fabric and towards their style of life, politics, and assertions of social order; how it achieved some pastoral relation to new groups like state school teachers and shopkeepers who put their stamp upon it and then involved it in their own obsolescence; how clergy shifted their own social location and politics from the old élites of law and the military towards the social location and politics of the social service professions. The underlying argument here would be that the sacred always extends its coverage to protect anachronism as well as to protect threatened values until they can be rediscovered. The sacred always provides cover for more than itself and so invites a comprehensive rejection, or at least a defensive scepticism and accusations of hypocrisy and partiality. That argument is important in helping to explain why some groups are within easy hearing distance of the messages offered by the church while others prefer merely to overhear those messages or to select different elements from them.

There is, however, one other major parenthesis which has to do with how in Protestant societies the tone of the élites and so of the command posts in media and education shifts from diffuse religiosity to diffuse secularity. In Scandinavia Social Democratic élites simply took over the command posts once occupied by state churches and redeployed them (and the church itself) for their own purposes. The centre held: the personnel and messages shifted. In England secular-minded groupings gained control of media and teacher education by turnovers of personnel and reorganizations which were slow enough and gentle enough not to alert coherent opposition. Christians were inhibited by liberal good manners and by the way a diffuse secular viewpoint evolved an amiable translation of Christian values in terms of peace, justice, welfare, human dignity, and public service. In particular in the schools this shift came about through a non-denominational approach drawing ethical conclusions from biblical material. This eased public faith away from profound issues of the human condition towards civic decencies.

At the same time, however, many of the leaders in media, teaching, and social science professions (collectively labelled in sociological terms as the 'knowledge class') had themselves moved on to embrace a more aggressively secular blend of moral relativism, self-expression, and therapeutic practice. They espoused a variety of multiculturalism specifically hostile to the historic culture of the mainstream traditions. So the scene was set for murmurings about disestablishment, which from one quarter drew sustenance from the resentment about the political critique of the clergy and the Church's presumed lack of concern for national and family values, and which from another quarter depended on deploying arguments from multiculturalism (undefined) and the limited active social constituency of the church. In other words these arguments represent precisely the collapsing of a social frame around which the vines of faith have historically been twined.

We return now to the problems of mobility and differentiation. As I suggested earlier, these are not so much special problems faced only by religious institutions. These are difficulties encountered by all voluntary organizations including parties and unions. As change and mobility accelerate it is bound to be difficult to retain identities to draw on taken-for-granted meanings and to reproduce values. Nor is it all that easy to match the attractions of media based on ephemera, on expendability and the pursuit of irony. Perhaps this is the point to mention the reassertion of the once discredited argument of a direct relation between rates of crime and rates of religious involvement by Professor Christie Davies.

POST-MODERN SOCIETY?

No doubt these various difficulties have existed through all the later stages of industrial society, but as everyone knows cultural commentators have identified certain other shifts as belonging to post-industrial society or to what some label post-modern society. These are fragmentation and an accent on immediacy and instant communication. Here perhaps I have to exaggerate and caricature in order to achieve some sharpness of definition. Thus it is important to get in touch: the world is tactile. Life is not viewed as a trajectory or framed in an all-encompassing narrative, whether that be sacred or ideological. Rather it is a thing of shreds and patches where things are mixed and matched. That implies a diminished sense of historical location, and the use of atmospheres of past times as heritage and as decorative items in a theme park. For many people there seems to be a slackened appreciation of the extended, the coherent, the long-term, the received, and the canonical. In particular the tragic appears as a random intrusion and is responded to *ad hoc*: the touching assemblages of memorabilia after Hillsborough (maybe), but also (maybe) a dredging around for confused fragments.[4] The world simply ought to be otherwise. Politics seems remote, not only because corrupt but because it deals in the fudged, the contingent, and the imperfect. It is even possible to see this political withdrawal as a religious or at any rate a utopian rejection of the world.

Clearly this is an accentuation of 'expressive individualism' with long roots in the romantic attitude. It brings to birth what has been called the 'me' generation and responds to so-called 'self religions' based on exploratory spiritualities and the search for inward and outward harmonies, without grasping the tragic dimension or the recalcitrance of the political problem. (Of course, it is evident that politicians feel obliged to collude in this evasion.) At the same time there is a growth of acquisitive individualism for which this world provides pickings for the taking. The race is to the strong, the self-sufficient, the survivors, and the main criterion is success. Neither this kind of

---

[4] Cf. Davie, *Religion*.

individualism nor expressive individualism accept any absolute character attaching to obligation or any notion like 'my station and its duties'. The implications for marriage and parenthood hardly need to be spelled out.

Nevertheless elements of spirituality and faith surface as fragments of meaning floating in the flotsam and jetsam of expendable and ephemeral signs. The largest of these fragments is perhaps a moral code, often cast in terms of social usefulness and personal convenience, which expresses dislike of exploitation of others, of taking what is another's and ignoring their dignity. This fragment is really the torn-off second half of the Decalogue and it links up with the desire for respect, given and received. This actually elicits a passionate righteousness. It is a matter of how you treat those you know, which means not so much society at large, but those who belong to your own group. The environment also is valuable and there has to be respect for the animal and plant world.

The sense of respect for self is linked to a desire for the healthy operation of self, physically and spiritually. The shelves of bookshops dealing with mind, body, and spirit or with vegetarian diet tell how extensive this is, though how many buy and read it is another matter. Sometimes this is merely magical manipulation, sometimes narcissism, sometimes self-exploration, sometimes genuine moral experience. Experience and meditation are the keys and wholeness and empowerment the goal. If there is a political concern it is in the extension of personal sensitivity to the variety of human kinds and preferences, sexual or aesthetic, and this is sometimes expressed in the codes of political correctness. There is also a yearning for community. If the world is out of joint people can come together for a festival. Your festival or celebration is a kind of faith but not a faith *in* anything, just 'faith' in general such as Prince Charles expresses.

One Response: Evangelicalism

If one sets out such elements they clearly both overlap and contradict a Christian understanding, but their prevalence helps explain the popularity of New Age spiritualities and also the impact of evangelicalism. So far as evangelicalism is concerned it may be as well to recognize that in many varied forms, above all in the form of Pentecostalism, it is proving the most vital response to the modern situation, very obviously in the moral turmoil of the Third World, but (less dramatically) even in the developed world. It takes individualism or self-expression and contains and incorporates them. A characteristic evangelical theme is the church family, but it endeavours to restore broken familial membranes or re-constitute them among the mutually supportive brothers and sisters. Alongside the brethren are the leaders in quasi-paternal roles who restore a sense of direction and mark out the moral boundaries and the boundaries of the group. This may mean in some cases erecting and patrolling a boundary between church and wider community which will inevitably raise the level of tension. In a few cases there is a reversion to literalism and fundamentalism apt to secure invulnerability at high cost.

All the modern tendencies are given some scope by evangelicalism: the need for the small cell-like groupings and the yearning for communal support, for tactile communications, emotional release, holistic healing, a fluid language of the body—and empowerment. In a term like empowerment we see the linkage of the Pentecostal cell and idea of the base community, and we also sense the dangers. Power can become concentrated in the 'shepherds' and can become inflated in self-delusion and denial of limits. 'Testing the spirits' becomes an arduous business as indeed it is in parallel situations in the non-evangelical world. The aim is to have 'power' in everyday initiatives and control over unruly spirits and personal indiscipline, but the encouragement of releases may make this difficult to secure. Clearly empowerment overlaps both expressive and acquisitive individualism and may deal in amoral potencies not 'buried in Christ' as well as in disciplined moralization. Empowerment may also sometimes share the modern evasion of cost, self-emptying, and at-onement, preferring instead a simple embrace of spirit and celebration. All options entail correlative costs and evangelicalism is no exception. Nor is the evangelical option likely to become universal.

All options encounter built-in limits, and again, evangelicalism is no exception.

SOCIOLOGICAL CONCLUSION

What by way of conclusion? A sociologist as sociologist ends not with a bang but with open-endedness. One aspect of open-endedness is the existence of opportunity and the non-existence of closure. The East German Church grasped crucial opportunities even though its active members were a mere 2 per cent of the population. The Hungarian Church registered a return flow of members ten years before the revolution of 1989–90.[5] But clearly there are certain difficulties for the church in what I have described and we ought perhaps most of all to be impressed at its survival. Christianity makes awkward recommendations which invite us to undertake scrutiny of our moral responsibilities, and it places the self under rebuke and judgement. It is judgemental and releasing. It has a vocabulary of regeneration and cost which centres around a death and around the compact resistance of the secular city to love's jurisdiction. It presents that death and that regeneration in a narrative which encompasses history and life as a whole; and it offers gifts in constant acts of commemoration. All this is not very grateful to the spirit of the age any more than it was in the first century in the arena at Ephesus or on Mars Hill.

In my view there is no possibility of a magisterial response to the challenge and yet another *aggiorniamento*. I do not even believe we can take an audit and come to an agreed policy. Things are simply much more various and experimental and they are carried by every member of the body of Christ. You might conclude from what was said earlier that we are greatly circumscribed by circumstance. Happily we are. Only a little rests on us, however much we may desire a more genuinely appalling responsibility. In the end it is a matter of guarding the heart of the mystery. That will mean, in practice, conservations

---

[5] Cf. Martin, David, *et al.* in Fulton, John, and Gee, Peter (eds.), *Religion in Contemporary Europe* (New York: Edward Mellen Press, 1994).

and retentions as well as releases and innovations, partial recoveries of unity as well as constant explosions of diversity such as we see today all over Africa, Latin America, and Asia.

Faith is constantly being reassembled and it presses in its multiplicity against the constriction of circumstances, seeking points of fit, niches of need, and occasions of confrontation. It does not follow, of course, that what slips successfully through the filter of circumstance, like the gospel of prosperity, is good, or that what is bound to failure, like the project of the Sea of Faith group, is on that account untrue. Again I would see it is a matter of such faithfulness as we can muster with the assistance of grace. The rest is not our business.

I see the Church from its very beginnings at Pentecost as a kind of underground explosion of the spirit on the far, unconsidered edge of the civilized world. Or to use gospel imagery it is a prodigal basket of all kinds of seeds, full of signs—many signs—of new life. Sometimes these seeds lie dormant for centuries, sometimes they achieve a distorted growth, sometimes in periods of turmoil they are hurled in every direction so that those who pick them up do not know their point of origin or recognize their Christian name. The signs of new life are infinite in their variety: a visionary city for the healing of nations; settled companies of friends peaceably sharing meat and drink; a wandering fraternity; an exalted handmaid, an isolated victim, and a resplendent victor. Think also of signs for wholeness of body and mind, signs for departing like pilgrims for destinations to discover a place of promise, signs for an attentive stillness awaiting a Deity within. Think of all the varied sorts and conditions of men and women who have received and nourished such signs of life.

None of these are trapped in the tentative mesh I have thrown over the social reality of the church, partly because they are not trapped by the church itself, only carried. The church is only a carrier and it is not the only carrier. And yet these signs are not so random as to be beyond all governance of rules, nor are they so socially disembodied as to be beyond scrutiny and discernment. Since we are ourselves made as ordered creatures we should always be alert for connectedness. After all, connectness is our one stay in an uncertain world. On it all creation depends—or, if you deny creation, then that just is the way things are.

NOTES TOWARDS A THEOLOGICAL RESPONSE

'Only connect.' Whereas social commentary may suggest possible ameliorations of this or that problem, the central task of theology is rather different. If sociology is the science (i.e. knowledge) of the possible, theology is the symbolization both of the ineluctable and the promissory. Theology seeks to uncover and discern in the recesses of our living where lies the secret analogy of Christ—the gestures that redeem and recover—and which enact our liturgy within the wider world beyond our delimited sacred space. Theology may also discern in the vaulting ambition for total autonomy, for which contemporary culture opens up so many opportunities, and so many temptations, a dangerous approach to the borders of nothingness or chaos or the demonic. It can also find a literal counter-action to all that in everything mirroring the Triune nature of God through the mutual creation of persons-in-relation. It may ask how different failures to include violate the universal scope of God's Kingdom.

Now, we at this present time retain in the church a particular kind of base in land and locality which opens out generously on to the people at large. Though one of our options is to withdraw into the safeties of the ghetto and into the gathered community and there tend the spirit, that is not the special genius of a national Church. It holds a door open for whoever wants to enter holy space or simply to overhear its messages from the outer court. However much it may be pushed from the centres of power, a national Church is a presence conveying memory and continuity. In it you find a special kind of commemorative re-presentation, not casual amnesia. Still it tries to answer the question put by any passer-by: 'What do these stones mean?' The passer-by asks also: 'Why do these people, the priests of the Church, tend this Sanctuary and its lights?' But the Church does something else: it endeavours to show by drawing on its whole rich history of sign and symbol that it is directly related to the reality of the world around it rather than offering a mere antique projection.

On Relating to a Fragmentary Spirituality

For the rest of my argument I take one or two elements in the spiritual flotsam and jetsam of today to which we may relate. I take first the concern with the material environment, and, second, the commonalities still present in the moral environment, and suggest how they are completed by an understanding rooted in the fruitful corruption of our nature and God's redemptive involvement in the narrative of death and regeneration. I am, then, talking about the relevance of the sacred narrative to the *disjecta membra*, the floating, unintegrated spiritualities of our world.

If we take first the kind of spirituality that is concerned with the natural environment, it corresponds to Genesis and to the connectedness of creation. If we then take the moral world it corresponds to the regulation and interconnectedness of right living found in the Decalogue. Beyond that it corresponds to the moral wisdom shared by the ancient world and the sentiment of neighbourliness exemplified in the Good Samaritan. In conclusion, I look at how the internal dynamic of the human story itself works itself out in the confrontations of the Passion and in the manifestation of the unmeasured love of God.

Allow me, if you will, to present these spiritualities through the standard device of typification. One major preoccupation of our time is care for resources, and for the integrity of the planet. People reject spoliation and abuse, respect the ecological balances, and seek to protect the brute creation and the variety of species. They take to heart the text from Revelation 'Hurt not the earth'. They see themselves as engaged in a quest for personal harmony worked out within the harmonies of nature, articulating an objection to dominance and exploitation and to any abuse of the material body of Earth. This special form of care is constantly recommended in the media and in the schools, perhaps because it is believed to be the heartland of our moral agreement, and the uncontentious core of consensus.

It hardly needs saying that there are sentimentalities present here not really consonant with a Christian understanding: both with regard to the pitilessness evident in the natural world and the proper requirement of material domination. But the main problem is that it ignores the geniune complexity of our human moral world and its permanent need for connectedness. It ignores the paramount need of respect for virtue and for regulative principles. But the moment anyone raises these they are regarded judgemental and as naïvely unaware of the supposed relative and subjective nature of moral judgements. That, however, may be changing. There may be an increasing recognition in the face of the unspeakable, say in Rwanda or in the individual English case of James Bulger, murdered by older children, that these contemporary sentimentalities, however amiable, do not cope with the range of evil or of good; they neglect both the range of murder and of sacrifice. In short, they do not cope with the persistent analogy of the Passion all about us.

That brings us from connectedness in Creation to connectedness in human relationships, and from Genesis to Exodus and Deuteronomy. We are subject to laws, both as manifest in the positive law and on our own account as moral creatures, exercising personal responsibility. Given the extent of the contemporary disintegration this recovery of the sense of laws may not be easy to achieve, but there are signs of a common moral spiritiuality to which we can relate, and in any case this is not the first moment in history when people have said that Christ and His Saints have slept.

One such sign is the horror aroused by the ungovernable and marauding destructiveness of young males, seeming to be almost without conscience, and abusive towards their mothers, their partners, and anyone in their path. Clearly they lack any anticipation of a secure social status, a proper male role, or personal validation. This is a deep-seated conflict in Western society brilliantly analysed in the book *Civil War* by Hans Magnus Enzensberger.[6] The other side of that is the pursuit of community recommended by Tony Blair as new leader of the British Labour Party.

What is interesting about this is its root in a Christian sense of being members one of another, and the way there is also a complementary affirmation that the individual achieves his personal fulfilment, which is acknowledged as important, in a network of relationship. Perhaps one piece of evidence that people are attracted by this call to community is that 60 per cent of people in England support prayers in school assemblies, which means in effect some inculcation of the basic duties and respects.

Yet another area of commonality is the language in which people express their moral anger at injustice and unfairness. The theme of unfairness is coming to join the theme of 'community' in our moral vocabulary, and it assumes a common point of moral reference. If people neglect to make certain arrangements whether it is installing seat-belts or taking proper care in offering medical treatment, they are regarded as culpable. In a similar way the increase in litigation over issues of negligence implies the moral requirement of redress. So, in spite of everything that may properly be said about how far disintegration has gone, there is a core of moral understanding present in a common language, and clustering around the Decalogue and injunctions not to steal, or injure, or kill, or covet, or lie. This is a very large fragment of the moral sense traditionally taught and recommended by the Church and it remains part of what people expect the Church to stand for: the basic difference between right and wrong, responsibility and irresponsibility.

For that matter, the Conservative Party has itself recently embraced this cause, encouraging a debate about responsibilities, habits and virtues, conduct, courtesy and manners. This has its own roots in the experience of the social costs of extensive disintegration and fears about crime and violence. It is plain that an untrammelled acquisitive individualism is at least as

---

[6] Enzensberger, Hans Magnus, *Civil War* (London: Fontana, 1994). On contemporary criminality and religion see Davies, Christie in Burnside, J., and Baker, N. (eds.), *Relationsl Justice* (Winchester: Waterside, 1994).

dangerous as the kind of expressive individualism that justifies everything in the name of the free expression of the self.

What seems to be happening here is a clash between the real dynamics of our moral nature and activity and the technological presumption that the main criterion as to how society should be run is effectiveness and efficiency. It is this that makes the manager and the accountant such key figures in our society. However, the costs estimated by this kind of accountancy leave out of the account the other and equally real costs in terms of divisiveness, moral disintegration, and the competitive war of all against all.

BEYOND MORAL WISDOM AND MORAL REGULATION

All that has been discussed so far is a straightforward moral wisdom and regulation such as found in the Decalogue and comparable codes in other civilizations. These are the guarantors of civility and part of what religion is about: the care for others inherent in civility and courtesy. But there is a third layer just as profound and as real. The categories of commonsense, ordinary decency, enlightened self-interest, well-adjusted harmonies, are not adequate for our situation. Nor are the kinds of abstract discussion of principles involved in moral philosophy, such as are found in David Hume's working out of the role of the passions, Kant's understanding of 'willing that which we would want to be adopted universally', or Bentham's principles of utility and happiness. These principles do not engage with the actual dynamics of the human story, or with the way our moral choices are corrupted and distorted and deeply infected with the inflation of the self. The resulting situation simply cannot add up and chains of cumulative distortion are set in motion. Our moral condition is persistently out of joint so that at some point or other there is going (in a truly profound sense), to be hell to pay. The competitive multitude of human projects cannot mesh without multiple trails of ruination. They create negative reciprocities, tit-for-tat, feuding, and a terrible meting out of measure for measure. They also have a demonic energy pushing them to excess and to an exploration of the depths of evil.

It is here, of course, that we are in the neighbourhood of redemption, because the Church's narrative incorporates this fundamental and universal process and invites our identification with it. God's Secret Agent seeks out, locates, and confronts the source of demonic energy and shows that our indebtedness cannot be met from our own moral resources. All the maleficent powers gather to ensure His elimination. And this is a crisis or public placarding of our condition which can only be met by unmeasured grace and measureless love. The imprisonment of the indebted soul—imprisonment for debt—is ended by a free justification, totally independent of the merits of our case. It is the persistent offer of this justification which is the final reason for the church's presence.

So, whatever the disintegrations characteristic of our times, these are the fragments we use on which to base our understanding of what is really happening in the world about us. From this unnegotiable citadel the Church speaks to contemporary society, whether heard or ignored.

Perhaps I may conclude with a quotation from a piece I wrote in response to a similar challenge:

We should remember both the resilience of traditions and their partial retention here and there as a base for future recoveries. And secularization is not some unavoidable destiny. It is related to particular historical and social conditions, which can be countered or utilised by human ingenuity and imagination.

What might be said from a Christian viewpoint of such a situation? I believe the everyday philosophy of neighbourliness and mutual friendship which constitutes the everyday idea of 'Christianity' is not to be despised. Anthony Harvey, in his discussion of the gospels, sees them as continuous with the everyday moral wisdom of the ancient world, and I think there is a similar continuity extending from the gospels to the modern world. I also believe that such wisdom misses the central note of Christianity, which lies in self-giving and sacrifice which reconciles, receives, and recovers our humanity. It turns on the recalcitrance of evil and the terrible costs of its encounter with goodness. I would suggest that out of the varied situations in which people find themselves there emerge dumb requests for those things which are already present in the sacred narrative and the repository of Christian sign and gesture. Men and women do want to have their isolation and alienation broken; they want someone alongside them taking up 'the trouble they're in'; they seek commendation, affirmation, even blessing; they want the miracle of their births recognized and the grief of their deaths assuaged; they want the wounds of creation and humanity healed; they have some sense that gift-giving and forgiving are the heart of the matter. The Christian narrative encompasses just those things, which means that implicit religion can also be implicitly Christian faith. Christianity is not some weird Palestinian oddity, made antique by science, and rendered remote by the modern situation, but a narrative of birth and death, anticipation and fulfillment, wound and restitution, disorder and recreation, which meets what is already there implicit in experiences.

In our human situations there is possible a persistent analogy of Christ. To hand on a Christian culture is simply to ensure that analogy can be both recognized and lived.[7]

---

[7] The conclusion of a piece printed in *Crucible*, Apr.–June 1944, pp. 59–64, which was originally a response to a conference at St George's House, Windsor Castle. For a discussion of the emergence of the Church's public voice and a critique of the notion of inevitable privatization see Casanova, José, *Public Religions in the Modern World* (Chicago: Chicago University Press, 1994).

SELECT BIBLIOGRAPHY

ARCHER, MARGARET, *Culture and Agency: The Place of Culture in Social Theory* (Cambridge: Cambridge University Press, 1988).

BANNER, MICHAEL, *The Justification of Science and the Rationality of Religious Belief* (Oxford: Oxford University Press, 1994).

BARKER, EILEEN, *New Religious Movements: A Practical Introduction* (London: HMSO, 1989).

BAUM, GREGORY, *Religion and Alienation: A Theological Reading of Sociology* (New York: Paulist Press, 1975).

BELLAH, R. N., *Beyond Belief* (New York: Harper and Row, 1970).

BERGER, PETER, *A Rumour of Angels* (New York: Doubleday, 1969).

——*The Heretical Imperative* (London: Collins, 1980).

BEYER, PETER, *Religion and Globalization* (London: Sage 1994).

BOWKER, JOHN, *Is God a Virus? Genes, Culture and Religion* (London: SPCK, 1995).

——*The Sense of God: Sociological, Anthropological and Psychological Approaches to the Origin of the Sense of God* (Oxford: Oxford University Press, 1973).

BUDD, SUSAN, *Sociologists and Religion* (London: Collier-Macmillan, 1973).

BYRNE, PETER, and CLARKE, PETER, *Religion Defined and Explained* (Basingstoke: Macmillan, 1993).

CASANOVA, JOSÉ, *Public Religions in the Modern World* (Chicago: University of Chicago Press, 1994).

DAVIES, CHRISTIE, 'Crime and the Rise of the Relational Society' in Jonathan Burnside and Nicola Baker, *Relational Justice* (Winchester: Waterside, 1994).

FLANAGAN, KIERNAN, *The Enchantment of Sociology* (London: Macmillan, 1996).

——and JUPP, P. (eds.), *Postmodernity, Sociology and Religion* (London: Macmillan, 1996).

FULTON, JOHN, 'Experience, Alienation and the Anthropological Condition of Religion', *Annual Review of the Social Sciences of Religion*, 5 (1981), 2–32.

GEERTZ, CLIFFORD, *The Interpretation of Cultures* (London: Hutchinson, 1975).

GILL, ROBIN, *Christian Ethics in Secular Worlds* (Edinburgh: T. and T. Clark, 1991).

—— *Competing Convictions* (London: SCM Press, 1989).

—— *Theology and Sociology* (London: Chapman, 1987).

—— *The Social Context of Theology* (London/Oxford: Mowbray, 1975).

—— *Moral Communities* (Exeter: University of Exeter Press, 1992).

HAMMOND, PHILLIP (ed.), *The Sacred in a Secular Age* (Berkeley: University of California Press, 1985).

HEELAS, PAUL, MORRIS, PAUL, and MARTIN, DAVID (eds.), *Religion: Modernity and Postmodernity* (Oxford: Blackwell, 1996).

HOMAN, ROGER, *The Sociology of Religion: A Bibliographical Survey* (New York: Greenwood Press, 1986).

KEE, HOWARD, *Christian Origins in Sociological Perspective* (London: SCM Press, 1980).

LACEY, MICHAEL (ed.), *Religion and Twentieth Century American Life* (Cambridge: Cambridge University Press, 1989).

LINDBERG, DAVID, and NUMBERS, RONALD (eds.), *God and Nature: Historical Essays on the Encounter between Christianity and Science* (Berkeley/London: University of California Press, 1986).

LYON, DAVID, *Signs of the Times: Postmodernity and the Futures of Religion* (Oxford: Polity Press, 1996).

—— *Sociology and the Human Image* (Downer's Grove, Ill.: Inter-University Press, 1983).

—— *The Steeple's Shadow* (London: SPCK, 1985).

MACINTYRE, ALASDAIR, *Whose Justice? Which Rationality?* (London: Duckworth, 1988).

MARSDEN, GEORGE, *The Soul of the American University* (Oxford: Oxford University Press, 1994).

—— and LONGFIELD, BRADLEY, *The Secularisation of the Academy* (Oxford: Oxford University Press, 1993).

MARTIN, DAVID, *The Status of the Human Person in the Behavioural Sciences* in R. Preston (ed.), *Technology and Social Justice* (London: SCM, 1971).

—— ORME MILLS, JOHN, and PICKERING, WILLIAM (eds.), *Sociology and Theology: Alliance and Conflict* (Brighton: The Harvester Press, 1980).

MITTON, C. L. *The Social Sciences and the Churches* (Edinburgh: T. & T. Clark, 1972).

PEACOCKE, ARTHUR (ed.), *The Sciences and Theology in the Twentieth Century* (Notre Dame, Ind.: University of Notre Dame Press, 1981).

PICKERING, WILLIAM, *Durkheim on Religion* (London: Routledge, 1975).

POEWE, KARLA (ed.), *Charismatic Christianity as Global Culture* (Columbia: University of South Carolina Press, 1994).

PREUS, J. SAMUEL, *Explaining Religion: Criticism and Theory from Boden to Freud* (New Haven, Conn.: Yale University Press, 1987).

REDEKOP, CALVIN, DE SANTO, CHARLES, and SMITH-HINDS, WILLIAM (eds.), *A Reader in Sociology: Christian Perspectives* (Scottdale, Pa.: Herald Press, 1980).

RICHARDSON, JAMES, T., ROBBINS, JAMES, T., ROBERTSON, THOMAS, GOODMAN, ROLAND, and JACOBS, JANET, 'Studying Controversial Religious Groups', *Religion*, 21 (Oct. 1991).

RICOEUR, PAUL, *Interpretation Theory: Discourse and the Surplus of Meaning* (Forth Worth, Tex.: Christian University Press, 1976).

ROBERTSON, ROLAND, *The Sociological Interpretation of Religion* (Oxford: Blackwell, 1930).

RUSSELL, RICHARD, *Reason and Commitment in Education* (Exeter: Paternoster Press, 1979).

SMART, NINIAN, *The Science of Religion and the Sociology of Knowledge* (Princeton: Princeton University Press, 1974).

SMITH, W. CANTWELL, *The Meaning and End of Religion* (London: SPCK, 1978).

STARK, RODNEY, *The Future of Religion: Secularisation, Revival and Cult Formation* (Berkeley: University of California Press, 1985).

STARKEY, ALAN, *A Christian Social Perspective* (Leicester: IVP, 1979).

SURIN, KENNETH (ed.), *Christ, Ethics and Tragedy* (Cambridge: Cambridge University Press, 1989).

THOMPSON, KENNETH, *Beliefs and Ideology* (London: Tavistock, 1978).

TOWLER, ROBERT, *Homo Religiosus* (London: Constable, 1974).

WALTER, TONY, *Funerals and How to Improve Them* (London: Hodder, 1990).

——*A Long Way from Home* (Exeter: Paternoster Press, 1979).

——*The Human Home: The Myth of the Sacred Environment* (Tring: Lion, 1982).

WHITELEY, D. E. H., and MARTIN, RODERICK (eds.), *Sociology, Theology and Conflict* (Oxford: Blackwell, 1969).

WIEBE, DONALD, *Religion and Truth* (The Hague: Mouton, 1981).

——SEGAL, ROBERT, STRENSKI, IVAN, and PREUS, J. SAMUEL, 'Explaining Religion: a Symposium', *Religion*, 19 (Oct. 1989).

WILSON, BRYAN, *Religion in Sociological Perspective* (Oxford: Oxford University Press, 1982).

WINTER, GILBERT, *Elements for a Social Ethic* (New York: Collier-Macmillan, 1966).

YINGER, J. MILTON, *Religion, Society and the Individual* (New York: Macmillan, 1957).

INDEX